FIGHTING RACISM

FIGHTING RACISM

Selected Writings

by Gus Hall

International Publishers
New York

© 1985 by International Publishers
Second Printing, 1987
Printed in the United States of America

Library of Congress Cataloging in Publication Data
Hall, Gus
      Fighting racism

1. Racism—United States—Addresses, essays, lectures.
2. United States—Race relations—Addresses, essays,
lectures.   Afro-Americans—Social conditions—Ad-
dresses, essays, lectures.   Communist Party of the
United States of America—Addresses, essays, lectures.
I. Title.
E185.615.H27   1985   305.8'00973   85-10923
ISBN 0-7178-0634-0
ISBN 0-7178-0626-X (pbk.)

CONTENTS

Acknowledgements

Writers are not islands unto themselves. Thus, no book is the product of a single mind.

Many have contributed to the thoughts in this book and getting it to the publishers.

Henry Winston, Elizabeth Hall, James Jackson, Barry Cohen, Len Levenson, Danny Spector, Carole Marks, Judith LeBlanc, George Meyers, William Patterson, Lorenzo Torrez, Jesús Colón, Joe Brandt and Laszlo Kubinyi are among those who, over the many years, have left their imprint on the thinking that went into this book.

FIGHTING RACISM

Introduction

A Winning Struggle

Some years ago a presidential commission on civil rights concluded that we have "two societies" in the United States—one Black, the other white.

By implication, the commission's report argued that that is how it has been, that is how it is, and that is how it is going to be.

One could also conclude from this report that the split between the "two societies" will continue to widen and the antagonism between them will inevitably sharpen and deepen.

Such ideas feed the misconception that racism is an inherent, inborn characteristic of people. They feed a pessimistic view that nothing can be done about racism, and even question whether anything should be done to fight it. They feed the dangerous idea that it is all right for white Americans to live with racial prejudice and support racist practices because that is how it is in two separate societies.

The "two societies" concept covers up the reality of a two-class society—the class of exploiters that is mainly white, and the class of the exploited that is Black, white, Chicano, Puerto Rican, Native American Indian and other racially and nationally oppressed minorities.

It covers up the real nature of class exploitation, an exploitation motivated solely by a drive for maximum profits for the richest corporate owners in our capitalist society.

It covers up the basic fact that racism is an integral part of and an instrument of the same system of exploitation, a tool used in the drive for corporate superprofits.

It covers up the fact that the roots of racism are imbedded in the system of capitalist exploitation and that the patron promoter of racism is the capitalist class.

Every time one thinks Ronald Reagan has told the biggest lie of his career, he opens his mouth again and outdoes himself.

This time he began his second term by accusing Black leaders of pushing the "two societies concept." He said:

> Some Black leaders in this cause are actually striving to build, for whatever reason, two Americas, a Black America and a white America. There's a tendency to keep the people stirred up, as if the cause still exists.

How treacherous and diabolical!

The material in this book approaches the struggle against racism from the very opposite direction. We believe the struggle against racism is a winning struggle.

We start from the understanding that racism is the most serious ideological pollutant in our land. Racism is not only an offense to human dignity, it is a sophisticated ideological and psychological instrument for making superprofits.

Racism is a special Big Business tool for preventing the unity of the working class and the unity of people in struggles against state monopoly capitalism.

Our Party joins with all people who are against racism because it is morally wrong, because it is unjust, a crime and a disease; because it is an evil concoction that has no basis in fact. Racism is social backwardness based on prejudice, bigotry and ignorance.

All these are important reasons to fight racism. But there is more to racism. We study and expose its very roots. We place racism into a historical framework. We see its relationship to all struggles of life. We view it as a part of the system of exploitation. We see the struggle against racism as special, important on its own merits.

But we also see its relation to the class struggle.

If civil rights leaders and the civil rights movement had accepted the "two societies" concept, or accepted the idea that racism is an inherent characteristic of all white people, or that racism is inevitable, there would have been no civil rights movements nor any advances in the fight against racism and discrimination.

The material in this book is mainly directed to people in our country who are influenced by racism. Much of it is focused on the working class.

The material argues the point that racism is not only wrong morally, that it is based on ignorance, but that it is against the self-interests of all workers and working people. To the extent white workers are influenced by racism, to that extent the rich get richer and the poor get poorer.

In an introduction to a Communist Party convention resolution, Dr. James E. Jackson, member of the Central Committee and Political Bureau, wrote:

> U.S. racism in doctrine and practice is a capitalist concoction compounded of prejudice and ignorance and was first administered on a mass scale to overcome the resistance to the introduction and maintenance of slavery.
>
> Slavery in the United States was a labor system based upon the capture and bondage of human beings from Africa, their shipment, sale and subsequent employment in the economy as human machines, work animals, sold and resold as chattel commodities on the capitalist market. The apologists of the slave merchants and cotton capitalists shamelessly developed the doctrine of the inherent supremacy of people of white skin and the inherited inferiority of people of black skin.
>
> Despite the terrible torture that the horrible hypnotic of racism has caused the nation—including the four years of Civil War—the monopolists still use this ideological rot to promote race conflict between the exploited and convert it into profit. (*The Afro-American Struggle*, 1979.)

Old capitalist Russia, ruled by the reactionary czars, was known as "the prisonhouse of nations." V.I. Lenin, the leader and architect of the socialist revolution that transferred political power from the feudal-capitalist class to the working class, also became the theoretical leader in the smashing of the demonic social, political and cultural prison in which the oppressed nations and nationalities were imprisoned.

The socialist revolution in Russia in 1917 freed more than 100 oppressed nationalities. For 67 years the Soviet Union has pursued policies of affirmative action, policies of equality, policies that have politically and economically raised all the nationalities to the level of the most advanced. The Leninist policy on the nationalities question has been proven correct, both in theory and in practice.

The policy and the practice in the Soviet Union rests on a principled and firm position against racism, chauvinism and anti-Semitism. In the "prisonhouse of nations" these ideological and political currents were extreme and violent, cresting in pogroms. The elimination of inequalities and ending ideological expressions of bigotry and ignorance in the Soviet Union must be seen as one of the extraordinary achievements, one of the great steps forward for humanity. It is proof that racism is not inherent, that it can be eliminated.

The Soviet experience provides invaluable lessons for all who support and are active in the struggle against racism.

In Lenin's words:

> The workers of the whole world are building up their internationalist culture, which champions of freedom and the enemies of oppression have long been preparing.
>
> To the old world, the world of national oppression, national bickering, and national isolation, the workers counterpose a new world, a world of the unity of the working people of all nations, a world in which there is no place for any privileges, or for the slightest degree of oppression of man by man.
>
> The national question must be clearly considered and solved by all class conscious workers.

No privilege for any nation or any one language! Not even the slightest degree of oppression, or the slightest injustice in respect of a national minority—such are the principles of working-class democracy. The capitalists and landowners want at all cost to keep the workers of different nations apart, while the powers that be live splendidly together as shareholders in profitable concerns involving millions. Class conscious workers stand for full unity among workers of all nations in every educational, trade union, political and workers' organizations. (V. I. Lenin, *Collected Works*, Vol. XIX, p. 92.)

It is one thing to understand the role of national pride, or the role of nationalism in the struggle for independence and freedom. It is quite another matter when we are discussing the need for a struggle for working-class ideology.

Lenin stated it very well:

Marxism can not be reconciled with nationalism, be it even of the "most just," "purest," most refined and civilized brand. In place of all forms of nationalism Marxism advances internationalism, the amalgamation of all nations in the higher unity, a unity that is growing before our eyes . . . The principle of nationality is historically inevitable in bourgeois society, and taking this society into account, the Marxists recognize the historical legitimacy of national movements. But to prevent this recognition from becoming an apologia of nationalism, it must be strictly limited to what is progressive in such movements in order that this recognition may not lead to bourgeois ideology obscuring proletarian consciousness. (*Collected Works*, Vol. XX, p. 34.)

Unless this is freely recognized and unless there is a constant fight for the dominance of the ideology of working-class internationalism, it can all too easily get out of hand. When it does, narrow nationalism replaces the working-class ideology of internationalism.

What both Marx and Lenin were dealing with is the privotal placement of the class struggle as a reflection of the main contradiction between the classes of exploiter and exploited. They were not placing the importance of one in opposition to the other, but rather placing them in dialecical interrelationship. Lenin concluded:

> In our times, the proletariat alone upholds the real freedom of na-
> tions and the unity of workers of all nations. (*Collected Works*, Vol.
> XIX, pp. 91-92.)

Discussing the question as it relates to the United States, especially the pivotal question of unity between Black and white workers in the class struggle, Henry Winston argues in his book *Class, Race and Black Liberation* against any notion that white workers don't have a stake in fighting racism.

He takes the position that,

> Of course, U.S. capitalism through all stages of development
> has perpetuated inequality between Black and white masses. But
> in order to do so it has had to perpetuate the illusion, from slavery
> to the present, that the white exploited have a "material stake" in
> Black oppression. And the survivals of racist "advantages"—orig-
> inating in the slave system—still lend credibility to the racist-fos-
> tered illusion that white workers on the assembly lines and in the
> unemployed lines have a "material stake" in the different degree
> to which monopoly exploits them as compared to Black workers.
>
> In reality, white as well as Black workers have a "material
> stake" in eradicating racism. To assert that white workers have a
> "material stake" in racism is to profoundly exaggerate monopo-
> ly's ability to sustain this illusion—particularly in the face of the
> deepening general crisis of capitalism. Such a concept is based on
> an overestimation of the strength of imperialism, and conse-
> quently an underestimation—in fact, a denial—of the intensifying
> contradiction between monopoly and the working class as a
> whole—Black, white, Chicano, Puerto Rican, Asian and Native
> American Indian. (P. 104.)

Incorporating this critical argument for Black-white unity and projecting the Communist Party's position on the struggle against racism in the United States, the Resolution on Afro-American Liberation adopted by the 22nd National Convention of the CPUSA states:

As the nation as a whole is class stratified, just so the Black component has an internal class structure. But the most important thing about the class stratification of the American Black people is its overwhelming working-class composition.

The principal class content of the Black people, therefore, is that reflecting its dominant class component—the working class. In the long run, it will be the requirements, needs, aspirations and ultimately the leadership of personalities from the working-class stratum of this people that will become reflected in the program, goals, strategy and tactics of the freedom movement.

Black workers know from their place in the production relations that it is not the white man in general who profits from the racist degradation and added economic exploitation to which the Black worker is subjected; it is the white capitalist who is the common exploiter of both Black and white workers.

The working-class influence will express itself in emphasis on building the movement on the basis of broad popular unity to maximum strength, in gaining working-class allies from among the white majority; in giving a democratic structure to its concert of leadership; in elaborating a strategy—a longer-range plan and associated tactics which further the realization of the basic goal and objectives. The influence of the working class upon policy and leadership makes for planned struggles carried out in a well organized and militant manner. Under its influence the movement reacts to spontaneous developments but it does not base its course upon them.

The capitalist class influence within and upon the Black people's movement reflects itself as policy that avoids struggle and appeal to the masses; invites compromise without struggle and accommodation to the conditions that obtain. It often projects the prejudices and hatred of the big capitalists into the movement, especially in opposition to alliance with white workers.

The influence of the non-working-class forces on the direction of the movement may cause sections of it to raise slogans for separation and national exclusiveness. These would have the effect of isolating the Black people's freedom cause and divorcing it from its natural allies in associated antimonopoly, anti-imperialist struggle.

The dynamic of the freedom struggle discloses more and more the fundamental unwillingness and incapacity of the monopolists to affect the kind of radical reforms which are required to secure a fair and equal level of civil and social equality, political democracy, material well-being and economic and cultural opportunity for the Black masses. State monopoly capitalism has no will to solve the problems of Black oppression; indeed it is the capitalist class which is the source of the problem.

The nation which has developed in the United States is a complex community of peoples drawn from a wide range of ethnic and racial types from many countries and all continents. This U.S. American nation can be likened to a national family of distinctive peoples who are more or less identified by the dominant traits of their respective earlier national origins. Identity with the nation is decisively determined by the economic values added to the wealth of its natural resources in the furtherance of its development. By this test no component element of the population has more claim on membership in the U.S. nation than Black Americans who have contributed their brawn and brains for the development of the economy of the nation, as slaves and as free persons.

The U.S. nation was reared in the cradle of the marketplace under the iron-fisted dictatorship of the class which has grown powerful from exploiting the value-creating labor of the working masses. The capitalist class always gave precedence to its own interest over that of the nation as a whole. It sacrificed the even and rounded development of the nation to its special class interests, whereas the true interests of the nation call for securing equality of status for every people, for each of its nationality component.

Under the hegemony of the capitalist class, the nationality composition of the nation was shaped on the basis of the racist concepts of superior and inferior peoples, on the foundation of white supremacy, on the imposition of discriminatory barriers against the Black people as well as the Chicano, Puerto Rican, Native American Indian and Asian minority peoples.

Progressive development of the nation requires that each of its component peoples enjoy full equality of rights and genuine democratic opportunity for participation with all others in determining the affairs of the nation. The rise of the American nation of the U.S. was marked by the near genocide of the Native American Indian and the brutally enforced exclusion of other peoples, most particularly of Black people, but also of the Chicano, Puerto Rican and Asian minorities.

The interests of the monopolist ruling class clash with the needs of the nation. The security and future development of this nation require the leadership of another class; that class which is not parasitic, but the most productive class of the nation—the working class. All future progress of the nation is related to the outcome of the struggle of the working class to bring about a timely replacement of the monopolists' class from the leadership of the nation. The cause of the nation, all the unrealized democratic and progressive needs and expectations which the respective peoples of the nation sought and fought for, become now the duty and responsibility of the working class to champion and to lead the nation in all and each of its component parts to victorious fulfillment.

The decisive social force objectively allied to the cause of Black liberation is the working class. It is bound by historical necessity to struggle ceaselessly for its own class emancipation from exploitation and ruination, to fight the ruling class of monopoly capitalism, the system that is the common foe, the system responsible for the racist oppression of Black Americans, as well as of the Chicano, the Native American Indian, the Puerto Rican, Asian and other oppressed minorities in the United States.

Unity and alliance with the working class—which is multiracial and multinational—is the vital link that must be welded by each people in struggle for freedom. Additionally, each of the oppressed nationalities should strive to strengthen fraternal ties with one another in the course of struggle against the common monopolist foe and overcome the design of the oppressor to foster competitive, antagonistic relations among minority peoples.

The violated civil rights of the victims of racism can not be simply equated to the common class exploitation and impoverishment of all workers. Racist oppression is an additional dimension of extra exploitation and double deprivation which state monopoly capitalism imposes upon Black people as a special mechanism in the total exploitative system. (Detroit, 1979.)

The thoughts in this book are based on and reflect the collective thoughts of our Party, the Communist Party, USA. It is clear that as a struggle develops, as more experience is gathered, concepts, formulations and expressions also go through a process of change. So it is with this book.

Thus, a conscious effort was made to make very few changes in the original articles and pamphlets. This provides the reader with not only an idea of how we reacted to events, but also an idea of the events themselves.

Communists have not only reflected the struggle and movements. We have had an influence both on those who are active in the struggle against racism and also on those who are influenced by racism. We have attempted to focus our efforts in the direction of convincing and winning those who are influenced by racism.

In this area of the struggle our Party makes a unique and decisive contribution. We have this focus because we are convinced that although under capitalism it is not possible to eliminate racism, it is possible to change how working people see and understand it; it is possible to blunt it and, yes, it is possible to eliminate it in the thought patterns of ever increasing numbers of people.

Most white Americans today consider themselves believers in equality and justice. They believe racism is wrong and injust, if not an evil that must be rooted out of our society. This atmosphere expedites the struggle against racism and discrimination.

This does not mean that they are no longer influenced by racism. It means the possibilities exist to reach and influence especially white workers to see their own self-interest in joining the active struggle against this poison.

Today, objective conditions also exist for making big strides in the struggle.

This book is dedicated to advancing that goal.   □

1

THE MOST DANGEROUS POLLUTANT

1971

The Nation's Most
Dangerous Pollutant

Just as we can not get away from breathing polluted air or drinking contaminated water, so we can not escape our polluted and contaminated ideological surroundings.

There are no thought-proof ideological shields or filters that can screen out pollutants and make it possible for us to inhale only clean ideological air—air that is not contaminated.

The ideological pollutants of the enemy are always present, and they penetrate wherever there is an opening. It is a fact of life that there is always some seepage of polluted ideology among people in our society and we can not isolate ourselves from them. In fact, we should not try. Such attempts are self-deceiving and self-defeating. We work with people who are genuinely influenced by the ideological currents of the enemy.

The way to struggle against wrong ideas is not to build walls between us and the masses or between us and the ideological currents which influence all honest people. In fact, the germs of enemy ideology multiply and grow in the stale and stagnant atmosphere resulting from isolation. An ideological struggle in isolation results in empty rhetoric, and enemy ideology is immune to empty rhetoric. Instead of walls of separation, we must build higher levels of resistance and immunity to enemy ideology.

But, as is the case with all resistance based on immunity, ideological immunity wears off. The level of resistance diminishes and the seepage increases. Because of this, there is always the danger of penetration—in fact, there is penetration. And so, as is the case of biological immunity, ideological immunity needs periodic booster shots.

The booster shots in ideology are constant struggle, endless vigilance, continuous criticism and self-criticism. It is a natural, necessary and integral part of the everyday struggle against capitalism. The struggle against the influence of enemy ideology within our own ranks is an inseparable element in the struggle against enemy ideology in general.

Today's discussion is intended to serve as the beginning of a series of booster shots to raise the immunity and the resistance level against the penetration and seepage of the influence of white chauvinism in the Left and within our Party. The level of penetration of any enemy ideological current is directly related to the struggle against it. There are no permanent lifetime shields.

White chauvinism remains the most persistent and widespread poisonous ideological current influencing the thinking of white masses. I use the word "remains" because, while it is the most persistent, we should not overlook the gains, though small, that have been made in the struggle against it. But it remains the deadly trigger within U.S. imperialist ideology. It adds a very deadly component to this ideology. It is the moving spirit and the ugliest segment of U.S. great-power chauvinism. It is the main obstacle to Black-white unity.

On the one hand, it is the main obstacle on the path to working-class unity, and therefore an obstacle to working-class victories. On the other hand, it is the main unifying element within the reactionary ultra-Right and fascist movements. What anti-Semitism was for German fascism, white chauvinism is for fascist movements within the United States. It is a most critical ingredient within all antidemocratic movements. It is the ideological fog behind which capitalism prepares its forces for fascism.

But above all, white chauvinism is the ideological pollutant that makes it possible for capitalism to sustain and continue the system of special oppression and exploitation of 25 million Black Americans. It is a most effective instrument of monopoly capital for extracting superprofits.

White chauvinism is the most formidable ideological roadblock to social progress in general, and to the transition to socialism. That, after all, is the reason why the ruling class so desperately clings to it and promotes it in every possible way.

Because of this, the struggle against racism, against white chauvinism, is the most crucial of all ideological questions for us. Because of its deep roots, the struggle against it is in may ways the most difficult of all tasks. Because it is the most persistent, our struggle against it must be the most persistent.

Before going into some of the problems in this struggle, permit me to digress for a moment to some other areas where there is seepage of enemy ideology. These are also areas where we must find time to administer some booster shots, though we can not do so at this meeting. However, today's discussion is very much related to the struggle on these other fronts because influences of white chauvinism feed weaknesses in the other areas, and because without a more effective and more consistent struggle against the penetration of white chauvinism, we simply can not effectively fight the other ideological currents and influences. The struggle against white chauvinism is the most crucial of all these struggles. Within these ideological currents white chauvinism is the catalytic agent. Therefore, let me just mention some of the other areas.

With the growth of U.S. imperialism, there has been a steady growth of U.S. great-power chauvinism. To one degree or another, this current affects most sections of our people. Is this not one of the putrid smells that permeates the events surrounding the My Lai massacre,[1] including the so-called trials? Large numbers of our people reject these influences.

But to one degree or another, millions are affected by them. The influence of great-power chauvinism dilutes the reaction of our people to the brutality of the massive bombings in Indochina. It is the main obstacle to the growth of anti-imperialism. In our emphasis on the economic and political side effects, we must never, even for a moment, forget the main thing: that U.S. forces are killing millions of Vietnamese men, women and children. White chauvinism is a big factor in great-power chauvinism.

The events in the Middle East[2] have set off new waves of both anti-Semitism and Jewish bourgeois nationalism in the United States. We must give much more attention to the struggle against anti-Semitism, and we are not giving the necessary leadership in the struggle against Jewish bourgeois nationalism. This is a reactionary current that has recently engulfed large sectors of the Jewish masses. It has seriously infected the Jewish Left. There are some expressions of it in our Party. White chauvinism is an additional factor in the chauvinist attitudes towards the Arab people.

The rise of the militant Black liberation movement has been accompanied by a rise of racial and national pride and consciousness. There is a new consciousness of history and culture. But there is also a rise of nationalism that feeds on the national pride. Again, we are not dealing with these problems.

There are problems in one band of the ideological spectrum. There is seepage in other bands as well. There is constant pressure from anti-Communism. It is not widely understood that there can be no anti-Soviet anti-imperialism.

However, this discussion will be pinpointed on white chauvinism and the struggle against racism as it relates to the struggle for Afro-American equality. This, of course, should not in any way be interpreted as a downgrading of the struggle against racism as it affects other sectors.

Closely related is the chauvinism directed against Chicanos, Puerto Ricans and Indian Americans. In each case there are special features. Each struggle needs special treatment. But the root of the question is the racism against 25 million Black Americans.

The interrelationship of the struggles must be seen within that basic context. Unquestionably, the lessons of our struggles and our discussions on white chauvinism as it relates to Black America must serve to raise the level of the struggle against chauvinism as it is related to the struggle of the other oppressed minorities.

The main danger is white chauvinism. Therefore, the main focus, the main emphasis, the sharp edge of the ideological struggle must be directed against racism in general.

For an effective struggle against white chauvinism, we must establish or, in some cases re-establish, some guidelines.

First, we must reject all slanders that our Party is a racist organization. We must reject the slander that the Communist Party is a white people's party. We must reject them publicly. They are falsehoods. We can not accept such language in silence. When faced with such slanders, silence on our part is itself opportunism.

We must also reject as untrue the implication that we are trailing other organizations in the struggle against white chauvinism, either within the Party or within the mass movements. Our Party's fundamental answer has different ideological roots from the answers of organizations on the Left which accept Black-white unity on the basis of some momentary factors. A few years ago, many thought we were trailing behind some of the Left groups. But when these met the hard realities of struggle, it was obvious that their concepts were surface manifestations and because of this their ideological seams began to come apart. The SDS theory of Blacks and whites going their own separate ways was a capitulation to racism. The emphasis of Progressive Labor and the Trotskyites on what they called a purely "class approach" turned into a fig leaf hiding white chauvinism.[3] Their denial of the racial and national character of oppression was a diversion from the struggle against racism.

We welcome and encourage all steps and all movements to eliminate the influence of chauvinism. But we must be able to differentiate between that which is real and that which is but a petty-bourgeois veneer covering up the influence of white chauvinism. We are not interested in covering up. We are not interested in false images. We are not interested in having a good record on paper. Our fundamental interest is in the elimination of the ideological pollution of chauvinism in the ranks of white Americans and the elimination of the seepage into our Party. To us the struggle against racism and chauvinism is rooted in the very fabric of our political, theoretical and philosophical makeup.

We have weaknesses. But in the struggle against racism in general, in the struggle for Black equality, in the struggle for Black-white unity, in the struggle against white chauvinism, our Party has stood and continues to stand far in advance of any organization on the Left. With all of our weaknesses, we are a vanguard organization in this struggle. With all of our weaknesses, we are the most formidable foe of racism. It is on this truthful estimate of our Party that we can base the most effective struggle against the weaknesses that do exist. A distortion of this truth can itself become an open obstacle to the elimination of these weaknesses. We must truthfully say what our weaknesses are without covering up, but also without exaggeration or slander.

Because of our advanced position, masses in general and Black Americans in particular rightly expect more from our Party than from any other organization. They rightly expect higher standards from us. Weaknesses that would go unnoticed in other organizations must be challenged as impermissible and dealt with as serious problems within our Party.

We have no racists or white chauvinists within our Party. In the first place, they would not join it. And in the second place, if discovered, they would be summarily expelled. Of course, we can not say that of some hidden enemy agents. We would be nave to assume that the enemy has not sent in agents who are specially trained to use every possible weakness on the ideological front. This, in fact, is their central concentration. They exaggerate weaknesses. They spread false rumors. They manufacture incidents. Their line of tactics is to create an image of our Party as being made up of white chauvinists and Uncle Toms. We must not play their game. But silence about our weaknesses or about expressions of chauvinism in the Party is also playing their game. Our answer must not be silence. Rather, it must be a critical but responsible examination of every such expression—a discussion that will result in higher standards and a firmer unity. An open, frank discussion takes the play away from the enemy.

The enemy agents not only take full advantage of weaknesses within the Party. They are an active ideological force, injecting ideological germs into the ranks of the Left and the Party. This is their central task today. It follows that we must give greater attention to ideological questions in general, but especially to the struggle against the seepage of white chauvinism. Influences of chauvinism are fertile soil for enemy agents.

As we said, we can not fight racism by trying to isolate ourselves from the masses who are influenced by racism. By the same token, we can not fight against its penetration into the ranks of the Party by making it an internal matter. We can not win the fight if we turn inward.

The struggle against racism is an integral part of the class struggle and of the struggle for social progress generally. It must be waged as a part of these struggles. The class struggle is not an inner-Party struggle. When we make it an inner-Party affair it means we are not fighting racism among the masses.

The struggle against racism, like all ideological struggles, must be concrete. It must be related to specific issues at each stage of the struggle. Without this it turns into empty rhetoric that actually hides the influences of racism.

The test in the struggle against racism is not in abstract rhetoric, not in the formulation of general demands. Even George Meany[4] does that. The test is carrying on concrete struggles on concrete issues. The test is winning these struggles. The test is our ability to convince white Americans, to mobilize them to end concrete practices that flow from the ideology of racism.

In a more general sense, the test is how effectively we are able to use these concrete struggles to destroy the ideological influence of racism among the masses and in building an immunity against its influence in our own minds. This is the yardstick. This is the test that we must apply to the work of every member of our Party.

The struggle for higher standards in the Party is in turn related to the new levels of struggle against racism in general. The problems in the Party are related to new levels of struggle against racism in general. The problems in the Party are related to new levels attained by the movements and struggles for equality.

These struggles are propelled by a deep determination not to accept either the status quo or tokenism in any area of human endeavor or relationships. It is a militant rejection of all old standards, values and priorities that are based on racism and inequality. These new standards and values have to do with Black-white relationships on all levels. In life, the struggle against the ideology of racism can not be separated from the struggle against its specific manifestations of discrimination and segregation. It can not be separated, it can not be postponed. This is the meaning of the struggle in specific areas.

In this sense there have been some changes in the trade unions. As yet they move reluctantly and only as a result of heavy pressure. There has been some progress in the ranks of the organized Left, in the student movement, in the peace movement. But they also are not on the level that is demanded by the realities of this day. Very often the struggle against racism gets sidetracked. In their own way the weaknesses in our Party are also related to this same challenge, and we must say honestly that our standards of struggle also do not meet the challenge of the moment.

There are many very important factors that compel us to take a fresh and deeper look at the ideological seepage of chauvinism into our ranks.

We are in the initial stages of a very important Party-building breakthrough. This breakthrough is the result of experiences of struggle. Tens of thousands have experienced struggle. They have experimented with different theoretical, organizational and tactical concepts. They have drawn some lessons. In significant numbers, they are now knocking at the doors of the Party. We have made some significant beginnings in the recruitment of Black youth into the Party. Others are members of study groups, studying Marxism-Leninism, studying the program and policies of our Party. These young people are the very best of the activists. They are coming into the Party as activists from the very struggles and movements that are now demanding new standards in all relationships. They are coming into the Party partly because of our higher standards in the struggle against racism. They are coming in because of our theoretical, political and tactical concepts.

But Communist standards of years back are not high enough for today. These young people are coming in expecting Communist standards that meet the level of the movements and struggles of the '70s.

To be able to recruit and to hold these Black youth in our Party is very much a part of our discussion of the influences of white chauvinism in our ranks.

We also have many new white youth coming into the Party. They, too, are the best activists, but they also need the Party's ideological concepts. It is necessary quickly to raise their understanding of racism. It is necessary to raise their resistance and immunity to this enemy ideology. Without such an ideological struggle, we can not hold these youth in the Party either. Many of them have considerable experience in the struggle against racism. Many are rejecting racism as a feature of the "old society."

Ideological weaknesses do not emerge from thin air. In the Party, they are not, as a rule, conscious or deliberate acceptance of enemy ideology. It is necessary for us to try to determine the causes of these weaknesses. Some of the weaknesses have roots in our history; others are reflections of current developments.

The decision of the Party to drop the slogan of the right of self-determination of a Black nation in the South was basically a correct decision. The old slogan did not reflect reality or the direction of developments. But hindsight now indicates that, while the change in policy was correct, we did not do enough to take care of the possible negative side effects of that change. We were not vigilant enough.

Among these side effects was the emergence of a somewhat mechanical conception of how the processes of integration would replace the struggle for self-determination of a nation in the South. To be sure, there were no such concepts in the Party's documents or position. But in the minds of many, the process of integration was seen as an evolutionary, peaceful development.

In this illusory framework, racism also became a vanishing ideological influence. This has been the position of white liberals for generations. It is the liberal reasoning behind tokenism. But in a fundamental sense, it is an excuse and a cover for living with racism.

The influence of this liberal position seeped into our Party. This resulted in a weakening of the struggle against racism. In this illusory context, the struggle against racism no longer has the same priority. In a world of peaceful integration accompanied by the evaporation of racist ideology there is no need for a special struggle against racism. This is part of the long-range seepage. It is based on an illusion. It does not see racism as an instrument of monopoly capitalism, an instrument of exploitation and superprofits. Such illusions arise from the concept that racism is an abstract moral and social issue unrelated to capitalist exploitation, therefore unrelated to struggle.

This seepage into our ranks resulted in a liberal attitude to influences of chauvinism. It influenced the Party to lower its guard. It resulted in complacency.

Our Party should have been forewarned about these possible side effects because we had had the experience of the opportunistic position, espoused by Browder,[5] that racism would disappear without struggle as a byproduct of overall social progress. With Browder, of course, all forms of struggle disappeared. The class struggle, the struggle against imperialism, the struggle against racism—all faded away, replaced by a classless society of love and tranquillity. Of course, as we know, the only thing that almost did disappear was the Communist Party.

In 1953, Comrade William Z. Foster[6] wrote an article entitled "Left Sectarianism in the Fight for Negro Rights and Against White Chauvinism" (*Political Affairs*, July 1953). Comrade Foster made a number of very important points. But the purpose of the article was to correct a specific, momentary one-sidedness in this struggle. Foster very correctly said: "In the fight for Negro rights, the main danger is white chauvinism and the main weakness is a failure to fight it." One must add, of course, that white chauvinism is a danger related to much more than the struggle for the rights of Afro-Americans.

Foster also said: "White chauvinism can not be fought as a thing in itself, by a separate campaign." This also remains a most important guideline. Then Comrade Foster added: "The Left sectarian tendency isolates the Party from the masses, makes a caricature of the fight against white chauvinism, considers white chauvinism as virtually ineradicable and proposes impossible disciplinary measures to combat it." This was intended to correct the specific one-sidedness that had developed.

This article was widely discussed in the Party. In a sense, it is the last real basic discussion that has been conducted in the Party on this question. But I think we can now say that because the Party again did not take measures to guarantee against wrong side effects, while Foster's article helped to correct a momentary one-sidedness, it became a factor in creating another one-sidedness. This is not so much a criticism of Foster's article. It is more a criticism of the Party for not guarding against or being vigilant enough against wrong side effects. This discussion became a factor creating a situation where the struggle against the influence of chauvinism was downgraded. This downgrading tended to create a vacuum. And as we know, wherever there is a vacuum, enemy class ideology penetrates, and thus the seepage increases.

There is one other inner factor that adds to the atmosphere of complacency. Because of our Party's history and record in the struggle against racism and the struggle against the influences of chauvinism, some have evidently concluded that we can rest and draw on that record forever, and therefore there is no special need to struggle against racism or its seepage.

This is wrong on every count. Ideology is not like stone, from which a piece can be permanently cut. It is more like sand: Only a constantly active counterforce can keep it from drifting and penetrating.

These are some of the longer-range influences in the Party creating weaknesses in the struggle against chauvinism. But there are more immediate factors that have their influences also. As a result of militant struggles, some victories have been won against specific practices resulting from racism. These include victories in the voter registration drive in the South, some headway in the struggle for political representation, some progress in some of the professions. These are not breakthroughs, but they are steps forward. In the total picture, they are still token. The latest government reports again show that the

Black community remains locked in the same bind, subjected to the same level of economic oppression, without any significant advancement. The income of Black families relative to that of white families is today on about the same level as it was 10-20 years ago.

Further, the present economic crisis has again exposed the true nature of racist oppression. The small gains made during the boom period have been totally wiped out in one industry and profession after another. When there is a general economic recession there is an economic depression in the Afro-American community.

It is not necessary to deny that some gains have been made. But the bigger error, an error of Right opportunism, is to overstate and to exaggerate these victories. This has been and is a strong tendency among liberals. It eases their conscience and provides an excuse for lessening their concern and their efforts. This was the excuse for the so-called liberal Moynihan's policy of "benign neglect."

This error of overstating victories in the economic, political and social arenas is compounded by transferring these illusions into the sphere of ideology. It leads to the opportunism of Browder. It leads to the notion that it is possible to de-escalate the struggle against racism.

Parallel to this position is the propaganda of the ultra-Right forces that "the Blacks are moving too fast and too far." But in the ranks of the liberals, this same thought is fed by the exaggerated statements of victories and gains. The ultra-Right condemns the gains. The liberals use them as an excuse for inaction. In the ranks of the Left and the Party, this seepage feeds complacency. It results in a low level of initiative.

There are many variations of this attitude on the Left. One that is widely accepted is: "Let the Black people carry on the struggle against racism. We will stand on the sidelines, or carry on struggle in other areas, and give whatever help we can." This concept of "let the Black people wage the struggle" is carried further in the advocacy of "armed struggle"—of course, by the Black people.

We live in a racist environment. As a Party, we can not isolate ourselves from it. In a capitalist society, racism is not only present, it is constantly in the process of production. Complacency, or a letup in the struggle against the influence of chauvinism, itself turns into chauvinism. Without a struggle, the ideological environment tends to engulf everything.

When we criticize wrong conclusions or wrong side effects in the history and record of our Party, we must not, of course, downgrade the real contributions our Party has made. To do that would downgrade the vanguard role not only of our Party, but also of our science, Marxism-Leninism. We need not say, as the generally good outline of the YWLL[7] on the struggle against chauvinism said: "We have no historical experience of our own to draw on for an answer to this question." Experience for a Marxist-Leninist youth organization did not start with the birth of the YWLL. That is an unnecessary and wrong downgrading of the previous contributions of our Party and of Marxism-Leninism. The YWLL does in fact have a very rich history to draw on.

There is an underlying theme running through most of these weaknesses—that racism is not related to exploitation and superprofits. It is a failure to relate racism to capitalism, and, therefore, to the class struggle. Racism is viewed as an abstract phenomenon of ideas and influences, as the product of a classless evil environment. Therefore, it becomes a subject for sermons and preachments, rather than a problem that must be dealt with in the context of struggle. This leads to yet another serious weakness. It leads to a sense of hopelessness. And hopelessness leads to inactivity—to passivity and an opportunistic accommodation to racism.

This, in part, is what has led petty-bourgeois radical groups to an accommodation with racism. In essence they say: "We are not racists. We understand the need for Black-white unity. But the situation is hopeless. It is impossible to convince white masses. So we will accept it. We will have to live with it and accommodate ourselves to it. We will have separate organizations now, with the thought that come socialism we will get together." This is a "Left" cover for chauvinism. But their acceptance of racism is also related to their rejection of the class struggle as the foundation for all progress. They take a no-struggle attitude toward racism for the same reason that they move into anarchistic channels—rejection of the class struggle. Any movement that does not relate to the class struggle is on a deadend course. Any movement that does not see racism as an instrument of exploitation, and therefore fails to see the fight against it in relation to the struggle against class exploitation, will end up in a pessimistic, opportunistic accommodation to racism.

No one in the United States can take a second step without encountering the iron heel of monopoly capitalism. The class struggle is the expression of this central, all-dominating contradiction in our lives. All struggle for social progress revolves around this contradiction. The main force that can resolve it is the working class. This is the path that is open—the only option that is open. To reject this path is to reject the only option available. Such rejection will lead only to dead-end situations—to hopelessness, passivity.

In our Party this results in living with the practice of racism. In a shop, school, neighborhood, trade union or other mass organization, it results in a low level of initiative. It results in not talking to white shopmates, coworkers or friends against racism. In a shop, if one can not relate it to profits and superprofits, it will remain an abstract moral issue. To be sure, it is a moral issue. But it is also related to the struggle for social progress.

Some comrades hide their inactivity by saying, "It's no use, workers are all racists." When placed in such sweeping terms this is a cover for opportunism, for inaction generally, and a convenient reason for accommodating oneself to racism in particular. Such a sweeping characterization is not true, and it is not true for all time. This "you can't do anything" excuse must be replaced by an attitude that says, in effect, that because all workers are exploited, because racism is a special instrument of exploitation, and because white workers are influenced by racism, it is necessary for us to take certain concrete steps. These steps must relate to specific problems of the class struggle, of racist oppression in a specific shop at a specific moment. Workers must be made to see the relationship between class exploitation and the special system of superexploitation based on racism.

To say that struggle against racism must be related to issues involving the self-interest of workers is in a general sense correct. But that, of course, is not the whole story. A white worker who gets some immediate advantage because a Black worker is discriminated against may see it from the viewpoint of his individual self-interest. We have to be able to show the shortsightedness of such a viewpoint. We must be able to show that it is against the best interest of the class as a whole, and therefore against the best interest of each member of that class. We must be able to show such a worker that he can not separate himself from his class or his class interests. We must be able to show him that such actions are in the interests only of the capitalist class. In accepting the momentary advantage he becomes an instrument for producing superprofits for the employer.

One of the new features of the class struggle of this moment of history is the militant role of Black workers. It is adding a tower of strength to the working class as a whole. For Communists not to see this is to miss a most important opportunity to add a new qualitative element strengthening the working class as a whole. This is the historic significance of the rise of the Black rank-and-file caucus movement in basic industries. These caucuses must be seen both in terms of how they strengthen the entire working class and how they add a significant element to the Black liberation movement. They are an important link between the working class and the Black community. It is of the greatest significance that the Black caucuses have not moved towards splitting the working class. Instead, they are a factor for unity on a higher plane.

In a very basic sense, the weaknesses in the struggle against racism and against influences of chauvinism within the Party are closely related to the overall influences of Right opportunism in the working class and in the Party. An accommodation to enemy ideology is opportunism. In most cases, it is Right opportunism. Those who can not see the working class as the major force in the struggle for social progress can not see the possibilities of the struggle against racism either. This leads to passivity and opportunism generally, and particularly in the struggle against racism. Right opportunism is a major obstacle in the struggle against racism. And racism in turn influences and, in a sense, feeds Right opportunism. Therefore, the two struggles can not be separated. The struggle against racism leads to a struggle against opportunism. The struggle against opportunism clears the board for a struggle against racism. Wherever there is opportunism there is bound to be racism—and wherever there is racism there is opportunism.

When we emphasize this basic relationship between the class struggle and the struggle against racial and national oppression, this has nothing in common with the Progressive Labor and Trotskyite positions of narrowing everything down to what they call "the class position." Their so-called "class position" is a fig leaf to cover up their accommodation to racism. With their "class position" they deny the racial and national character of the system of special Black oppression and exploitation. We not only recognize the special national and racial nature of this oppression, but we raise it to top priority by demonstrating its relationship to the class struggle and to capitalist exploitation. In reality the PL-Trotskyite position is a Right opportunist accommodation to racism, covered by a "Left" fig leaf.

Our position gives us confidence in the possibility of victories against racism. Because we have confidence in the working class, we have confidence in being able to win against racism. Our confidence in the working class is not fatalistic or romantic. It is determined by our basic understanding of the laws and processes of capitalism. The developing working-class consciousness is, therefore, the ideological framework for plowing under all ideological currents designed to support every type of exploitation and oppression.

The sharpening of class contradictions creates objective propellants that stimulate the development of class consciousness. This consciousness, based on real class interests, tends to overcome all alien class ideological influences. Class consciousness leads to a higher level of social consciousness, it leads to higher moral concepts. These higher levels of consciousness are all involved in the struggle against racism. There is a dialectical interchange of cause and effect between the struggle against racism and the rise of class consciousness. Class consciousness has a built-in limitation unless it takes up the struggle against racism. This is the meaning of Karl Marx's profound thought that "Labor in a white skin can not be free as long as labor in a black skin is branded." The other side of the truth is that the struggle against racism has a built-in limitation if it is not related to struggles that give rise to class consciousness.

Because we understand the relationship between the class struggle and the struggle against racism, we also understand the crucial importance of the struggle against racism in the ranks of white workers. Racism is an important ideological current that diverts white workers from the path of class consciousness. In the ranks of the people as a whole, it is the poison that diverts them from the path of anti-imperialist consciousness. The struggle against racism is, therefore, crucial for the development both of working-class consciousness and anti-imperialist consciousness. For the United States, racism is a most formidable obstacle to socialist consciousness.

We must clearly see the relationship between these ideological currents. There can not be racist working-class consciousness. There can only be class conscious workers who may be influenced by chauvinism. Only capitalist class consciousness and racism mix. We can not have racist anti-imperialist consciousness. Very quickly, they will clash. We do have anti-imperialists who suffer from chauvinist influences. And without antiracist consciousness, we can not have working-class unity or anti-imperialist unity. And without such unity, there can be no real social progress. There can not be a successful long-range struggle for democracy if it does not take on the struggle against the racist ideology of the antidemocratic forces. There can not be an antimonopoly coalition that does not take on the racist ideology and practice of monopoly capitalism.

Thus, the struggle against racism is inextricably linked with the most basic processes of the class struggle, the struggle for social progress and the struggle for socialism. The fight against the influences of chauvinism in the Party is therefore a struggle to remove every possible obstacle that in any way hinders our Party from playing its full role in the fight against racism, against reaction, against imperialism and in the battle for socialism. The struggle against these influences in the Party is the struggle to make it possible for the Party fully to play its vanguard role in this revolutionary and explosive period of history. The working class can not play its strategic revolutionary role without a struggle against racism.

In our Party, influences of chauvinism do not show up as resolutions or speeches. It would be easier to deal with that kind of weakness. The appearance is more indirect and subtle. In our Party, it results more from unconscious influence than from conscious chauvinism. In our Party, it appears as insensitivity, as sickening paternalism, as an inability to deal with problems related to the struggle. It appears as a lack of initiative and a lack of continuity in the struggle against racism. It appears as silence, omissions, rather than overt acts of chauvinism. It appears as passivity.

Its most visible results are that our Party is not fully mobilized, that it is not hitting on all cylinders in the struggle against racism, both as ideology and practice. We simply are not doing nearly enough in any of these areas.

There is a new upsurge in the class struggle. The rise of the rank-and-file movement in the trade unions is a reflection of it. This moment presents great new possibilities in the struggle against racism. The 1930s were such a moment. The class struggle at that time resulted in a rank-and-file push for militant industrial unions. The overall class issues of that day were related to the struggle to break down the bars against the hiring of Black workers. With the direct participation of our Party, the struggle resulted not only in militant industrial unions, in union victories against the large monopolies, but also in victories against the corporations' practices of discriminatory hiring. These resulted in a new level of Black-white unity in general, and particularly in a new level of Black-white working-class unity.

We are at one of those historic moments again. The working class faces new problems because of new levels of exploitation. If the moment is to result in a victory for the class, if it is to result in a new level of class unity and a new level of class consciousness, then the present struggle and the overall class issues must include concrete actions and demands directed toward ending all forms of racism and tokenism in the upgrading of Black workers to skilled jobs. It must include a struggle for safeguards against their being the first to be fired. This new level of class unity will be reached only if the trade unions themselves put an end to tokenism in electing Black workers to their leadership and policy-making bodies.

In this sense, to raise the struggle against racism to a new level is bound up with and a crucial feature of the efforts to raise the class struggle and class consciousness to a new level. It is clear that this is a struggle against Right opportunism. We are the only force that can give this kind of leadership.

I use this example because it presents the greatest potential, because in this area there are developments of the greatest significance. I use it because new levels of Black-white working-class unity are being achieved and because we are an important factor in these developments. I use it because, in spite of the good work, there are serious weaknesses. I use it because the way in which this problem is handled will go a long way in determining where and how far the historic rank-and-file movement is going. How well we fight against the influences of chauvinism in our ranks is measured by how we combine struggles against racism with issues that give rise to this rank-and-file movement.

The Free Angela Davis movement[8] has emerged as one of the truly great people's movements. It has become symbolic of all the issues involved in the struggle against racism, including its interrelationship with the struggle against anti-Communism. In general, our Party has shown great initiative and boldness. The movement would not have emerged on the present scale without our Party's contributions. But the movement has also exposed some serious weaknesses that can be attributed only to influences of chauvinism. Not all sections of the Party have shown an understanding of the significance of this case. Here also there are altogether too many hesitations—hesitations that can be explained only on the basis of ideological seepage.

Some who are close to the Party and who are active in the struggle for democratic rights have said: "We must be cautious about getting into the struggle to free Angela Davis." This advice is given in private conversations. Instead of being initiators, the people who give it become obstacles to the development of a mass movement. Is not such "cautiousness" an expression of chauvinism? It is chauvinism and Right opportunism. It is a capitulation to racism, coupled with opportunistic capitulation to anti-Communism.

In some cases, happily not too many, comrades have said: "How do we know Angela Davis is not guilty?" Behind the question lurks chauvinism. Chauvinism narrows one's vision. In that narrow field of vision, the Angela Davis case does not emerge as an integral part and dramatic symbol of 300 years of struggle against the most brutal and inhuman racist oppression. Racism and the racist system do not appear as the real villains. The slums and the faces of hungry children, the rat-infested houses, the degrading insults, the early deaths, the life sentences to prison for misdemeanors, the racist executions and beatings by prison guards and the endless acts of racism do not stand out in sharp focus. We can not afford to be "cautious," any more than the victims of racism can. Those in struggle can not afford to be so "careful." Such carefulness is opportunism; it is chauvinism.

The important point is that we do know that Comrade Angela Davis is guilty of fighting racism, that she would not be facing the gas chamber if she had accommodated herself to racism. This is clear if one's vision is not blurred by the influences of racism. The indictment against Angela Davis is racism. The struggle for the freedom of Angela Davis can and must result in victories against racism generally, and it must serve as a vehicle for the elimination of chauvinist seepage on the Left. How we succeed in the struggle against chauvinist penetration will be measured by how well our Party moves fully into the struggle to free Comrade Angela Davis.

There are other examples of this weakness in the Party. There are numerous cases in which white trade union comrades have resisted even calling together the Left and radical trade unionists to discuss how the Angela Davis case can be raised in the shops and trade unions. There has been some resistance at different levels of the rank-and-file movement. The scope of the opportunism appears in the resistance to giving Angela Davis' political identity as a Black woman Communist leader. The resistance to raising the Free Angela Davis struggle is the clearest expression of the interrelationship and overlapping of Right opportunism in the struggle against anti-Communism with influences of chauvinism.

There are cases where white comrades remain silent in meetings when non-Party people express racist ideas. There are cases where Black comrades have to take up the challenge when white comrades have remained silent. This is more than insensitivity. It is capitulation to racism. It is opportunism.

We have new people coming into the Party. By and large, they are the best. But we know they bring with them ideological prejudices, especially racial prejudices. The question is: How do we help them to shed these influences? Are our educational programs geared to this struggle? We are not giving our clubs either the leadership or the materials to guide them in this struggle. We are neither giving this leadership in the case of new members nor are we raising the level of immunity among the old members. This lack of educational material is a measure of the priorities we are giving to this struggle.

There are also some open expressions of racism, not directly in the Party, but in institutions that are particularly close to the Party. We do not now control the editorial policies of *Glos Ludowy*, a Polish Left paper, published in Detroit. Most of its readers, however, believe it expresses our viewpoint. There are Communists who work with the staff. In the January 15 issue it published an openly racist piece. Most language newspapers would not dare to publish such open racism. That the writer is not a Communist does not change the seriousness of the crime. The article was about the changes taking place in the old Polish neighborhood in Chicago. Let me quote from it:

> In the former Little Poland from which the Poles are forced out . . . a 21-story skyscraper was erected in which 70 per cent of the residents are colored people.
>
> Noble Square and this skyscraper are a symbol of the policy of

ethnic liquidation which proceeds under the slogan of racial integration. . . .

This situation was aided by the fact that due to the pressure of the colored population large numbers of Poles began to flee from Little Poland. . . .

The Polish firms and institutions are disappearing. The only Polish bank in that neighborhood, the National Manufacturer's Bank . . . was quietly sold to a Jewish-Italian company . . . and today it also has colored people among the employees who once were all Poles. The post office in Little Poland on 1635 West Division Street has so changed that of its 170 employees more than half now are Negroes. (Once they were 100 per cent Polish.)

There has also been this change: White employees have now taken the positions formerly held by Negroes; that is, they do the heavy work and the Negroes do the easy jobs and earn more. At all the tellers' windows where the public is served and which is still white and in its majority Polish, one finds Negro men and Negro women. Before the holidays one could observe the following scene in this Polish post office: A mass of white people, mostly Poles, is pushing about, and the officials are Negro women. Among the crowd of whites a young, pretty Negro woman with an armband entitled "Miss Zip Code" walks about and this was done for propaganda purposes apparently to stress the Negro achievements in the Polonia.

In conclusion, still another sad news item from Little Poland, a news item of a scandalous character and perhaps for this reason it is ignored by the present Polish press. The old symbol of Polonia patriotism, the building of the Polish Sokol on 1062 North Ashland Avenue, where the recruitment for the Blue Army was conducted, has been sold to Puerto Ricans.

The article in its basic sense is an open expression of white chauvinism. But as you can see, it also has expressions of anti-Semitism, chauvinism against Puerto Ricans, and drags in an anti-Soviet draping by glorifying the World War I Blue Army that was made up of the dregs of society organized to fight the young socialist republic. This is not seepage. This is an act of racism.

I suggest we take direct action on this open expression of racism:

- We condemn it in a public statement.
- We demand a retraction and a campaign to undo the racist filth it spread.
- We use the material in this struggle in a campaign with other national group papers.
- We ask the Review Commission and the Michigan District leadership to investigate what responsibilities, if any, members of our Party had in this affair. If any member of the Party had any kind of responsibility for this act, we demand that proper disciplinary action be taken.

We can not have an easygoing attitude to this incident, because we in the Party have had critical discussions about chauvinism and anti-Semitism with the people involved on one or two occasions before.

We are a united Black-white Party. All of us have overall responsibilities. But we also have special responsibilities. Our Party, as a whole, must take on the struggle against racism and white chauvinism. But in this struggle, white Communists have a most urgent special responsibility. That responsibility is to take the lead in the struggle against racism wherever and in whatever form it appears. This is an ideological, political and moral responsibility. In the struggle against Black nationalism, our Black comrades have a special responsibility to take the initiative. A special responsibility of our Jewish comrades is in the struggle against Jewish bourgeois nationalism. And so on.

I would like to emphasize that these special responsibilities are not Party assignments in the usual sense of the word. They are not in the area of usual divisions of work. These are special responsibilities which we accept because of our ideological convictions. We carry them out not because of a Party decision, but because of our own decision based upon our own convictions. Our weaknesses in carrying out our special responsibilities are not for lack of Party assignment. We can not take refuge in not having an assignment from the Party. The weaknesses flow from lack of ideological understanding, ideological conviction. The lack of sensitivity to the influence of chauvinism is not related to Party decisions. A Party decision can not make us sensitive to influences of racism. The weakness is related to ideological seepage. The collective responsibility of the Party is to raise the level of collective sensitivity and struggle. Conviction will determine how each of us carries out his individual responsibility. Ideological struggle is collective, but it is also very personal.

There are some who equate white chauvinism and nationalism as twin evils. This is but another excuse for accommodation to racism. This equation is based on a totally wrong understanding of the nature and roots of chauvinism. Nationalism is a reaction to national oppression. It is related to the struggle against this oppression. When it is directed against oppression, it can serve a just and progressive cause. Chauvinism is, in all its varieties, ideological support for oppression. Because it is an instrument of oppression, it is reactionary, in all its varieties at all times. Under no circumstances can it be a progressive force. Thus, there can be no accommodation with it. There can be no equal treatment of the two. In the period of imperialism, nationalism has been on the right side of history. It can be misused, as Zionism is misusing Jewish nationalism. When it is being misused we fight it. But there can be no equation of the nationalism of those fighting oppression with racism, with chauvinism.

In the Party, we have special responsibilities. But we are not creatures of departments and inhabitants of special cubby holes. We must reject any concept that only white comrades can raise and deal with the problems of racism and white chauvinism and only Black comrades can raise and deal with problems of nationalism. The logical conclusion of such departmentalization would be the syndrome of "each doing his own thing."

For a successful struggle against the influences of racism, we must put an end to the atmosphere in our Party in which influences of chauvinism, as well as other ideological weaknesses, are treated as a family would treat leprosy—as something we do not talk about. This undeclared silence becomes an obstacle in the struggle against the penetration of chauvinism and nationalism. The most effective way to raise the level of immunity is by comradely, critical discussion. The starting point is not the levelling of charges or resort to administrative actions. These follow only when other methods do not succeed and, of course, when the actions involved are openly chauvinistic.

In our Party and especially on the leadership level of our Party, the question of Black-white oneness must be on a different level than is the case in other organizations. It is on a different level because of our ideological oneness. It is on a different level because of our theoretical, political and tactical oneness. It must be on a different level because we are the leadership of a revolutionary working-class Party. We are the embryo, the prototype of the coming society, in which the pollution of the ideological environment will be ended and the basic source of the contamination eradicated. On this level, the words "equals" or "equality" somehow fall short of giving the essence of the inner oneness of our Party. To meet these standards is a challenge. It demands an unrelenting struggle. The struggle against the penetration of the influence of white chauvinism is at the very heart of this challenge.

Our priorities must reflect the fact that white chauvinism is the main danger, that it is the most serious obstacle in the struggle for class unity and for the full effectiveness and unity of our Party. The success of our struggles in other areas will depend, in a basic sense, on the success of our struggles against racism and the influences of chauvinism.   □

[Pamphlet, *Racism, the Nation's Most Dangerous Pollutant*, New Outlook Publishers, New York, 1971]

2

WORKING CLASS UNITY

The People
Must Act!

One of the new factors in the struggle around the Vietnam War has been the activization of some elements in the construction trades, and the gathering of other Right-wing forces under the banner of "construction workers." This group is not yet very large. But we must see the inherent danger in this development. There are some 20,000 construction workers in the Wall Street area where the demonstrations have taken place.[1] At the high point of this mobilization only a small sector were involved. Yesterday's demonstration was organized by all of the ultra-Right and fascist organizations, Birchites, city policemen in plain clothes and other reactionary elements. The actions were not spontaneous. They were organized secretly with the help of outside forces. Money from some big corporations went into the operation.

These are the facts. But it is necessary for us to ask, how was it possible to organize this reactionary assault with the participation and in the name of construction workers?

There are, of course, general ideological weaknesses, jingoism and misled patriotism, that influence many. But this development is related more specifically to the nature of some of the unions involved and the nature of some of the workers in these trades.

Of course, the cover for all this is the reactionary, war-supporting policy of George Meany. The top AFL-CIO leadership is out to organize a mass movement in support of the war policies. However, with proper work, this attempt by the forces of reaction can be defeated. We must take it seriously, but we must not permit this to become the basis for wrong, anti-working-class conclusions, which are totally unjustified.

There are some special problems in developing the struggles further. There are areas that need special approaches, special attention. While greater numbers of workers than ever, both Black and white, are now taking part in mass actions against the war, and while a wider section of the leadership has responded, it is nonetheless necessary to continue special efforts in this area. This is necessary as long as the top leadership of the trade unions remains an active pro-war force. It is necessary until the working class assumes its rightful place at the head of the parade of progress.

The most successful approach is that which li ks eco nomic interests, class issues—wages, jobs, taxes, rents, prices, housing, discrimination, which have all been aggravated by the war—to the moral and political issues of imperialist aggression. This path will raise understanding to the level of anti-imperialism and to higher levels of class consciousness.

While large numbers of Afro-Americans, especially workers, are taking part in demonstrative actions, it is necessary to continue pressing for special approaches, special efforts, in this area also. Here again, the question of intermediate forms of organization, of intermediate forms that the people respect, has come into sharp focus.

Special efforts are necessary because there are special problems. For the Black community, the war and its escalation is a serious additional matter, on top of the escalation of racist oppression at home. There is murder in Vietnam, Cambodia and Laos; and there is murder and hunger in Mississippi, Alabama and Georgia, in Chicago and Los Angeles, and in ghettos throughout the USA.

The Black community is not going to trust or work with peace committees which, for show, invite some way-out Black speaker who in most cases represents no one.

There has to be a struggle for a new approach, a new attitude, by those in the leadership of the peace movement. It is necessary to cleanse from its ranks chauvinism dressed in "Left," radical phrases. In the Black community the most effective leadership is that which can show the connection between racism, imperialist aggression and capitalist profits. In the white community the most effective leadership is that which convinces the community that the struggle against racism is essential to the struggle against policies of imperialism and reaction.   □

[Report to National Committee, May 1970]

Hard Hats
And Hard Facts

Here is a big question of interest and concern to each construction worker about which there is much misconception: How about opening up the skilled trades to Black and Puerto Rican workers, ending the rotten racism that splits workers in all industries, including construction?

Building-trades union officials have gotten many building trades workers to believe that their conditions are improved by keeping jobs for white workers and excluding Black workers. In the first place, this is socially immoral, economically false and historically impractical. It is a big lie which is used to keep wages down. It is a crime against fellow human beings and violates all human ethics. It is a violation of our own Declaration of Independence, which says, "all men are created equal."

In addition to violating the laws of humanity, it violates common sense. It won't work. It is a losing game. In the long run there are no winners. For one group of workers to maintain job security by oppressing other workers is a modern version of gladiators fighting each other for the profit and enjoyment of the aristocratic rich.

The only path to victory, to job security for all, is a united struggle against the present-day aristocratic rich, the owners of big corporations. The struggle must be for whatever economic changes are necessary—a six- or four-hour day without a cut in weekly wages; government projects—changes that will provide jobs for all at union scales. Let job security come from the billions the corporations make in profits.

You are told you are "protecting" your job and your interest by keeping Black workers from employment on construction jobs.

Let's examine that a moment. The record shows a vastly different picture. Racism hurts white workers too.

Here is a good example. Take down South. Discrimination is much worse in the South than in the North. Black workers are kept out of good jobs much more completely there. Southern Black families earn 54 per cent of what white families earn, whereas in the North, Black families earn 72 per cent of what white families earn.

If racism benefited white workers, they would be better off in the South.

But look at the facts. In 1967 the average white family in the South earned $1,212 less than the average white family in the North. That means a total loss of $15 billion for all the Southern white families—most of whom are workers, of course.

Why? Because the employing class pegs wage standards to the lowest brackets, and therefore wages are lower in the South for both white and Black workers.

Because wages are lower in the South for both white and Black, more and more industry is moving to the South. Northern workers are losing their jobs because of this.

Even worse, U.S. multinational companies pay Asian workers one-twentieth or even as little as one-fiftieth what they pay American workers for the same work. Racism-colonialism is leading to the international runaway shop that is taking so many jobs from American factory workers.

Already residential construction in New York is practically dead, killed by the war. Sooner or later the racist runaway shop will be felt in heavy construction, office and industrial building too.

The only way to halt that is to end racism.

The building trades workers have the biggest possibility and the biggest responsibility of all labor.

If the building trades end racist practices, if they provide jobs for Black workers and Puerto Rican workers on a basis of complete equality and proportionality at all levels—this will be a decisive breakthrough in the general conditions of minority peoples in New York, who are about one-third of the population.

The end of racism in the unions, the end of swollen military budgets, would make it possible to win the struggle for decent housing for the millions of New Yorkers living in slums and ghettos.

It would make it possible, through struggle, to provide uncrowded and well-equipped schools and hospitals.

It would make possible expansion and improvement of the transit system, so badly needed.

This, plus shorter hours, would create such a demand for construction labor that it would be difficult to find enough construction workers, white, Black or Puerto Rican, and so require a vast expansion of training programs, a big increase in wages and improvement in conditions, in order to attract young people in enough numbers to the industry.   □

[Pamphlet, *Hard Hats and Hard Facts*, June 1970]

1975

Monopoly's Hammer
Against All Workers

The economic crisis magnifies and brings into sharp focus all the contradictions of capitalism. This is a moment to lay bare the class roots of economic and political policies. The crisis brings out the cruel and inhuman character of monopoly capitalism.

The present plant closings, layoffs and elimination of second and third shifts in many industries highlight the 200-year racial pattern of last-to-be-hired and first-to-be-fired. For proof of racist patterns one has only to note the overwhelming number of Black workers in many factory departments where the work is dirtiest and hardest, the large number of Black workers in the most dangerous occupations, and the greater number of white workers in skilled and higher-paid jobs. Because of all this, the economic crisis is deeper and will last longer for Black, Puerto Rican and Chicano workers.

It does not take a depression to convince the victims of racism that they are oppressed and exploited. They are aware of this every moment of their lives. The problem is not to convince Black workers that they are victims of racism. The real problem is to convince white workers that so long as they are carriers of racism, so long as they acquiesce in or support racist practices against Black workers, they are themselves victims of racism.

The crisis makes it easier to prove that the source of racism is the capitalist system of exploitation for corporate profit. The crisis presents new possibilities to convince white workers that racism is against their interests.

This is one of those moments when racism can be dealt a devastating blow. To land the blow, the struggle against racism must be integrated into the fabric of the struggles and issues arising from the economic crisis.

Certain elementary truths must be repeated at every turn of events. The class nature of racism is one. Racism is an ideological poison that induces white workers to act against their own interests. It is acceptance of rules set by the class enemy. It is letting the enemy con you into believing that you are better than your fellow workers. Racism is a device, a means by which corporations make extra profits from the work of the racially oppressed. It is also a means of increasing the rate of exploitation of the whole working class, squeezing higher profits from all workers. This is the starting point, the foundation upon which the struggle against racism can be built.

The decadent rich of the Roman Empire entertained themselves by having gladiators fight each other. It is not so different now. Wealthy U.S. capitalists enrich themselves by having workers fight each other over jobs, housing and education, and now over layoffs and seniority. It is a basic truth that so long as workers fight each other they will not be in the strongest position to fight the bosses. So long as white workers support policies and practices of discrimination based on race against their fellow workers, there will be no class unity.

Unity is possible only on terms of equality, based on the old maxim that "an injury to one is an injury to all." This is a fundamental starting point of a working-class outlook. The idea is elementary but basic.

White workers must draw some special lessons from this economic crisis. One such lesson is that past compliance with racist practices against their Black, Puerto Rican and Chicano brothers and sisters in the unions and shops has not given them job security. Millions of white workers are being laid off without any ceremony or compensation, despite their acquiesence to racism. They are joining Black workers on the unemployment lines. Support of racism has not stopped the escalation of prices and rents. On the contrary, their rents and taxes keep going up. Their real wages, too, are cut by inflation; they too work in unsafe conditions; most white workers are victims of the same deteriorating urban conditions. While racism divides the workers, the corporations speed up production. The production line does not slow down where white workers toil.

Racism is one of the key factors making it possible for U.S. corporations to maintain the highest rate of exploitation and highest profits in the world.

The gap between the average annual income of Black and white households has now reached the astronomical figure of $4,640. Multiply this by the total number of Black households, and it is easy to see that this superexploitation results in something like $35 billion in extra profits each year. These superprofits go into the coffers of the corporations which oppress the entire working class. By not fighting racism, white workers help the corporations pocket these extra profits. However, the extra profit monopoly capital rakes in as a result of racist policies and practices is greater than $35 billion.

The steel industry is a good example. Wages are based on job classification. Classifications one to eight pay between $4 and $5 per hour. Higher classifications pay around $7 per hour. There is no reasonable explanation why some jobs are in one or another classification. The system is a perfect structure for racist policies. Most Black workers are in the one to eight classifications. The Black workers—and also the white workers—in these classifications work for $4 to $5 per hour. This is clearly a case where the steel corporations get extra profits from racist exploitation of Black workers, and also to a degree from white workers. It would serve the interests of white and

Black workers to join in a struggle to put an end to the racist classification structure.

Increased exploitation and racist patterns in the steel industry are closely related to the toadying, class-collaborationist policies pursued by Abel and his gang in the leadership of the steel union.[2]

Workers in the North and West of our country face the old problem of runaway shops moving to the South. Corporations move their operations to Southern states because of the 200-year-old wage differential between North and South. Southern wage scales are lower because Southern workers are largely unorganized. They are unorganized mainly because of the influence of racism among white workers.

Because of racism, class consciousness is at a low level. There are few trade unions, which are a basic requirement for a struggle to wipe out the regional wage differential, which in turn would then put an end to runaway shops.

The Southern wage differential is a source of extra profits from Black and also from white workers. Lower wages are paid both to Black and white workers in the South.

A new problem U.S. workers face is the transfer of production facilities to lower-wage areas of the world by multinational corporations.

The dual culprits are imperialism and racism. The winner in both cases is the corporations.

Many changes are taking place in the South. There is significant progress towards working-class unity. Black and white workers are uniting in local trade unions. But even during the last months there have been elections in some big unorganized shops where the issue has been between a union and no union. The votes have been close. But in a number of cases the workers voted for no union. Racism still blinds many white workers to their class interests. When white workers vote against unions, they are victims of their own racism.

What is the working-class approach to resolving the problems that have surfaced during the economic crisis?

The "gladiators" must unite and turn the struggle against the corporate monsters. The working class must take up the battle against all layoffs. This must include the demand for a shorter workweek with no cut in pay. It must include a prohibition on the closing of plants. Let union committees run the plants! Workers must fight to establish a limit to speedup. There must be a united struggle for government programs to build houses and apartments, schools and hospitals. Such programs would not only create jobs, but would provide decent housing for every family, quality, integrated schools and hospital beds for all who need them. Such a struggle is in the interest of the entire working class. It would turn the struggle against the real foe—monopoly capitalism.

This would create the basis for unity, but it would still not eliminate racist inequality.

In order to wipe out the effects of racism, white workers must join in the fight for special adjustments. There must be special steps taken to erase inequalities due to past hiring and promotion practices. Workers must fight to end the maneuvering by the bosses and many trade union leaders to bypass the Fairfield decision.[3] They must fight to reject any "consent agreements" which leave overall racist patterns intact. In order to wipe out discrimination in housing, all workers must fight for a government program that will make a decent house or apartment a reality for every family, wherever they choose to live. In order to carry out such adjustments it is necessary to work out concrete steps that meet the problems in each situation. How to approach these adjustments is a key question in molding working-class unity.

The economic crisis has brought these questions into sharp focus. The capitalist establishment is definitely not interested in their solution. They continue their racist policies. They rejoice in the fact that layoffs are creating new obstacles to labor unity and stimulating new racist attitudes and divisions.

Next year will mark the 200th year since the people of

the colonies declared their independence from British colonial rule. It will also be the 200th year of oppression of the Black community in this country—first under slavery and then under a special system of discrimination and ghettoization. The question is not only to end discrimination. It is necessary to establish true equality, to wipe out the effects of 200 years of discrimination. There must be special adjustments to compensate for the centuries of racist oppression.

In industry, adjustments must be made in hiring, training and promotion. The economic depression has made this question more urgent.

These are not simple matters. But it is easier to convince white workers of the need for special adjustments when it is placed in the overall framework of the struggle against monopoly capitalism. When the overall struggle is against the class enemy; when the basic demands go in the direction of making the corporations pay; then it is easier to help white workers see their class interest in the fight against racism. Then it is easier to help white workers see the need for special adjustments that also call on them to make personal adjustments.

On the basis of this working-class approach to the struggle against racism in the economic structure, it is possible to simultaneously take on the ideological monster of racism. Once white workers see racism as a tool of the corporations, a means to exploit the working class as a whole, they will see racism as their enemy as well.

This struggle against racism is very much in keeping with the patterns of world developments. Peoples throughout the world have made great strides in repelling racism. The United Nations resolution condemning racism in all its forms reflects the growing strength of the antiracist forces—in the first place the countries of socialism.

The economic crisis of world capitalism brings into sharp focus the fact that there are no economic crises in the socialist countries. Socialism eliminates the causes of crises. The socialist countries stand out in sharp contrast to capitalism because they have not only erased racism, but they have destroyed its roots. The socialist countries are setting an example of life without race prejudice or race hatred.

Struggle is a stimulant of thought. A confrontation compels one to ask: Who is my enemy? What is the ideology, the politics of my enemy? The answers lead workers to a deeper class consciousness. Struggle forces workers to think in terms of class unity, and to recognize obstacles to unity, such as racism and class collaboration.

Each experience with class battle is a spark, a spur to class consciousness. But left to itself the spark never ignites into a flame, the tendency never reaches its potential. By itself the process is one of trial and error.

The crisis makes working-class unity an absolute and urgent necessity. The main obstacle to this unity is racism. It is the most effective weapon that monopoly capital has against the United States working class. This is the moment to uproot, to reject this poison brewed in the ideological cauldrons of Big Business.   □

[Report to National Committee, 1975]

Equality Is
A Class Issue

Based on our experience in this period, it is necessary to see rank-and-file movements as key factors in the struggle for Black-white unity—the unity of a multinational working class. No matter what the original form of a rank-and-file group, in this period they have all gravitated towards being multinational.

Therefore, besides all the specific issues which are reasons to organize rank-and-file groups, we should take the initiative to organize them for the specific purpose of conducting a struggle for class unity based on the fight against racism and chauvinism. They should serve as caucuses in the struggle for multinational unity in union locals and in international unions. Rank-and-file groups can persuade unions to conduct antiracist campaigns, and, in case they can not convince the union to do so, can organize their own educational campaign.

A central task for such caucuses today is the struggle against the racist pattern of crisis layoffs. There are some tendencies to speak about the contradiction between the racist patterns of layoffs and preserving established seniority systems, but to do nothing about this problem. In practice, this kind of behavior supports continuation of the racist cycle of last-to-be-hired and first-to-be-fired. In these situations the monopolies, the exploiting corporations, with great glee, are saying: "We are neutral. We will do whatever you say. Fight it out among yourselves."

We must work to build a force that puts the issue squarely: It is a class issue, but it is affected by generations of corporate policies of racial discrimination. The struggle must be raised in the framework of demands that there be jobs for all and no layoffs. But this must not become a framework for general talk about no layoffs and jobs for all, while doing nothing about the racist layoffs that are going on. The struggle must get to the specifics of breaking the racist cycle. It must get to the specifics of special adjustments and of preferential hiring and layoffs.

Once white workers are convinced of the necessity of these adjustments, there are concrete ways in which they can be implemented. For example, Labor Research Association, in its publication *Economic Notes*, presents an idea. The idea comes from trade union leaders with a long history of struggle. The proposal is that instead of laying off younger workers with least seniority, among whom minorities are concentrated, older workers be furloughed. On furlough, they would be paid 95 per cent of their wages and continue to receive Social Security and pension credits, and also be fully covered by the existing medical plan. When the economy picked up and the company began to rehire, they would return to their jobs. This would stretch out the lifespan of the older workers and strengthen the unions by gaining the support of the younger workers. It would also promote union solidarity because it would end discriminatory layoffs.

The furloughed workers would receive their wages from state unemployment funds plus a federal supplement, including upward adjustments when wages are raised. There would be no time limits on these payments and no need for biweekly reports, only an initial registration.

The struggle against racism must be worked into concrete demands and concrete plans for struggle. And it must be placed within the context of the fight for working-class and trade-union unity. Then it can be concretely related to the self-interest of all workers.

In these last years, there have been some important legal victories, such as the Fairfield decision,[4] that have helped in the struggle against racism. It is important to use such victories in every way possible. They have created cracks in the wall of racism. However, as is the case with all partial victories, especially when they come from the courts, and even more so when they do not specifically strike at the roots of the system of racism, or when they apply only to individuals, we must be careful that we expose the limitations of such measures. Not to do so leads to illusions that the struggle against racism has been won, and therefore the struggle can cease.

Our Party has for some time placed special emphasis on our activity among the working class and trade unions. We should be self-critical about weaknesses in our policy of industrial concentration. But it is also necessary to draw the positive lessons. We are now seeing the beginning of a new period. Because of our working-class emphasis during the past years, we are on the ground floor of this upswing. Because of it we are an integral part of this important development.

We have made important headway against the seepage of racism and white chauvinism into our Party's ranks. But we can not afford to be complacent, for many reasons.

The influences of racism exhibit, dialectically, two sides: new opportunities in the struggle against racism, as well as continuing efforts by the ruling class to inject this poison into the bloodstream of our society. As crisis contradictions sharpen, racist pressures increase. This sharpening of contradictions gives rise to struggles, which exert pressure for greater unity, which in turn helps to create conditions in which the fight against racist pressures can be more successful.

To meet this situation it is necessary for the Party to raise to new levels its role among the white sections of the working class and other white masses, to win them to struggle against the oppression and discrimination against

Black and other nationally oppressed peoples, and against the influence of ruling-class racism. This is a condition, a necessary feature, of a successful struggle against reaction in general; it is in their own best interest. To be able to exert leadership by example, the Party must raise sharply its own level of understanding, and struggle against all manifestations of white chauvinism in its own ranks.

The primary test of whether we are measuring up to the demands of the times is the initiative taken with respect to racism by white Communists among white masses on today's decisive front—jobs and the economic crisis. This means setting concrete goals, followed by checkup on implementation, placing demands and winning over white masses to support them. Such demands include special job creation programs for the victims of racism; modifying seniority rules to break the last-to-be-hired, first-to-be-fired pattern, etc. It means rejecting liberal and Social Democratic pressures to place the demand for full employment in such a way that it becomes an excuse for not fighting for the special demands of Black workers.

The ruling class is making the fight against busing for school desegregation their main front to divide and divert white working masses. This calls for new initiatives by our white comrades among white masses as a concrete test of our progress.

At the same time, our internal educational work on matters from basic class analyses of racism and the national question, to forms of expression of white chauvinism in our ranks must be raised to a new level. To tolerate manifestations of white chauvinism, to have a liberal attitude toward acts of chauvinism, is to increase the seepage of the poison. The task is not only to put an end to the manifestations, but to burn out the ideological influence of white chauvinism in the first place.   □

[Report to 21st Convention of CPUSA, 1975]

The Wage Differential Rip-off

Things you can't see or touch rarely make the news. But one invisible thing did recently make headlines—the mysterious "legionnaires' disease" in Philadelphia. It killed 30 people, but no one has been able to locate the cause.

I'd like to talk about something that has destroyed more lives and ruined more cities than the Philadelphia disease. Though it goes by different names, "the Southern differential" is the link between unemployment in the North and the open shop and runaway plant in the South.

If I am elected President we will propose to Congress a law prohibiting wage differentials except for skill, difficult or dangerous work, bad climatic conditions or night work. It would bar the following:

• Wage differentials between one region and another, between big and small cities.

• Differentials between white, Black, Chicano, Puerto Rican and Native American Indian workers.

• Differentials between men and women.

Wage differentials and the runaway shops are the road to the open shop, to unionbusting injunctions, to the murder of union organizers, to antilabor "right to work" laws.

The lowest factory wages in the country are paid in North Carolina, the home of the unionbusting J.P. Stevens textile empire and the revived Ku Klux Klan, where Ben

Chavis and the Wilmington Ten[5] are imprisoned, where scores of Black and poor white prisoners are on death row. It is the state with the lowest percentage of union membership.

Last year the average weekly wage of employed factory workers in North Carolina was $116 less than in Michigan. That adds up to $6,000 per year. That means $6,000 of extra profits per worker for the corporation that runs away from Michigan to North Carolina. It means $4.5 billion extra profits from the 750,000 factory workers employed in North Carolina.

Let's see what that means for Michigan. Last year a materials handler in Saginaw, Michigan, averaged $3.64 per hour. A company running away from Saginaw to Memphis would make an extra $4,100 on that single job. That is one of the reasons Detroit and Flint still have an official unemployment rate of 10 per cent—it's actually double that—far higher than the national average, despite the fact that automobile production has recovered and profits of General Motors are back in the billions.

Let's look at the automobile industry. In large factories in the North, class B assemblers average $6.12 per hour. In large factories in the South they average $3.37 per hour. That is a differential of more than 40 per cent, worth $6,000 per year to the company that moves the work South (1974 figures).

But that isn't all. There was just as large a differential in the North between large shops and small shops. More and more, big companies subcontract work to small-town subcontractors, who pay substandard wages and chisel on safety and health provisions and fringe benefits, in order to sell parts or subassemblies to the Big Three cheaper than the big companies can make them—and still eke out a small profit. That is why General Motors closed down the Fisher No. 23 die-building plant in Detroit and distributed the work among ten plants scattered around the United States.

The extra profits from these regional differentials are

growing each year. To protect these extra profits, extracted from low wage labor, an assassin was hired to murder the Reverend Martin Luther King, Jr., in Memphis, where he was assisting the struggle against non-union, low-wage conditions of the Black sanitation workers there. Rev. King became an effective spokesperson for all the exploited and oppressed.

The tens of millions of dollars necessary to elect a Ford or a Carter to protect the Southern differential are peanuts compared to the profit payoff to the corporate capitalists who put up the election funds.

In 1975, the per capita income of Black people was $2,500 less than that of whites. Applied to the 25 million Black people in the country, that means a loss in purchasing power of $70 billion. When the loss of purchasing power of Puerto Ricans, Chicanos, Native American Indians and Asian Americans is added in, the total is more than $100 billion.

There is on the books a federal Equal Employment Opportunity Act and similar state laws; there are government commissions and fair employment clauses in union contracts. But the laws are not enforced and most union leaderships do not insist on positive action to make equality a reality in the shops.

A Black auto worker is much more likely than a white auto worker to be unemployed. Because the auto industry is cyclical, the last-to-be-hired, first-to-be-fired rule applies with particular force. The otherwise strong seniority system won by the workers becomes a mockery for many Black workers because it lacks special provisions necessary to break this vicious circle.

If I am elected President, we will propose legislation ensuring that the principle of compensatory seniority be applied. As even some courts have begun to recognize, it must be taken into account that many Blacks, other minorities and women would have had greater seniority were it not for brutal discrimination in hiring.

It is the corporations that have made profits from these

discriminatory practices. The corporations must be made to pay for correcting the situation. For example, rather than lay-off workers strictly according to seniority, workers with more seniority could be given paid sabbaticals to rebuild their health and learn higher skills.

To return to the auto industry, every auto worker knows that Black workers are still disproportionately assigned the worst jobs—the hardest stations on the line; the paint department that ruins the lungs; the jobs in the pits; the hot, heavy, dangerous foundry jobs. Add to worse working conditions lower wages and more unemployment time, and you have a many-sided racist pattern. All this was created by design of the auto manufacturers.

The strategy is simple enough. Its aim is to make extra profits. And its aim is to make white workers, who feel safe and superior, feel that their security is threatened not by capitalism, not by the company, but by Black workers trying to take their jobs and their homes.

Any such feeling is an illusion. When the crisis hits, Blacks are laid off first, but white workers are also laid off. Right now tens of thousands of white auto workers laid off in 1974-75 have not been rehired.

Speedup hits white as well as Black workers, shortens white lives as well as Black. The worst speedup in the auto industry was in the Lordstown, Ohio, GM plant, which was nearly all white.

If a company is permitted to practice racial discrimination, it will move its operations where racism is worst. Economic discrimination against Blacks is still worse in the South than in the North.

One must look at the South to see what racism costs white workers. In 1969, the income of Southern white workers was one-eighth less than the income of Northern white workers. Racism pulls down their wages more than it does the wages of Northern white workers. Applied to all whites in the South, this came to a loss of more than $20 billion in 1974, and it is growing constantly.

White, male factory operatives in the South make 23 per

cent less than those in the North, and 18 per cent less than Black operatives in the North. Yes, they make much more than Black operatives in the South. But because of the Southern differential, they make less than Black workers doing the same work in the North, who are themselves discriminated against.

General Electric, Ford, General Motors and many other big companies are moving more and more of their work to the South, setting up new factories under nonunion conditions. The auto companies agreed with the United Automobile Workers to automatically recognize the union in new Southern factories. But they are violating that agreement, fighting the union throughout the South. Most auto plants in the South are nonunion.

Along with wage differentials go tax giveaways. Capitalists in small Southern towns cash in on subcontracting from the runaway shops. States and cities give tax exemptions to lure runaway factories, and the workers of these states pay in higher taxes and curtailed municipal services. Now Northern states are beginning to compete with Southern states in tax giveaways, with the same harmful effects.

Wage differentials against Black and other minority workers are matched by discrimination against women. Average earnings of women working full time are 40 per cent less than those of men. This costs women workers the enormous sum of $150 billion a year. Taking advantage of the sex differential, employers replace men with women at lower wages in occupation after occupation.

A related development is the vicious attempt of Big Business, with the aid of both Democrats and Republicans, to take advantage of the huge volume of unemployment among youth by legalizing the hiring of young people at less than the mimimum wage. They hope thereby to crack the entire wage structure.

All this, however, doesn't take into account international runaway shops. Profits of multinational corporations are highest of all from their operations in low-wage countries. More and more work is being transferred to these countries. Sales of U.S. companies from foreign plants and mines came close to $400 billion in 1974, four times what it was eight years earlier.

Workers of the United States are beginning to struggle against these differentials. In a number of cases, militant unions have defeated attempts to move shops, preventing employers from moving out machinery. Such fights can be won through militant actions, through forcing action by local government officials and members of Congress.

In the South, Black workers with organizational experience in the civil rights struggle are showing outstanding leadership in the struggle to establish trade unions. Some big Westinghouse and General Electric plants have been successfully organized, with a high degree of Black and white unity. This is also key to the ultimate victory of Southern textile workers.

The struggle of the trade union movement against international runaways is just beginning.

Let me explain the Communist program for dealing with this evil. I have already said that we would propose legislation eliminating wage differentials except for skill, hardship, etc. I've mentioned steps we would take to assure real equality of employment for Blacks, other minorities, and women. We would also raise the minimum wage to assure that youth and all unorganized workers got decent wages.

That isn't all. We would propose to Congress that federal, state and local tax systems, including income taxes, be consolidated. Tax revenues would be distributed according to a formula reflecting the need at different levels. This would put an end to competitive tax giveaways, which encourage runaway shops and help Big Business shift the tax burden to workers.

Finally, we would put an end to the international runaway shop. We would insist that Congress revoke all tax privileges for foreign investments. We would withdraw all troops from foreign bases and return the U.S. fleet to home

waters. And we would declare a 100 per cent embargo on
the racist South African and Rhodesian regimes,[6] with severe penalties for companies that did business in violation
of the embargo.

How does the Communist program against wage differentials fit in with our jobs program? Elimination of wage
differentials against Blacks, Chicanos, Puerto Ricans, Native American Indians and women would directly increase
wage and salary income by more than $100 billion. This ad-
ditional mass purchasing power would generate five million jobs in consumer goods industries, trade and services.

Slashing the military budget by 80 per cent and using the
funds to build houses, schools, hospitals, mass transit and
recreational facilities for the people would add another
three million civilian jobs.

Ending trade discrimination against socialist and developing countries would provide an additional two million
jobs.

From these sources, then, the total increase in jobs
would be 10 million.

What about our basic demand to reduce the workweek to
30 hours without reduction in pay? This is an appropriate
demand, considering the high level of productivity of
American labor and the intensity of labor in industry. U.S.
production workers produce $3.50 in added value for each
dollar they receive in wages. Even with a 6-hour work day
and the same total wages, they would still be adding $2.60
of value for each dollar they receive in wages. Clearly, not
only can the country afford a shorter work week, the country needs it.

Thus, the Hall-Tyner[7] program provides for a much
higher level of employment and total income and much
higher living standards than ever before.

To vote for Ford or Carter is to vote against yourself.
You would not elect your boss as your shop steward. So
why vote to put his man in the White House?   □

[Election campaign speech, 1976]

The Million Conspiracies
Of Racism

Racism, in everyday life, is a million conspiracies. The racists resort to conspiracies and camouflaged maneuvers because racist practices violate established legal, constitutional and moral norms.

The Supreme Court decision on the Bakke case was deliberately wrapped in a maze of seemingly contradictory statements. The legal gobbledygook was meant to obscure and hide the racist essence of the decision. This is a feature of many legal conspiracies.

The full force of the Bakke conspiracy emerges in the dozens of cases embodying similar challenges that have been filed in courts in many parts of the country. A clear example of the conspiratorial, dirty tricks nature of racism is the Weber case. The Weber case was hatched in a Kaiser Aluminum and Chemical Corporation plant in Gramercy, Louisiana.

About 40 per cent of the adult work force in the city of Gramercy is Black. But in the Kaiser plant only about 15 per cent of the workers are Black. Of the 290 skilled workers in the plant, 5 are Black. Of the last 28 workers admitted into the skilled trades at the Kaiser plant only 2 are Black.

Some time ago the corporation set up an on-the-job training program for skilled workers. The United Steelworkers' local representing the workers at Kaiser and the management of Kaiser negotiated an agreement taking the first steps to counteract the obvious effects of generations of racist practices in hiring, promotion and training at the plant. This agreement was designed to open the training program to workers based on seniority, but also based on the concept of "one to one," admitting an equal number of Black and white workers selected from two established seniority lists. This was clearly a minimal approach to affirmative action.

But before the program even got started, Brian Weber, a white worker, filed a suit which challenged the legality of the program on the basis that a Black worker, with less seniority than he had, had been admitted to the on-the-job training program ahead of him. Within a matter of days the legal conspiracy was fully developed. Attorneys and legal documents appeared on the scene as if from nowhere. The conspiracy had been hatched before the case hit the court docket.

On the basis of the challenge, the district court and the court of appeals decided that because there was no evidence presented about past discrimination, there was no need for the program of affirmative action. And this is where the wider conspiracy began to emerge. Because the affirmative action agreement was made between the union and the Kaiser Corporation, they were both named as defendants in the case. Weber charged them with "reverse discrimination." But neither the corporation nor the union presented evidence of past discrimination. In fact, Kaiser lied. It claimed to have always "hired and promoted workers on the basis of the most qualified."

They neglected to explain, of course, how it came about that of 290 skilled workers, only 5 were Black. Neither the union nor its attorneys said anything about this. Whether by design or otherwise they became partners in the conspiracy of racism.

The tentacles of this conspiracy of silence reached even into the Officers' Report read to the last National Convention of the United Steelworkers. The written report said: "We want to do the fair thing, so we have to sit it out and let the courts decide what is fair." That's the racist element of the policy of class collaboration.

This is a conspiracy of silence against Black workers, because there would have been no problem presenting plenty of evidence of past discrimination to justify the affirmative action agreement. But it is also a conspiracy of silence about the violation of some very basic trade union rights. In their decisions the district and appeals courts have, in effect, ruled that trade unions have no right to negotiate affirmative action agreements. Their rulings seriously limit the process of collective bargaining.

In his opinion dissenting from the Supreme Court's Bakke decision, Justice Thurgood Marshall clearly stated the implications of the case when he wrote:

> [I]t is more than a little ironic that, after several hundred years of class-based discrimination against Negroes, the Court is unwilling to hold that a class-based remedy for that discrimination is permissible. . . It is unnecessary in 20th century America to have individual Negroes demonstrate that they have been victims of racial discrimination; the racism of our society has been so pervasive that none, regardless of wealth or position, has managed to escape its impact. (Justice Thurgood Marshall, "Dissent in the Bakke Case," *Freedomways*, No.3, 1978, pp. 133-134.)

We must alert the working class and the people to the dangers inherent in these conspiracies of racism. We must not permit the Weber case to silently establish legal precedents for racism. There must be a storm of protest demanding that the Weber case be sent back for review, where evidence of both racial discrimination and conspiracy can be presented.

The members of the United Steelworkers must demand that the leaders of their union end their conspiracy of silence and take up the struggle for affirmative action on behalf of Black workers, in defense of basic trade union rights for all workers.

"To do the fair thing" the leadership of the United Steel-workers must be forced to give up its present "sit-it-out" policy and get out and mobilize against the racist conspiracy.   □

[*Daily World*, November 16, 1978]

1978

How to Stop
The Monopolies

An increased role of the government in this period is reflected, among other ways, in the reactionary role of the Supreme Court and its actions in defense of racism.

The ruling class, and especially the federal apparatus, has been actively working to establish a climate in which a definite level of racism is acceptable. This is reinforced and legalized by the Bakke decision, which is being followed up by the Weber case[8] and many others. There is no question that monopoly capital correctly anticipates a mass fightback by workers and the people against its offensive in general and, of course, Carter's economic policies in particular.

But they also know that Black people as a whole, and Black workers in particular, are going to respond to Carter's austerity measures, and to the sharpened racist cutting edge of the monopoly offensive, with a new level of mass upsurge. It is for this reason that the state and its political and ideological instruments are pushing such concepts as "reverse racism," "reverse discrimination" and "deracialization."

The struggle against racism must be placed in the context of today's developing antimonopoly struggle, in the context of the class struggle at this time in history. This is not the old phoney-Left idea that the class struggle replaces the struggle against racism.

It is necessary to see the new context, in which the majority of Black Americans are part of the working class. Not only a part of the working class, but a very active part. Millions of Black workers participate in the class struggle in addition to the struggle against racism.

The class enemy understands this new relationship. That is why, whenever they launch an anti-working-class offensive, it is also a racist offensive. To struggle effectively against racism and for class unity, we also must understand this new context and apply its lessons.

We have to place questions of class unity, of Black-white-Chicano unity, in this context. The policy of the ruling class in this period, seeking to undo previous gains toward Black equality and increasing the use of racism, will put new strains on working-class unity. These developments add urgency to the task of molding firm unity between general class demands and concrete demands for affirmative action. This context emphasizes the fact that class unity must be directed against the main enemy—state monopoly capitalism.

For Black candidates and Black elected officials, some old problems have reemerged in the new context of the state monopoly offensive. What has clearly come to the surface is the fact that there are very real racist obstacles and limitations for Black candidates, especially those running for state or national office within the two-party system. The fraudulent concept of "reverse discrimination" has been extended into the field of electoral politics. There is a concerted effort to reverse previous gains in electing Black officials. In this past election campaign, funds and endorsements were often denied Black candidates. Political support from Democratic liberals like Governor Brown and Senator Kennedy, and from people around the Carter Administration, was either cut off or kept on a minimal and formal basis. For many Black candidates this meant the difference between victory and defeat.

To a large extent, Puerto Rican, Chicano and women

candidates received the same kind of treatment. As a result there was a decline in the number of new women candidates and women newly elected to office, and new difficulties for Chicano and Puerto Rican candidates.

In addition, there was also undeniably a national campaign of frameup, political harassment and entrapment against Black officeholders. This is definitely a national racist pattern.

This harassment brings to mind an experience we had in the early 1940s. I was one of a number of Communists who were arrested and sentenced for witnessing election petitions as collectors, when in fact we had not collected the particular signatures ourselves. My case was in Youngstown, Ohio.

After sentencing me to a 90-day jail sentence, the judge told my wife Elizabeth: "The truth is that Gus did not do anything other than what all the candidates running for public office have been doing for 100 years. But when Communists do it it's different. Because of the great pressure, I had to give Gus three months."

The harassment of Black elected officials has a clear racist tone and aim. There are literally thousands of laws that lie dormant and are resurrected for special use only when they serve reactionary or racist purposes. Instead of getting hung up on legal technicalities, we must expose the fact that this is a nationally directed and organized racist campaign. It is a continuation of the notorious FBI campaign against Rev. Martin Luther King, Jr., by reactionary forces in today's setting.

A feature of current developments is the emergence of new pressures and questions in the ideological field. As always, when monopoly capital feels cornered it goes on an ideological offensive. There is a new boldness in its racist propaganda.

The Supreme Court has given racism a new legality. The concept of "acceptable limits of racism" has opened the doors to greater racism in the mass media. In industry this concept is used to continue racist discrimination in hiring, upgrading and layoffs.

There is a need for the Party to take a hard look at how to counteract in our own ranks the influence of this racist ideological poison all around us.

Speaking for monopoly capital, the editors of the *New York Times*, in their frustration, recently spewed out their ideological poison. In an editorial on the UN resolution on the role of the press, they wrote, "let us put the matter bluntly, as our diplomats should have: to Americans, there can be no free speech unless those who advocate racism and apartheid and, yes, war are also free to speak." (November 27, 1978).

Clearly it is not the working people of the U.S. who need or want to speak for wars of aggression, racism or apartheid. It is the *New York Times* and Big Business who insist on having that "right." They should have added they also want the "right" to slander and lie about the Soviet Union and real socialism and distort everything related to the working class and the struggle for national liberation.   □

[Report to Central Committee, 1978]

Worse Than
'More of the Same'

For the Afro-American, Puerto Rican, Chicano, Native American Indian and Asian-Pacific peoples—the 50 million Americans who suffer racial and national oppression—the start of the '80s is worse than "more of the same."

The late '50s and '60s was a period of hope and promise. Black and other racially and nationally oppressed people made a number of important gains. They won the right to vote, to be elected to public office, to attend integrated schools. Transportation, restaurants and other public facilities were desegregated.

But the '70s ushered in a decade of disappointment and frustration. Many of the rights won in struggle were weakened in practice and in some cases all but nullified. Tricky redivision of voting districts was used to reduce the impact of nationally oppressed peoples' votes. Private schools and other devices were used to thwart school desegregation. In many parts of the North segregation actually increased. Cross-burning and other forms of intimidation increased where Blacks moved into previously all-white neighborhoods.

The failure to solve the problem of equality for Black and other oppressed people in hiring, job upgrading, housing and health care stands as a formidable roadblock to all social progress.

Consider the employment situation. Last year, according to government figures, the unemployment rate among whites averaged 5.1 per cent, while for the category "Black and other" it averaged 11.3 per cent. And these official figures lie by not including those workers who are no longer "actively seeking" work because they have given up hope of finding any. The true rate of unemployment among oppressed people, particularly Black people, is closer to 20 per cent. For Black teenagers the figure is a catastrophic 50 to 75 per cent in some areas. For oppressed people unemployment has been at the depression level of the '30s for many years.

In the '70s the courts set up legal barriers to affirmative action and school desegregation.

President Carter's corporate-profits-first economic policies have a sharp racist edge. They call for a reduction in the standard of living and quality of life for all of us. But these policies hit oppressed people, whose standard of living is already the lowest, with special force. They are policies of official racism.

More than ever, an effective attack on the superexploitation and oppression of Afro-Americans and other oppressed peoples now requires a clear understanding of the source of the problem. It requires a strategy that can bring about progress not only in civil rights and civil liberties, but in jobs, housing, health care and other economic rights.

What are the basic causes of racism? Historically, racism in this country originated with slavery. The slaveholders attempted to justify the monstrous, antihuman institution of slavery with racism, bigotry and prejudice. Today the main upholder of racism is monopoly capital—the giant corporations that dominate our country's economy, government, mass media and educational institutions. The owners of these corporations are the main beneficiaries of racism; they maintain it, stir it up, use it to make huge superprofits and to divide and rule over the people.

The corporations make billions each year by paying artificially low wages to racially oppressed workers. Job classifications are manipulated to define certain jobs as worth less than others, not because they require less skill, but simply because they are occupied mainly by Black, Chicano, Puerto Rican and other oppressed workers. White workers must understand that keeping down the wages of racially and nationally oppressed workers also keeps their wages down.

Landlords, real estate agents and banks make billions by deliberately fomenting racism in housing. They divide the housing market into racial compartments. Redlining is rampant. Not only does this severely limit people's freedom to choose where to live, it also forces Black people to pay outrageously high prices for miserable ghetto housing, and raises the rent of other people.

In plants and offices, racism is used to pit one group of workers against another. It divides the trade unions and holds back the whole working-class movement. It is an instrument of class rule—the main weapon of Big Business to control the country, politically and economically.

It is absolutely crucial for the solution of the pressing problems of our country that white Americans recognize their self-interest in fighting racism; they too lose by it. Racism is an obstacle to a better life for all the people, to social progress generally.

The overwhelming majority of white people—those not tied to corporate interests—do not benefit from racism. This becomes especially clear in times of economic crisis like the present. The people of the United States suffer from out-of-control inflation. Unemployment is high and rising. Workers' real spendable earnings are lower now than 15 years ago. Last year alone real wages fell by 7 per cent. The government declares regularly that working people's standard of living must be reduced.

What racism does is to divert attention from real problems, from the true causes of these problems, and therefore from the necessary solutions to them. What racism does is to divide people so they are unable to mount an effective fightback.

All this does not mean that a white worker may not gain some particular, immediate advantage from discrimination against a racially oppressed person. But in most cases this advantage is obtained at the cost of sacrificing bigger, more fundamental interests.

For example, some white construction workers may gain some immediate advantage in obtaining jobs as a result of discrimination against racially oppressed workers. But how much does this help construction workers, especially in a situation where the government is deliberately choking the construction industry, and building trades unemployment is soaring? The true interests of white construction workers lie not in discriminatory practices, but in fighting for the economy to be run in such a way that there are jobs for all. Racism has greatly weakened the building trades unions and construction workers have been forced to take wage cuts.

The problem is basically one of class solidarity. Scabbing may bring a person immediate advantage. However, most workers have always despised scabbing. Gaining an advantage from discrimination is like scabbing. It sacrifices the interests of the whole class for momentary, individual, selfish gain. We need to build up a tradition against benefiting from racial discrimination that is as strong as the tradition against scabbing.

Just as it is crucial for white people to recognize racist poison for what it is and to fight against it, so it is important for racially and nationally oppressed people to know who their potential allies are, who the enemy is, and what stands in the way of unity and progress at this point.

To begin with, there is the question of solidarity between Black and other oppressed peoples. The ruling class works tirelessly to sow division among Blacks, Chicanos, Puerto Ricans, etc. They shrewdly use differences in historical background and customs to foster disunity. But regardless of such differences, oppressed people are all in the same boat. They all confront the same oppressor. Pride in one's background is natural, but it should not be allowed to serve as a wedge between peoples.

The Black, Chicano, Puerto Rican, Native American Indian, Asian-Pacific and all other nationally oppressed peoples in the United States total more than 50 million—some one-fourth of the entire population. Strongly and solidly united they can become a potent, major force.

But even solid unity among the oppressed peoples is not enough. Unity with white people and above all with white workers is indispensable. This is especially true in the current situation.

Basic economic progress for oppressed people, progress in improving their jobs, wages, housing and health care, requires turning the priorities of the whole country around. It requires slashing the military budget, reversing foreign policy and cutting into corporate profits. Without these changes there can be no economic progress.

But these changes can only be compelled by a broad coalition of the great majority of the people. The basis for such a coalition already exists in embryonic form. What is needed is to broaden and strengthen it. The basis for this coalition exists in the mutual interests of its parts. It is in the interest of the racially and nationally oppressed—and working people generally—to seek out and act on these overlapping interests.

The ruling class seeks to bring to the fore the contradictory features of the relationships within the coalition of the people. In order to wipe out the effects of racism it is necessary to take special steps, to implement affirmative action, especially in hiring and upgrading. Together with such steps, workers can unite and fight against speedup, for shorter hours and for higher wages.

Taking on monopoly capital is a big job. But there is no way around it. Without an all-out, unified fightback against the monopolies there is no way our country's problems can be solved. The job can and will be done precisely because there is no other way to solve our problems. The people of our country are not going to sit back and watch things get worse and worse. More and more, they are going to unite and fight. And unity requires first and foremost mounting a determined fight against racism and discrimination whenever and in whatever form they rear their ugly heads.   □

[*Daily World*, April 10, 1980]

1983

The Class Basis
Of the Struggle for Equality

Some say that in order to understand and to know the working class it is first necessary to know its separate parts.

It *is* necessary to know the component parts of the working class and the specific and unique problems they face. However, we must not, as Karl Marx warned, stand things on their heads.

We must always keep in mind that what gives the working class a sense of oneness, what moves it toward class unity, what gives it class consciousness, what forces it to move to the head of the line of march, and what propels it as a class to consider revolutionary action, is class exploitation at the point of production.

It is understanding and recognition of this basic premise that must become the starting point and framework for consideration of all questions relating to the working class and the class struggle.

The fact that we must keep emphasizing that our working class is multiracial, multinational, male-female, young and old, is itself an indication that there are special problems that relate to each component of the class.

Therefore, the struggle against inequality is a basic question simply because not all members of our class work and live under conditions of equality.

The Afro-American component of our U.S. working class is exploited, as are all workers. But they are additionally discriminated against and exploited based on racism. Black workers, men and women, are exploited on the basis of the class of which they are a part. They are further exploited on the basis of race. And they suffer many-sided discrimination because they are members of an oppressed nationality.

It is estimated that the racist cut in wages is $70 per week, or an average of $3,600 per year. Racism is a big factor in the fact that 20 per cent of Black workers are unemployed and that 25-30 per cent of Black workers in basic industry are unemployed. Most are suffering from long-term unemployment.

There is also a distinct pattern of racism in upgrading and job classification. The racist pattern in hiring and firing of Black workers remains in full force.

The Reagan cuts in food stamps and all social and economic programs have a special, sharp racist edge against Black workers and their families. Because of past discriminatory practices, pension, retirement and social security benefits are smaller for Black workers.

Black workers and their families suffer from the discrimination and racism directed against the whole Afro-American community—poor housing, education, medical and child care, cultural oppression, as well as political under-representation.

Thus, the struggle for working-class equality must begin with the struggle to eliminate the $70 per week wage inequality. It must start by doing away with discrimination in upgrading and job classification, in hiring and firing practices.

The gap created by racist inequality is a major obstacle to working-class unity. A true measure of the class consciousness of all workers—but, in a special way, of the level of class consciousness of white workers—is the level of Black-white unity. Black-white working-class unity is a fundamental precondition for working-class unity in general. The struggle for Black-white working-class unity is key to building alliances.

A critical arena for the struggle must be jobs and affirmative action. The struggle for equality in unionized industries can be conducted by way of affirmative action clauses in labor contracts. This must become standard for all labor contracts.

But some of the most serious racist inequalities are in unorganized industries and shops. Therefore, the struggle for equality and against racism in general raises the need for organizing the unorganized and for more binding affirmative action legislation that would be applicable to the unorganized service industries. It also raises the need for enforcing the law and increasing the minimum wage.

The inequalities suffered by other nationally oppressed components of our working class are all patterned after the system of racism against the Afro-American community. The racism against Black America feeds the national oppression, discrimination and chauvinism against other nationally oppressed minorities.

The oppression that other national minorities suffer is not the same. But it is fed by and is closely connected with the racism that permeates all phases of our life.

The struggle for equality of the Chicano-Mexican component of our working class is also key to working-class unity, especially in a number of regions and in some industries. About 50 per cent of Chicano-Mexicano workers are in basic industries such as metal, mining, steel and auto. And some 20 per cent are low-wage agricultural workers.

Most of the people without legal documents are also workers in low-wage and largely unorganized industries. Most, if not all, live below the poverty level.

Therefore, the struggle for equality of the Chicano-Mexican component of the working class must start with elimination of the wage differential. This must include the struggle to end the non-legal status of workers without documents and the struggle for their full economic, trade union, political, civil and human rights.

Puerto Rican workers are another important component of the U.S. working class. The Puerto Rican people in the United States are overwhelmingly working class. They are a key sector of the class in industries like garment. They are an important sector of the working class in many industrial centers, including in some steel communities.

The result of policies of racial and national discrimination is widespread poverty. In many areas, the Puerto Rican workers are among the lowest paid and unemployment is disproportionately high.

The struggle for the liberation of Puerto Rico from colonial oppression is a struggle against U.S. imperialism. Therefore, the racial and national oppression of Puerto Rican workers and people is closely linked because in both cases the class enemy is the same.

The struggle for equality of the Puerto Rican component of our working class must also start with the struggle to wipe out the wage gap and the discriminatory practices in hiring, firing, job promotion and classification.

As in the case with Chicano-Mexican workers, the refusal of the corporations to consider using Spanish in the workplace becomes an instrument of inequality. This is especially a contributing factor in the refusal to conduct bilingual classes for learning skills and trades. Such classes must become a union contract demand.

The relatively smaller number of Native American Indians in the U.S. work force is itself proof of the old policy of discrimination in corporate hiring.

The extreme poverty and, in some cases, total unemployment in the slums of reservations force many to move to urban centers where Native American people face the new Reagan cuts in social services. In these industrial centers they meet head-on the special, long-established corporate policies of discrimination against Native American Indian workers.

The problems faced by the Native American Indian workers are closely related to the monopoly-corporate rip-off of the energy and water resources on the reservations.

Their problems are closely connected to the struggles for return of stolen lands and to the policies of genocide, including sterilization.

Therefore, the starting point in the struggle for equality of Native American Indian workers is the struggle to put an end to the age-old ban on hiring. The goal must be to eliminate the wage gap and open the trade schools to Indian workers, especially youth.

There are millions of other members of our working class who are victims of similar practices and policies of racial and national oppression. Most of them are in the low-paid, unorganized industries.

There are Filipinos, Japanese, Chinese, Korean and other Asian-Pacific workers. There are Iranians, Dominicans, Jamaicans, Haitians and others who, to one degree or another, are all victims of racial and national oppression.

Here again, as components of the working class, the starting point in the struggle for equality is a struggle to end the wage gaps and the inequalities in working and living conditions.

As you can see, I have dealt with the struggle against racial and national oppression and the struggle for equality as they are reflected within the working class, as a feature of the class struggle.

This does not encompass all aspects of racial and national oppression, and is not meant to substitute for a full examination of these questions. What is most important is that it does deal with the basic class roots of racial and national oppression. This way of placing the question takes into consideration a number of factors.

The great majority of the racially and nationally oppressed are workers and therefore components of the working class.

Placing the question in this context more clearly lays bare the role and responsibilities of the trade union movement and the working class in the struggle for equality, since the basic inequalities originate in the work place.

This framework correctly makes the connections between our emphasis on the working class, the concentration on workers in the basic mass production industries, and the struggle for equality.

This lays the basis for a better understanding of the key role of Black-white unity. It makes it easier to show concretely and to convince white workers why they must take on the struggle for equality, which is a struggle for equality in their class.

On this basis it is easier to see the necessity to develop working-class consciousness as an important ingredient in the struggle for equality.

This emphasis lays the foundation for the unity of racially and nationally oppressed peoples with the working class.

It makes clearer the necessity for the working class to seek unity with the oppressed minorities.

It places a needed emphasis on the economics of racism—its relationship to corporate profits and to class exploitation. It places the capitalist system as the root and ultimate source of all racism.

As its class consciousness deepens, the working class will see itself more clearly as a class. It will fight for the interests of the class more consistently. It will see more clearly that the problems are rooted in class exploitation.

However, as this consciousness deepens the working class must learn that to be able to fight for the best interests of the whole class it must take on the special struggle against the inequalities faced by the components of the working class.

This approach more clearly focuses on the special and unique contributions that Communists must make in the struggle for equality.

This framework also provides a stronger foundation for and an added dimension to the general human, civil and moral aspects of the struggle for equality.

Because the cause is just and because it is in its class interest, the trade union movement must be convinced to accept as its major responsibility the struggle for equality for all components of the working class in every area of life.

This can become a firm basis for the struggle against racism, national oppression and chauvinism in all areas of life—in housing, in public education, in medical and child care, in social services and political representation.

The position of the working class in the line of march continues to change. There have been significant advances since our last convention. Our class has moved closer to the front of the line.

This should not surprise us. We should expect it. We should hail and nurture it. But, above all, we should understand the significance of it.

We must view all these developments from a rose-colored, partisan, class perspective.   □

[Report to 23rd Convention, CPUSA, November 1983]

1984

A Glorious History
Of Struggle and Victory

The struggle against racism is a long way from final victory, but there have been significant gains in it.

Just as in the struggle against the exploitation of labor, the battle has not been won. But none can argue that there have not been significant victories.

In judging the effect of mass struggles on the course of history, we have to place the question: Where would we be if there had been no struggle? Struggle is an inseparable part of the existence of all living things, including the social existence of people.

The history of the Afro-American people is one of heroic struggle and bittersweet victories.

Slavery did not leave the stage of history voluntarily or passively. Abolition was won in a historic battle involving the entire nation. The right to vote, breakthroughs in employment in basic industry and in access to education and housing and the decrease in open racist slander are, like the abolition of slavery, results of struggle.

The bark of Bull Conner[9] and his police dogs in Birmingham, Alabama, was silenced by mass struggle. The disappearance of "whites only" signs was won by picket signs carried in mass protests. The struggles for equality have left their positive, indelible imprint in greater human rights and democracy and higher wage scales.

However, exploitation of the working class still exists. Class, racial and national oppression and exploitation of the Afro-American people still exist. Racial and national oppression continue to exist because they are integrated into the economic and political structure of U.S. state monopoly capitalism. The motive, as in the case of exploitation itself, is maximum corporate profits.

The total eradication of racism and its uprooting from all phases of life, like the elimination of exploitation, will require a revolutionary transformation of production relations on the basis of public ownership of the means of production. Socialism eliminates the private profit motive and thereby does away with the instigator of ideological diversion and coverup.

There have been gains, and new victories can be won. But the struggle has not yet been won. Indeed, because of the Reagan Administration's antilabor, racist policies there have been defeats and setbacks.

The income gap between Black and white families continues to widen. In housing, education, health care, child care and many other areas the gains of past years are being eroded. Afro-American unemployment remains at depression levels. The underlying antihuman nature of U.S. capitalism is most clearly evident in the racial, national and class oppression and exploitation of Afro-Americans.

The present stage of the struggle for equality focuses on elimination of racial differentials in wages, employment, income, housing, education, health and representation in government. It seeks equality in the arts and culture as well as in the mass media.

The triple tiers of racial oppression are all affected by the triple-layered crisis of U.S. capitalism—the recurring cyclical crisis, the structural crisis and the overall general crisis of decay of capitalism.

Because most Afro-Americans are workers, they are affected by the cyclical crisis. The layoffs resulting from the crisis have a racist impact because Black workers are laid off in disproportionate numbers. And this history of discrimination in hiring and promotion is reflected in lower unemployment benefits.

The structural crisis, with its plant closings and abandonment of entire industries or sections of industries, like basic steel production, devastates working-class lives and communities. But the structural crisis also has a racist wrecking ball. These are the industries where Black workers have won some breakthroughs in hiring. Because of racism, Black workers who become unemployed remain unemployed longer, or become permanently unemployed.

The third layer of crisis—the overall crisis of decaying capitalism—affects most workers. But cutbacks in industrial and trade expansion decrease job opportunities, and so become another domain where racism does its dirty work of discrimination.

The racist policies of the Reagan Administration add another dimension to the exploitation and oppression of Afro-Americans.

As the basis of capitalist relations decays, all its contradictions become sharper. This is true of the contradiction between the two opposing classes—the working class and the capitalist class. All other contradictions and forces are influenced by the sharpening of this contradiction.

These developments are forcing the victims of capitalist exploitation to think more in terms of unity in struggle against a common enemy. As contradictions continue to sharpen it becomes easier to see that monopoly capital, the monopoly corporations, are the source of all these problems. It becomes easier for white workers to understand that not only is unity a necessity for struggle, but that the ideology of racism—the poison of white superiority—is based on a lie. It becomes easier to see that racist poison is consciously injected into the thought patterns of the nation to create divisions and disunity in their class ranks.

There is a growing awareness of related interests. As class consciousness deepens among the workers, they become more aware of the multiracial, multinational, male-female, young-old composition of their class and of the necessity to reject racism and inequality in all its forms.

There is a growing class consciousness, and with it a growing sense of class unity. From this follows recognition of the need for alliances among all victims of monopoly capital. And the most logical allies of the working class are the racially and nationally oppressed, women, youth, small farmers, professionals and small-business people.

There is a growing awareness that while each group has some special interests, there are also widening areas, issues and needs—like peace and economic well-being—where their interests overlap and are joined.

There is a natural sense of pride and unity in the Afro-American community. But there is also a realization that it is necessary and possible to win allies and forge alliances in the struggle against racism.

The intermingling of interests and the growing unity have emerged as the key ingredients in the struggle against the Reagan offensive. To strengthen this unity it is necessary to boldly promote the truth that all struggles and movements have built-in limitations if they do not include the struggle against racism.

The struggles of the working class and trade unions are limited if they do not take up the struggle for equality. And it is a hard fact that there can not be equality today without concrete measures of affirmative action, adjustments to make up for inequalities of the past. It is another hard fact that the superexploitation of part of the U.S. working class intensifies the exploitation of the whole class.

The struggle for democracy will be limited and will flounder if it does not take up the struggle for those whose democratic rights are most brutally violated. Racism is a built-in feature of the system of capitalist exploitation. It is a means by which the monopoly corporations squeeze maximum profits from their workers. It is a system of superprofits. U.S. capitalism has been racist from its very inception. Its origins coincided with the bloody genocidal campaign against the Native American Indian peoples.

The oldest of all Big Lies is that of "inferior races" and "superior races." It accompanied the forcible uprooting of peoples from Africa to work as slaves on the cotton, sugar and tobacco plantations. When slavery was abolished, racism was integrated into the system of capitalist exploitation.

The U.S. is a nation with sharp class divisions and contradictions. It is multiracial and multinational, as is the working class. It is a nation of many cultures and religions, each retaining its own heritage and traditions, but also integrating into the common life of the nation.

But because of the practice of racism, the different racial and nationality groups of the United States are not living as equals. Racism distorts and slows down the objective, progressive process of intermingling of different peoples into a single national entity. But there is an overlapping of basic interests of all the people of our country, and therefore a tendency to unite in struggle. It is most important to be aware of and to take advantage of the opportunities this presents.

In the struggle against racism and for equality, the Afro-American question is a unique national question. It will not be resolved simply because other questions are posed for solution. There is a distinct relationship between the class struggle and the struggle against racism. But it would be a serious and most harmful mistake to in any way submerge or set aside the struggle against racism. The struggle for Afro-American equality is a unique and special question that demands unique approaches and forms of struggle. The struggles must deal with the specific questions of an oppressed national minority. They must deal with the class question. And they must be responsive to the questions arising from racial oppression.

These are central to achieving working-class unity, to winning working-class victories. They are central to building an all people's front against Reaganism. Just as we must take on the struggle against monopoly capital's triple-layered crisis, so we must see the struggle against the tripled-tiered exploitation and oppression of the Afro-American people as an indispensable, integral and special aspect of all struggles. Without specific approaches to the struggle for equality and against racism, we can not mount united struggles and win new victories.   □

[*Daily World*, February 16, 1984]

3

STRATEGY
AND TACTICS

Welcome
Dr. DuBois!

Following is the letter from W.E.B. DuBois to Gus Hall, apply-
ing for membership in the Communist Party, USA, and Gus
Hall's response.

Gus Hall
Communist Party of the U.S.A.
New York, New York

On this first day of October 1961, I am applying for admission to membership in the Communist Party of the
United States. I have been long and slow in coming to this
conclusion, but at last my mind is settled.

In college I heard the name of Karl Marx, but read none
of his works, nor heard them explained. At the University
of Berlin, I heard much of those thinkers who had definitely answered the theories of Marx, but again we did not
study what Marx himself had said. Nevertheless, I at-
tended meetings of the Socialist Party and considered myself a Socialist.

On my return to America, I taught and studied for six-
teen years. I explored the theory of socialism and studied
the organized social life of American Negroes; but still I
neither read nor heard much of Marxism. Then I came to
New York as an official of the new NAACP and editor of
The Crisis magazine. The NAACP was capitalist-oriented

and expected support from rich philanthropists.

But it had a strong socialist element in its leadership in persons like Mary Ovington, William English Walling and Charles Edward Russell. Following their advice, I joined the Socialist Party in 1911. I knew then nothing of practical socialist politics and in the campaign of 1912 I found myself unwilling to vote the Socialist ticket, but advised Negroes to vote for Wilson. This was contrary to Socialist Party rules and consequently I resigned from the Socialist Party.

For the next twenty years I tried to develop a political way of life for myself and my people. I attacked the Democrats and Republicans for monopoly and disenfranchisement of Negroes; I attacked the Socialists for trying to segregate Southern Negro members; I praised the racial attitudes of Communists, but opposed their tactics in the case of the Scottsboro Boys[1] and their advocacy of a Negro state. At the same time, I began to study Karl Marx and the Communists; I read *Das Kapital* and other Communist literature; I hailed the Russian Revolution of 1917, but was puzzled at the contradictory news from Russia.

Finally in 1926, I began a new effort; I visited Communist lands. I went to the Soviet Union in 1926, 1936, 1949 and 1959; I saw the nation develop. I visited East Germany, Czechoslovakia and Poland. I spent ten weeks in China, traveling all over the land. Then, this summer, I rested a month in Rumania.

I was early convinced that socialism was an excellent way of life, but I thought it might be reached by various methods. For Russia, I was convinced she had chosen the only way open to her at the time. I saw Scandinavia choosing a different method, halfway between socialism and capitalism. In the United States, I saw Consumers Cooperation as a path from capitalism to socialism, while England, France and Germany developed in the same direction in their own way. After the Depression and the Second World War, I was disillusioned. The progressive movement in the United States failed. The Cold War started. Capitalism called communism a crime.

Today I have reached a firm conclusion:

Capitalism can not reform itself; it is doomed to self-destruction. No universal selfishness can bring social good to all.

Communism—the effort to give all men what they need and to ask of each the best they can contribute—this is the only way of human life. It is a difficult and hard end to reach—it has and will make mistakes, but today it marches triumphantly on in education and science, in home and food, with increased freedom of thought and deliverance from dogma. In the end communism will triumph. I want to help bring that day.

The path of the American Communist Party is clear: It will provide the United States with a real third party and thus restore democracy to this land. It will call for:

1. Public ownership of natural resources and of all capital.
2. Public control of transportation and communications.
3. Abolition of poverty and limitation of personal income.
4. No exploitation of labor.
5. Social medicine, with hospitalization and care of the old.
6. Free education for all.
7. Training for jobs and jobs for all.
8. Discipline for growth and reform.
9. Freedom under law.
10. No dogmatic religion.

These aims are not crimes. They are practiced increasingly over the world. No nation can call itself free which does not allow its citizens to work for these ends.

W.E.B. Du Bois

Dear Dr. DuBois:

In reply to your letter of October 1, in which you make application for membership in the Communist Party of the United States, allow me to relate the following:

I read it before our National Board on October 13th, where it was greeted with the highest enthusiasm and responded to with many heartfelt testimonials to the titanic

labors which you have performed over a glorious span of
60 years of dedicated services and leadership in the cause
of human progress, peace, science and culture.

Already in 1906 in your historic "Address to the Country
of the Niagara Movement," you had perceived the main
line of development of our century, and wrote these pro-
phetic words:

> The morning breaks over the hills. Courage brothers! The bat-
> tle for humanity is not lost or losing. The Slav is rising in his
> might, the yellow minions are testing liberty, the Black Africans
> are writhing toward the light, and everywhere the laborer is open-
> ing the gates of opportunity and peace.

And so it has come, and is coming to pass. And knowl-
edgeable people everywhere are mindful of the fact that
your selfless labors and mighty works have been a powerful contribution to the dawn of our new epoch, the epoch of
the final triumph of man over all manner of oppression,
discrimination and exploitation.

You (the first Negro to receive the Doctor of Philosophy
degree from Harvard University in 1895) are the acknowl-
edged Dean of American letters and most eminent living
American scholar.

As editor, sociologist, historian, novelist, poet, publicist,
lecturer and organizer you have made enduring contributions. Your life is a monumental example of achievement
for all Americans.

For 50 years you have been a tireless champion of the
national liberation of the African peoples and new Africa's
wise counselor and "elder statesman."

For more than 60 years you have been the foremost philosopher, theoretician and practical organizer of the Negro
people's glorious freedom struggle.

You have authored numerous books, each of which is a
weapon against colonialism, racism and imperialism, and
for the victory of the cause of peace, freedom and brotherhood of peoples.

You have raised your voice powerfully and incessantly

against war machinations, for world peace and disarmament, for friendship with the socialist countries and coexistence between the two world social systems.

Your act of joining the Communist Party at this time not only expresses that recognition of the new world reality, of the great turn of the people of the world toward socialism for the solution of mankind's need for peace, brotherhood and well-being, but it constitutes an invitation and a challenge to men and women of science and culture, to creative thinkers of all countries, to the Negro masses and their outstanding leaders, both here and abroad, to avail themselves of the social science of Marxism-Leninism and the fraternity of the Communist Parties to give new wings to their cause and their works.

You have chosen to join our Party precisely at the time when with brazen effrontery to the trends of the times, the most backward, ultra-reactionary forces in our country's national life have temporarily dragooned the Supreme Court's majority into upholding the most flagrantly unconstitutional thought-control laws—the McCarran and Smith Acts—designed to muzzle free speech, ban freedom of association, persecute Communists and suppress our Party.

This is symbolic of the personal courage and heroic exercise of social responsibility which have characterized your service and leadership to the people's cause throughout your long life.

Dear Dr. DuBois, welcome into the membership of our Party! The title of Party member is an honorable and worthy title, worn with pride by the most dedicated and farseeing, the best sons and daughters of the workers and peoples of all lands in the first ranks of the struggle for mankind's happy future.

With comradely greetings,

Gus Hall

A Question
Whose Time Has Come

History has reached a threshold marked: "End colonialism now." This is not an idle wish. Rather, ending colonialism has become a practical possibility and an absolute necessity. Because of the point reached in the balance of contending forces in the world, nothing can prevent this step in the march of civilization. The anti-imperialist coalition of the socialist world, the national liberation movements, the working class of the capitalist countries, and all progressive mankind, with their ideology of liberation, independence and internationalism, is now stronger than ever before relative to imperialism, with its ideology of great-power chauvinism, racism and jingoism. Civilization is confronted with the urgent task of abolishing colonialism. And all mankind will benefit from it.

With the emergence of new independent nations in Africa and Asia, the evil ideology of racial superiority has suffered a shattering blow. The United States is not insulated from the fires of freedom and independence burning abroad. The U.S. is directly affected on two fronts. As the main world center of colonial exploitation, it is forced to adjust to this development and give ground. Further, the United States must, in the context of this world situation, address the most explosive issue on the domestic scene, namely, the policies of discrimination and segregation inflicted on 20 million Black citizens. We as a nation must take a fresh look, reevaluate, achieve an understanding of this question commensurate with an epoch that is witnessing the end of colonialism in all parts of the world.

Colonial oppression and discrimination against Black Americans are very close relatives. The oppressor is the same: U.S. monopoly capitalism. Hence the slogans, "End colonialism now in the world" and "End segregation in the United States" are twin slogans. The latter corresponds to the balance of forces in the United States, and is therefore a realistic outlook.

The Afro-American people's movement for full equality continues to gather force. Its militancy and dedication are an inspiration to all Americans.

There is also a slow but continuing advance in the understanding of sections of white Americans of the inevitability of ending racist practices and their own interest and need to enter this struggle.

Recent events at the University of Georgia[2] reflect all these factors. The calm confidence and heroism of two young Black students, Charlayne Hunter and Hamilton Holmes, are symbolic of the heroism of the Afro-American people and their movement. The viciousness of racism is written in the faces and actions of the rock-throwing hoodlums. The growing understanding of some sections of white Americans is symbolized in the petition signed by over 300 of the faculty of the university, as well as by the petition signed by a sizeable section of the students. These petitions call for the return of the expelled students and a return to law and morality in Georgia. This is the beginning of something new and important in the South.

To keep up with the rest of the world, segregation must go! Our people must surmount many political as well as ideological obstacles to accomplish this task. We Communists must become a more effective force helping our people to destroy these barriers. We must help the working class, Afro-American people, youth and intellectuals to see the new elements in the picture, the new policies and tactics needed to use the objective possibilities presented by the present epoch.

In the very center of this new understanding must be the recognition that for all of us—Black and white—freedom, equality, dignity, standard of living, happiness and security are indivisible. As our 17th Convention (December 1959) resolution, "The Negro Question in the United States," says: "Not only the working class, but all social classes and currents which are in any way restricted in their democratic development by the reactionary monopolists have a stake in the cause of Negro freedom."

The new balance of world forces and especially the position of the United States itself have made clearer who is the central adversary, the main culprit. Developments in this epoch tend to focus the attention of all the victims on the identity of the oppressor. The tentacle that prolongs colonialism in the Congo, the tentacle that foments war in Laos, or supports the colonial powers' desperate efforts to hold on to their possessions, the tentacle that upholds the Dixiecrats[3] and in fact the whole racist system, the tentacle behind the layoffs, speedup and high taxes, the tentacle behind the generals who advocate military buildup and war—all these are in fact attached to one body, that of U.S. monopoly capitalism.

We must do more to bring home the lesson: when one tentacle is destroyed, it weakens the grip of the rest. Conversely, if one is strengthened, it strenghtens the grip of the others. We must bring home the lesson that white workers and trade unionists can not make headway or even preserve their hard won gains if they overlook and sacrifice the rights of their Black brothers. They can not ward off blows to their own heads if they turn their eyes away when blows are rained on their Black brothers. A union that closes its eyes while Black workers are laid off because of automation is helpless when layoffs hit other sections of workers. It deprives itself of the unity and strength which it needs to fight. The simple truth is that white workers can not form an alliance against the monopolies that oppress them if they permit these monopolies to oppress Black Americans.

The new epoch brings hard struggles. U.S. capitalism is striving to pass on its setbacks in the form of speedup, wage cuts, layoffs, inflation and high taxes. And no appeasement by the unions or white workers when the blow is directed against Black workers will change this. The only effective protection against monopoly capital is unbreakable unity of all workers, and not least, unity of Black and white.

Hence the inherent self-interest of the working class in the struggle for Afro-American equality. And the Afro-American people need the support of the working class in their struggle for equality. Objective developments make it easier in this period to hammer home the lesson that the working class needs unity with the Afro-American people. The sameness of the enemy and the common interests of the victims become clearer and clearer.

This period also places new questions before the leaders of the Afro-American people's struggle. They have spoken out militantly, courageously for equal rights in the United States. But this has been weakened by some who support the foreign policies of the very oppressors of the Afro-American people. This contradiction is now becoming more evident. It is increasingly difficult to ignore the identity of the body to which are attached the various tentacles of oppression. The support U.S. trade unionists give to U.S. foreign policy seriously weakens the struggle in the class struggle arena at home.

It is more true than ever, as we said in our 17th Convention resolution, "The Negro movement's need and possibility for sympathetic alliances do not end with the nation's borders. . . . The international aspects of the Negro question are of major importance in the struggle for equality at home, favorable to wresting concessions from the ruling class." And we urged that: "The Negro movement will be further strengthened as it forges bonds of conscious alliance with the rising colonial, semicolonial and newly independent nations of the world, the peoples of Asia, Africa and Latin America." We added, "the Negro people must come to look with favor upon the socialist world," which has ended for all time national oppression and enmity between people, and wiped out discrimination on national, racial or color lines. The socialist world has been the best friend and most reliable ally of the oppressed colonial peoples, contributing immensely to their rapid advance to freedom and independence.

We have always understood that the interests of the working class, youth, intellectuals and farmers are in close harmony with the historic task of ending racism. But now objective developments make it easier for the great masses of Americans to understand this. We, as a vanguard party, must accept the responsibility of bringing this deeper understanding into the broad ranks of the people and raising the struggle to end racism to new heights.

The Democratic Party and President Kennedy made far-reaching promises on civil rights in their election platform and campaign. This won Kennedy the votes of the overwhelming majority of Black voters, notwithstanding his selection of Lyndon B. Johnson as candidate for Vice President. The votes of the Afro-American people and labor were decisive in his victory.

It is imperative that these promises be kept! There have been retreats, compromises and capitulations before on the question of Afro-American freedom. This brought only disaster to our country. It must not be repeated. All democratic-minded people must insist that the reactionary policy of "not antagonizing the South," on the spurious ground that struggle with the Dixiecrats would divert from so-called domestic issues, be abandoned. Afro-American equality is also a domestic issue—in fact a central one. The sooner this is realized and the sooner the Dixiecrats and racists who lead the main committees of Congress are challenged, the quicker will progress be made in the sphere of social welfare and other domestic needs.

The President of the United States has full authority as well as historic precedents to end legal segregation now by executive order. And the executive arm of our government has a clear-cut mandate of the people to take bold and decisive steps to do so.

The precedent was set by President Lincoln when he issued the Emancipation Proclamation. The authority flows from our Constitution, and additionally from such laws as the Reconstruction Statutes passed in 1871. These state that whenever insurrection, violence or unlawful combinations or conspiracies so obstruct the execution of the laws in a given state that any group is deprived of its rights, and whenever the authorities of a state are unable or fail to protect these rights, "it shall be lawful for the President, and it shall be his duty, to take such measures, by the employment of the militia or the land and naval forces of the United States, or of either, or by any other means as he may deem necessary, for the suppression of such insurrection, domestic violence or combinations."

The mandate for such action was reaffirmed in the Democratic platform, as well as promised in the Republican platform.

Only this kind of resolute action would be in keeping with the era in which we live. The concept of gradualism was always wrong, but there is reason today to be even more sharply critical of it than in the past. In fact, in the framework of today's situation, to defend gradualism is to protect segregation, to shield it. It would be an odd contradiction indeed, while colonialism is being ended, to look on ending segregation as a process which will take ages.

The executive orders should start with a complete and absolute guarantee of the right to vote and hold office. Suffrage is closely connected with the right to hold a job, to get an education. It is no accident that areas of industrial desolation are often areas where the majority of citizens are denied the right to vote.

Two examples should suffice to nail down the importance of this question. For the first time, Kennedy carried some Southern states only because of the heavy support of Black voters, and this is also true in several key industrial states of the North. Second (and this shows how keenly the Dixiecrats understand the potential of this issue), there is the hysteria and the inhuman ejection of Black farm families from the land in Tennessee for the sole crime of indicating their intention to exercise their constitutional right to vote in the local and presidential elections.

The question of the right of Black people in the South to vote is of cardinal importance to every section of the population.

This year most states are reapportioning electoral districts based on the 1960 census. The politicians are busy plotting the most brazen gerrymandering in our history with the aim of making it impossible for Black people, as well as other minority groups and the working class, to elect their own representatives. This further demonstrates how indivisible are the rights and interests of these sections of our people. There is no rhyme or reason in permitting Southern states to have representatives in the halls of Congress who presumably represent their people but in actual fact are chosen in elections from which large sections of the people are barred.

There is no dearth of laws on the statute books that guarantee equal rights to all citizens. What is wrong is that most of these laws remain on paper. What is needed is to demand unconditional compliance with these laws. There is no reason why there should not be a Secretary of Civil Rights in the President's Cabinet. For most of these laws to have any meaning there must be suitable enforcement bodies in each city and state.

A central task at the present time is the fight for jobs. This is obvious from the figures on the high rate of Black unemployment. It is essential to have an overall national program, as well as programs for specific areas. The fight for jobs for Afro-Americans is, of course, related to the general struggle against the growing economic crisis and unemployment. But any general program to cope with these must include particular demands regarding the needs of the Afro-American people, which must receive the utmost consideration, especially as to their implementation.

Let me cite some examples:

The federal government gives billions of dollars of business to corporations. Why should not the federal government publish the names of corporations which do business with the government so that people's committees could police compliance with federal laws barring discrimination?

City governments, like New York and others, also carry on extensive business with corporations. Why should they not do likewise?

Fair employment practices laws already on the books in many cities and states should be enforced, and the unfinished job of enacting a federal Federal Employment Practices Commission should be completed.

There is the fight, carried on since the Great Depression, for jobs for Black people in the corporations and commercial establishments that carry on extensive trade in Black communities.

There is the question of opening up new job possibilities in depressed areas, both South and North.

There are questions of seniority rights, apprenticeship training and many others.

School desegregation remains a major task. While every assistance must be given to the central battleground—the South—where desegregation is opposed with savage violence by the state and city governments in defiance of the Constitution and the Supreme Court, this fight is not a Southern struggle alone. Desegregation is an issue in the North as well. It is an issue in New York City and surrounding areas, in Philadelphia, in Chicago and a host of other cities.

There is also the struggle against discrimination in housing, the effects of which are becoming more and more acute as Black people are increasingly crowded into shameful ghettoes in our cities. This discrimination, which also serves as the excuse for school segregation in the North, has become a primary issue in one Northern industrial city after another.

Our Party has made and is making important and unique contributions to the struggle for equal rights. Our task as a vanguard Party is to disclose the deep wells of strength on which this struggle can draw, to show the oneness of this movement with the movements of other forces, and to help keep all eyes on the center of the enemy forces.

We can do this best if we are an active part of the struggle for jobs, if we take an active part in the campaign for proper reapportionment, if we are part of the struggles for FEPC laws[4] and, finally, if we are part of the mass campaign for executive action to end discrimination. In short, we can fulfill our responsibilities if we are an integral part of the Afro-American people's movement and the struggle for complete equality.

It is essential to lift the level of our work. We must concentrate on this task, which means that all the main forces of the Party must regard the fight for Afro-American rights as of crucial importance. It is not a subsidiary task, not "another" task; it is a primary, fundamental, front-rank Party task of the highest order.

We must restore the full crusading spirit of our Party on this issue. It is essential for the Afro-American freedom struggle and for America that more and more Communists be in that great battle. Communists help to bring clarity and direction where there is confusion as to the line of march. They contribute resoluteness and militancy where there is timidity and uncertainty. They bring unity—unity among Black people, unity between Black and white, unity of Black people with labor and all democratic sections of the population.

Communists have no interests alien to the Afro-American people's aims and struggles. They regard the unity of all strata of the Afro-American people as essential to victory, even while they consider it necessary to increasingly bring forward the weight and leadership of workers, who are the largest stratum of the Afro-American people, who are employed in heavy industry and who, with 2,000,000 union members, are the best organized.

Communists work to carry out the programs of the Afro-American people's organizations. True, they have differences with the policies of some Right-wing, reformist leaders who fear mass struggle and tend to limit and curb it. They criticize such policies in the interests of victory. But at all times, they seek to present constructive measures which aid the struggle and which build the Afro-American people's organizations and their unity.

Communists seek to convince Black workers of the need for socialism, to bring to Black workers the great ideas of Marxism-Leninism, which have already emancipated millions. The more such class conscious workers there are, the better for the struggle.

Communists can be counted on to wage a continuous, unyielding ideological battle against racism, against every manifestation of white supremacy, against all forms of white chauvinism, including its subtler forms which find reflection at times even in our ranks. We also oppose narrow nationalist views in the Party and thereby work for the firmest unity of Black and white.   □

[*Worker*, February 10, 1962]

Afro-American Freedom
The Cause of Every American

Nothing is more powerful than an issue which social development has placed for decision. Its resolution can no more be prevented than the rising of the sun.

In 1776, such an issue was independence for the colonies. And independence was won. In 1863, it was freedom for the slaves. And slavery was abolished. Victory in each of these momentous struggles was assured by the fact that great numbers of Americans, even though they did not fully grasp the significance of the issue at hand, were nevertheless compelled by their own interest to join in the battle.

In our day, a central world issue that has come up for decision is the ending of imperialist oppression of peoples and nations. The world system of colonialism is already disintegrating. In our country, the key issue on the agenda is eradication of the system of segregation and discrimination against 20 million Afro-Americans. Just as the United States could not have progressed without the people resolving the questions of independence and emancipation, so we can not move ahead now without putting an end to a system that keeps 20 million of our citizens half slave and half free.

The destruction of this system of discrimination and segregation is in the most fundamental self-interest of the great majority of Americans. It is crucial to the preservation and extension of democracy. It is vital to the working class in its economic struggles. It is a question that influences decisively the relations of the United States to the rest of the world. On its resolution rests the moral and ethical standards of our people. For a people can not tolerate the national oppression of 20 million of citizens without a corresponding corruption and warping of moral standards.

Our most basic interest as a nation, therefore, calls for a national coalition and a united crusade which will put an end to the system that blocks progress, corrodes human relations and warps moral standards.

It is ten years since the Supreme Court declared school segregation illegal and unconstitutional. Since then there have been hundreds of other court decisions. Millions of Americans—Black and many white Americans, tens of thousands of the clergy, hundreds of thousands of youth—have marched, sat in, demonstrated and picketed, gone to jail and suffered beatings and the pain of cattle prods, all in the struggle for minimum human decency and equality. Men, women and children have died as heroes and victims in this struggle.

But after all these militant struggles, what are the results? There have been positive results. Not to see them would be wrong and a disservice to the struggle. Many of the solid walls of segregation and discrimination have been broken down. There has been some progress in every area of struggle. But progress has been painfully slow and limited. To fail to see the stubbornness of the resistance would also be a disservice.

In the Southern states the main pillars of this evil system still remain. And the refusal of city and state governments in the North to take measures against de facto segregation of schools testifies to the resistance to any real breakthrough there.

The question is: What force so stubbornly resists and obstructs the peaceful, nonviolent resolution of this question?

Why the tenacity with which this evil system hangs on?

Its basic source is not the open, active opposition of the masses of white Americans. Thus, in the South the violence and terror unleashed against the struggles of Black people have been primarily the work of the police, not of white mobs. While a substantial sector of the white population is afflicted with outright racism, the majority do not offer the kind of active, violent resistance which would explain the slowness of progress.

This resistance flows rather from the fact that the system of discrimination and segregation against Black Americans is imbedded in the very fabric of United States capitalism. It has been, and is today, the policy of every major corporation in America. The system of oppression is the creation of Big Business.

Consider, for example, the following rather typical situation reported from a midwestern steel mill:

> There are no Black women workers in the offices. There are no Black bricklayers, pipefitters, millwrights, boilermakers, carpenters, plumbers, machinists, engineers or metallurgists. There is one Black foreman—in the sanitation department. Most of the Black steelworkers are in classes 1 to 4. These are the unskilled departments. Most white steel workers are in classes 5 to 11.
>
> The shops have a system of seniority. When layoffs take place, anyone with higher seniority can bump men in classes 1 to 4. Because classes 5 to 11 are the skilled categories, the system of shopwide bumping does not apply there at all.
>
> When Black steelworkers take a test for a higher-rated job, they are not shown the results. The management merely tells them they failed to qualify.

This system of special oppression is a tool of capitalism to squeeze maximum profits from the labor of all who toil. It is an instrument for maintaining in the halls of Congress, and in state and city legislative bodies, reactionary blocs of antidemocratic, antilabor and anti-Black politicians. It is an effective device for keeping the working class divided. White supremacy, the ideological foundation of the system of discrimination and segregation, is a central pillar in the ideology of U.S. capitalism.

In short, these roots are imbedded in U.S. capitalist economics, capitalist politics and capitalist ideology. It is this that explains the stubborn persistence of discrimination.

What stops U.S. Steel or General Motors from putting an end to the system of discrimination practiced in every one of their plants? Very simply, it is because this system is profitable. This is its purpose. It keeps workers divided. It helps to keep the less skilled workers in the hardest jobs, with the lowest pay. A not insignificant part of the two billion dollars in profits that General Motors is making this year is made possible by this system of discrimination.

Who in Birmingham, Alabama, are the masters of the economic complex that is the basis for the whole system of inequality and discrimination? U.S. Steel and similar corporations dominate the scene. If these corporations were to discard their policy of discrimination, very quickly the nature of the struggle would change in Birmingham.

Big Business moves plants to the South because workers there can be hired at lower wages. In February 1964 the average hourly pay for production workers in the South was $1.83, compared to a national average of $2.43. In Mississippi it was $1.75, in contrast to $3.07 in Michigan.

The cause of these lower wage scales is obvious. The system of oppression of Afro-Americans reduces the wages of all workers, Black and white. And as long as the system of racist discrimination keeps the working class in the South divided, wage scales there will remain lower.

The special oppression in the South affects the jobs and wages of white workers in the North. It affects those who are left on the relief lines when the plants move South. There, ironically, they find themselves united with their Black class brothers. In many instances the wages of Northern workers are kept down, and sometimes even cut, through the threat to move plants South. In other ways as well, the existence of lower wage scales in the South acts as a drag on the wages of workers throughout the country.

Working-class unity and organization of the unorganized in the South will become possible only when the white workers in the South and the North understand that this system is the product of Big Business' drive for profits at the expense of all, and that their interest as workers lies in putting an end to it. White workers who support the system of oppression, whether actively or by their neutrality, actually support Big Business and are acting against their own interest.

That the root of the system of racial oppression lies in Big Business is further demonstrated by the huge sums it passes on to every kind of racist organization. A series of articles appearing last year in the UAW publication *Solidarity*, on the subject "How Big Business Finances Right-Wing Extremists," speaks of a "sinister network of subversive racists, hate peddlars, antilabor extremists and neofascists" and says

> Acting as "angels" for these lunatic fringe extremist groups are a large number of "respectable" and well-known Big Businessmen. These highly-paid corporation executives form a virtual "interlocking directorate" for many of the ultra-Right-wing groups, providing unlimited funds and the necessary facade of respectability.

Among those listed are present or former executives of such corporations as General Electric Company, Sun Oil Company, Jones and Laughlin Steel Company and the notorious Kohler Company, heads of Southern textile mills, former presidents of the National Association of Manufacturers, and numerous others. That is why these outfits, which are both racist and antilabor, never suffer for lack of money.

At stake in the civil rights issue is everything progressive, all the past gains made by our people. The stubborn resistance by the forces of reaction to its democratic resolution is unifying and strengthening the ultra-Right reactionary coalition. The aim of preserving the evil system of oppression of Afro-American people, with its vicious ideology of white chauvinism and racism, is now bringing together all of the most reactionary, bigoted and fascist-tainted organizations and movements in the country. The nuclear war maniacs, the rabid antilabor crowd, the anti-democratic, pro-fascist gangs, the professional anti-Semites, the anti-Communist racketeers—all are gravitating towards unity with the Dixiecrat White Citizens Councils, the KKK and their ilk,[5] thus forming an evil alliance which menaces all that is progressive in our land.

Here is a polarization of reaction, a crystallization of an evil alliance that can open the gates to fascism. And open racism flows through all their veins.

Each of these groups has its own reactionary goal. Each calculates that the civil rights issue will demoralize and paralyze enough people to create the opening through which it can ride to power, just as in Germany the various reactionary groups gravitated toward the fanatical anti-Semitism and anti-Communism of Hitler fascism.

This cabal emerged as the organizer and the shock troops of the campaigns of Alabama's racist Governor Wallace in Wisconsin, Indiana and Maryland. Most of the Wallace-appointed electors were members of the John Birch Society.[6] Every possible pro-fascist group joined in, including many of the reactionary refugee groups. The antilabor corporations financed the campaign. The nazi groups financed the goon squads. Wallace furnished unsurpassed demagogy. Each group made its contribution to the evil alliance, whose ultimate aim is the destruction of democracy in our country and the resort to nuclear weapons in an attempt to plant the iron heel of U.S. imperialism on the neck of all mankind.

This reactionary coalition, which is the main force behind the Goldwater campaign,[7] now controls the Democratic and the Republican parties in the South, has made serious inroads in other states. This makes the menace of the ultra-Right all the more imminent.

Here is a new challenge to the democratic forces. How it is met has both immediate and long-range significance.

Just as resistance to civil rights brings together the evil powers of this coalition, so support for civil rights can bring together the democratic forces. Reaction has forced the civil rights issue into the very center of the struggle for a democratic future for America.

To the extent that the forces of this evil coalition are successful, how will the self-interest of specific groups of Americans be affected?

1. Democratic rights. The 80 per cent disfranchisement, the use of electric cattle prods and vicious dogs, the brazen acquittal of the murderers of small children, the lynchings, the rapes, the cynical destruction of all democratic rights now prevalent in Alabama, Mississippi, Georgia and other Southern states, will become the pattern for all of America. Just as these states have now set up large concentration camps for those who fight for civil rights, so will the federal government, if it falls into their hands, set up such camps for those who fight for civil liberties, peace and higher wages.

2. Trade unions. The unionbusting policies of the Southern states, the anti-union policies of the corporations who now finance the ultra-Right, the antilabor "right-to-work" state laws that these reactionary groups now promote—all this would become the law of the land. The Landrum-Griffin and Taft-Hartley[8] Acts were concessions to these forces. Their avowed purpose, if victorious, is to cut wages, speed up production, eliminate all hardwon fringe benefits, and permit the big corporations free rein to use automation to destroy jobs and working conditions.

More than this, their victory would threaten the most elementary democratic rights of unions, won in long, bitter struggle. In the pamphlet "Equal Rights For All," AFL-CIO President George Meany says:

Unions were created to fight against injustice. They were instruments of protest, deplored by public officials and much of the citizenry. They were often accused of flagrant civil disobedience.

For example, many trade unionists no older than middle age can well remember when local ordinances or court injunctions forbade the holding of a union meeting, even on private property owned or rented by the union. The "right of the people peaceably to assemble" often had no local standing, despite the Constitution.

Today the denial of such rights to Afro-American people in the South fighting against injustice is all too common, as in Tuscaloosa, Alabama, where Afro-Americans were driven out of their own church with tear gas and fire hoses. But equally important is the fact that elementary rights of unions are to this day also grossly violated in the South.

For example, at the 1961 AFL-CIO Convention, delegate John Chupka of the Textile Workers Union told of the use of traffic and trespass laws in South Carolina to arrest union organizers for distributing leaflets. He told of beatings of organizers and others by company thugs and the subsequent arrest and conviction of those beaten on charges of "inciting to riot," citing dozens of such cases in North and South Carolina, Georgia and Alabama.

The lesson is clear: The leadership of the AFL-CIO should do more in the struggle against racism.

This is happening in the South now, not a generation ago. And it is a direct consequence of the system of oppression and persecution of Black people. If the evil coalition could have its way, this would happen to unions throughout the country.

Clearly, therefore, the struggle for civil rights is also a struggle for the rights of labor.

3. Social Security. Most of these ultra-Right, racist groups are publicly opposed to all phases of social security. They are against old age pensions, unemployment insurance, veteran benefits, etc. Thus, one of the first acts of the Right-dominated state legislature in Wyoming was to cut unemployment compensation. The struggle for social security is thus inseparable from the struggle for civil rights.

4. World Peace. To the extent that this reactionary coalition is successful, its openly proclaimed advocacy of nuclear war will become national policy. General Walker[9] is only one of the military maniacs who are at the heart of this ultra-Right crystallization. The unity of the fanatical

pro-nuclear war forces and the racists in the struggle against civil rights has thus made the struggles for world peace and for civil rights indivisible.

5. Poverty. The same bigoted forces that have united to preserve Black oppression are equally united against any and all measures to fight poverty. Because so many of those forced to live in poverty are Afro-American, to fight poverty is to fight discrimination. It is to fight the evil coalition. Racism and poverty are twin products of capitalism.

How is this grave challenge to be met? Some argue that Afro-Americans should slow down, not rock the boat. Some say, let us keep things as they are. These are counsels of defeat. The one reality, on which all Americans must take a stand, is that the system of discrimination and segregation must go now, and is going to go now because its time has come. To compromise with it in any way is to compromise with the very foundation of the evil coalition that menaces our country. Segregation and discrimination are like a disease-breeding swamp which, if not removed, will destroy us.

The civil rights struggle, therefore, is a central arena of battle. It has become inseparably joined with the entire struggle for progress. It can not be bypassed. It must be resolved.

How is the fight to be waged? The experiences of the last ten years prove once again that progress results only from militant mass struggle. Therefore, if white Americans are to meet the challenge of Right-wing reaction, they must start by actively taking part in the civil rights struggle. This is in their own basic interest.

The struggle takes many specific forms. There is the attempt to strangle the Civil Rights Bill in Congress, an attempt only recently blocked by the closure vote in the Senate. Some people become greatly disturbed over sit-ins as a means of protest against discrimination. Yet in the Senate there is a small group of racist bigots, illegally elected, who have been able repeatedly to stop the machinery of the highest elected body of our government. And this is generally regarded as an accepted feature of the legislative process. The closure vote must be theforerunner not only of passage of the Civil Rights Bill but of the complete elimination of the Dixiecrat sabotage of the democratic process.

There is also the struggle to desegregate the public schools. It is in the self-interest of white parents to join with the parents of Black children to fight together for a system of integrated schools of a caliber that measures up to the demands of this nuclear age.

There are struggles for housing, lower rents, repairs, open occupancy.

These are all very important arenas of struggle for equal rights. But the crucial arena is the struggle for jobs and equal job opportunity. There two sectors of our people who are the key elements in the struggle for progress meet—the Black people and the working class. The two are natural allies. A large section of our working class consists of Black workers, and a very high percentage of Black people are members of the working class. Hence there is a large area in which the interests of both converge.

A path to the realization of these mutual interests must be found. Toward this end, it is necessary to put the question of jobs into proper perspective. It must be viewed within the following broader framework:

1. Because it is based on securing maximum profits at the expense of the earnings and living standards of the workers, and because the introduction of technological improvements is always designed to get rid of workers, capitalism inevitably tends to create a mass of jobless workers. Unemployment is a built-in feature of capitalism.

2. U.S. capitalism has always had a policy of discrimination. It has been applied against the foreignborn, against Jews and against Catholics. But this is relatively minor compared to the extreme degree of discrimination against Black Americans. The Black workers have been the last to

be hired, and have been habitually confined to the hardest, dirtiest and lowest-paid jobs.

3. In the hands of Big Business, automation spells disaster for millions of workers. But in the first place it displaces unskilled workers. Therefore it has been above all Black workers who have been laid off. Automation, controlled by Big Business, has only multiplied the effects of discrimination and has become a weapon for racism.

4. After scores of years of working without protection of any kind, the workers in basic industry organized unions. After decades of militant struggle, these unions won a measure of job security. This was a big step forward for the working class. But the union contracts were superimposed on the results of hundreds of years of racial discrimination, and they inherited the evil effects of this employer policy. In fact the unions, in many cases inadvertently, became the protectors of these effects. This is exactly what the corporations want. They sit back, manipulate the strings and watch the workers fight one another. All this adds to their huge profits.

The most urgent task for the unions is to find ways workers can separate that which is in their interest from corporate policies of discrimination, which are only in the corporations' interest. The starting point must be the understanding that Black Americans and the working class are not enemies, but natural allies who must have the closest unity in struggle for their mutual interests.

The main obstacle to such unity has been the stubborn resistance by some union leaders. True, the AFL-CIO has declared: "The AFL-CIO is for civil rights—without reservations and without delay." And: "In the labor movement even a little discrimination is too much." (*Equal Rights for All*, AFL-CIO Publication No. 133, 1964.) But such statements must become guidelines to action, otherwise they become demagogy.

The trade unions face a serious problem of working-class unity. The victims of automation become disappointed in unions when these fail to take on their fight. The young generation sees the unions as being unconcerned with their inability to get jobs in industry. Nor can Black workers who are suffering discrimination and layoffs enthusiastically support unions if they do not take up their fight.

This adds up to a big problem. The solution clearly is a militant, united struggle for all these sectors of labor who are the direct victims of the policies of capitalism. To lay the basis for such a struggle, it is necessary to recognize the need for making certain adjustments.

For Black and white workers to fight over existing jobs is no solution. But for white workers to refuse to make adjustments to offset the effects of a hundred years of discrimination at the hands of Big Business, to refuse to make adjustments for a condition they inherited, is to close the doors to united struggle on all issues in the interests of all workers—Black and white. For the unions to be the guardians of the corporation policy of discrimination is to be a pallbearer at the funeral of labor unity.

What kind of adjustments need to be made?

1. The perpetuation of the present inequality in employment must be fought by forcing the corporations to hire Black workers to replace all those who retire or pass away. This is not a total solution, but it would be an important beginning. While seeking further solutions, this would set the stage for Black-labor unity in struggle.

2. Adjustments need to be made in the application of the seniority system. This would not destroy the system. Adjustments have been made in it before—employment of veterans or promotion of younger skilledworkers, and in some unions hiring of skilled refugees. Once there is agreement on questions of adjustment in hiring and upgrading, then there can be a united struggle for demands of mutual interest, such as a shorter work week, lower retirement age, longer vacations, cutting down on speedup, more rest periods, control of automation, etc. These struggles would in turn become avenues of further steps toward

ending the inequalities suffered by Black workers and raising the standard of living of the entire working class.

A working class thus united would then be in a position to raise a further question: Should not the corporations that make billions of dollars in profits provide jobs for all who want to work? And if the corporations will not take on this social responsibility, then should not the government be forced to tax these huge profits and use the proceeds for creating useful employment? These proceeds, added to the 50 billion dollars which can be transferred from war production, would provide ample funds for a broad program of building schools, roads, housing, hospitals, conservation and power projects and other job-creating and needed public works.

Thus does one step lead to another. But the first step must be a readiness to fight for adjustments to overcome the effects of discrimination.

The Big Business ideology of bigotry is like a poison gas, deliberately designed to incapacitate all opposition. Like such a gas, it distorts reality and brings on a state of confusion. A friend appears as an enemy, an enemy as a friend.

Nowadays we read stories of witchcraft with disbelief. But is not the witchcraft of racism, if anything, more fantastic? Moreover, while the old witchcraft affected hundreds, the witchcraft of racism affects millions.

U.S. capitalism took over fostering the ideology of white supremacy from the slave masters and the ideological upholders of slavery. They refined and further developed it, and made it more subtle and penetrating. Its purpose is to imbue masses of white Americans with race hatred by creating in them the illusion that they are superior. In this ideological stupor they become instruments of oppression of other people whom they consider inferior—in this case Black Americans.

Under the influence of this ideological drug, their own lives of toil, debt and hardship, in comparison with the lot of their Black neighbors, seem somehow transformed into a superior existence. While they rant against their neighbors with black skins, they temporarily forget their own empty cupboards and lack of security. In such a state of mind they can not distinguish their real oppressor—the oppressor of both Black and white workers. Through the action of this ideological drug, Big Business, which exploits both Black and white, the source of the bigotry, becomes the enemy forgotten.

Not all are affected to the same degree by the poison of white chauvinism. The spectrum runs all the way from the rabid racists to those who are for civil rights but do nothing about it.

The struggle against this poison will be a protracted one. Its effects will disappear by virtue of the experiences gained in struggle. But even then it would be an error to think that it will disappear automatically. An essential weapon against the influences of chauvinism is education and discussion. We will free ourselves from the influence of this witchcraft only through struggle, through experience and through education.

If the roots of the system of discrimination and segregation are deep within the profit system of capitalism, is it possible to eliminate racism before capitalism is discarded as the outmoded system that it is? As the stubborn resistance to civil rights continues, this question is asked more and more often.

Of course, it is not possible to dig out all of the roots while capitalism exists, since the evil is inherent in the very nature of capitalism, which constantly generates pressures for its revival. But it is possible to sever many of the roots and to destroy offshoots and branches even while the tree of capitalism still stands. Such victories are a realistic goal now. In this sense it can be said that the time for resolution of this issue has arrived. Otherwise, one would have to wait to resolve it until socialism arrived in the United States—a time which clearly is not at hand now.

Secondly, can larger sections of white Americans be

won to take an active part in the civil rights struggle even before they are freed from the poison of white chauvinism? The answer is very definitely—yes. Most white Americans will be impelled to participate in the civil rights struggle because they see their own interest riding on its resolution, even while they continue to be influenced to one degree or another by the ideology of white chauvinism. This is why serious leaders must seek out and explain the areas of convergence of self-interest.

When the question is placed in these terms, it may jar those who look upon such matters from a viewpoint of idealism or romanticism and who see the issue simply as a moral one. They suffer from what Marx and Engels described in *The German Ideology* as "the old illusion that it depends only upon the good will of people to change existing relations and that the existing relations are only ideas." (*Reader in Marxist Philosophy*, Howard Selsam et al., International Publishers, 1963, p. 280.) But this overlooks the material basis of the struggle. It is precisely because they see their own interest involved that these workers, in the process of fighting for civil rights, will develop a new and higher sense of class unity and class consciousness, new moral and ethical standards and a new sense of ideals that will replace the old influences of bigotry and chauvinism.

Americans of Puerto Rican origin, Mexican-Americans and the inhumanly oppressed Native American Indians have all been stirred into action against their own oppression by the civil rights struggles of Black Americans. They have become convinced of the possibility of gaining allies among Black Americans, trade unions and other progressive forces. All these movements start on the basis of self-interest, but they are already moving into alliances with other sections of the population, and the scope of the struggles is far beyond the narrow limits of self-interest.

Such is the logic of all mass struggles. One must view these struggles in terms not only of where they stand at a given moment but also of where the logic of struggle will lead them. The advice Karl Marx gave the American people one hundred years ago following the Civil War is still valid and very much up to date:

> If you fail to give them citizens' rights while you demand citizens' duties, there will yet remain a struggle for the future which may again stain your country with your own people's blood. We warn you, then, as brothers in the common cause, to remove every shackle from freedom's limb, and your victory will be complete. (*Minutes of the First International.*)

It was also Marx who said: "Labor can not emancipate itself in the white skin where in the black it is branded." (*Capital*, Vol. I.)

Winning a life of full equality for all of our people comes up for achievement at a new moment in the history of mankind—at a time when the development of science and technology has made a world without want or the fear of want a realistic possibility. The material base for a world without want can also be the basis for a world without wars, without bigotry or prejudice, without oppression of individuals, peoples or nations—a world where at long last the practice of man's inhumanity to man will be no more.

This goal is within the grasp of humanity. The obstacle to its realization is capitalism. Big Business and its greed for maximum profits is the one great hurdle civilization must overcome before it can proceed to a world finally free of want, oppression and wars. The new social order that has discarded the greedy motive of private profit is socialism. One-third of the world's people are now building this new society.

As the people of the U.S. unitedly struggle against poverty, insecurity and racism, they will eventually arrive at a point where they too will decide to discard the evil system of monopoly capitalism and reorganize our country's life along socialist lines. With that act, we will have joined the mainstream of mankind's march to a better life.   □

[Pamphlet, 1964]

1967

The Civil Rights
Containment Policy

Reverend Martin Luther King, Jr., Julian Bond, Floyd Mc-
Kissick[10] and others have eloquently documented the relationship between this unjust war and the unjust system of
discrimination. It is clear why the closest relationship exists between the two phenomena. Both are instances of oppression of a people, in both cases, of a colored people.
Both have the same roots in the capitalist system, are the
work of the same oppressor class and have the same aim—
extra profits.

It is the nature of capitalism to place its burdens on
those least able to afford them. Not just some but all of the
antipoverty programs that could have some effect on the
problems created by the system of discrimination have
been drastically cut or scuttled altogether. These projects
were the first to be sacrificed on the altar of war. The number of unemployed in the ghettos, both North and South,
has increased. There is more hunger. There is less hope.
There is a deep sense of frustration and anger.

As we stated in our open letter to the President,[11] the so-
called war on poverty has turned into a harsh policy of containment—a policy designed to contain the struggles, the
poverty, the slums, the unemployment, the anger and frustration. To the old system of oppression is now added containment by force, by preventive terror.

The war and its aftermath—the rise of the ultra-Right,

the silence of the federal authorities and the policy of containment—are giving rise to a new level of racism. In many cities there is open racist agitation, not only by the ultra-Right, not only by such organizations as the KKK, but by city, county and state officials. The containment conspiracy is based on a racist concept. The policy is to "contain Negroes." This racist policy extends to industry, not only to those firms that directly finance the racist groups, but to industry in general. It is intended to confine Black workers to specified jobs and departments. The same containment policy is practiced by many unions. Its purpose is to keep Black workers out of the unions and to contain those that find their way in.

The strength of the civil rights movement arises from the fact that so many of its leaders understand its relationship to the fight against the war policy. Herein lies the strength with which to destroy the containment policy.

There is no strength for civil rights in the Wilkins-Young[12] policies. Their close relations with the Administration lead to the same weakness as the trade unions suffer from.

The indispensable instruments of victory in social struggles are unity, organization and mass action. This is the only kind of power that the forces of reaction recognize. For Afro-Americans such unity and organization are both a prerequisite to victory and a path to alliance with other forces on the basis of equality. Unity and organization appear ominous only to those who seek to perpetuate the policies and practices of white supremacy.

Diversity of form and organization serves a useful purpose when there is a basic community of interests, and when such diversity is approached with the idea of strengthening the unity of all forces of progress. Of course, if diversity is used to split, to divide, to promote antagonism among different sections of the forces of progress, then it serves reaction.

The key to progress in the United States is unity in struggle of Black and white. This is the key to progress in every arena. It is a basic, rock-bottom foundation of our reality.

The path to future successes, to victory over the containment conspiracy, is the same for the civil rights movement as for labor. It is, in both cases, the path of unity, organization and mass action. This path is being charted by numerous Black leadership conferences; for example, at the Negro American Labor Council (NALC)[13] convention in Washington, D.C. The open letter we sent to the President should serve as a backdrop for a summer of activity and struggle.

The ruling class, seeking to preserve its undivided power and add to its profits, has continued to demonstrate its commitment to the all-sided exploitation and oppression of the 22 million Afro-Americans. Because of the advance of the Black freedom movement, it combines terror with minor concessions to sustain the system. Toward this end, a new use is being made of some white liberals.

In alliances, relationships change as the level of struggle changes. Some white liberals who have in the past aided the Black people's movement for freedom and equality now often exploit and abuse their positions in the coalition of allied and associated forces. Many who in the past played a positive role are now guilty of attempting to hold back the militant mass thrust of the movement. They impose heavy demands on Afro-American leaders to endorse or support causes which are diversionary and unrelated to their primary allegiance as the price for support of specific programs of struggle for Afro-American rights. They use their financial resources to dictate to and seek to dominate the Afro-American movement.

Very often these forces play the same role in relation to the Afro-American freedom movement as social democracy plays in respect to the labor movement. Similarly, the weight of these liberals is cast on the side of conservatism, tokenism and elitism, against mass involvement, mass action, mass methods and tactics of struggle. They often divert from programmatic emphasis on the needs and demands of the masses.

These elements exhibit a curious admixture of humanitarian concern and paternalism. Actually they represent a certain cut of white supremacist presumptuousness and prejudice.

I single out these manifestations of prejudice and white chauvinist practices on the part of some liberals because this expression of prejudice is currently an obstacle to the consolidation of the required bonds of mass unity and confidence within the peace movement and the movement for independent progressive political action. It is no less the case in the trade union movement and it is an urgent question in the youth movement as well. To suggest that white Americans take on the task of organizing and mobilizing white Americans in the struggle for civil rights is not necessarily an argument against Black-white unity. Winning white America to the cause of equality is an absolute prerequisite to ending the system of racial and national oppression.

We need to sharpen our vigilance, refine our sensitivity to violations of the norms of equality, brotherhood and mutual confidence which must characterize all relations between Black and white in our Party.   ☐

[Report to National Committee, June 1967]

1968

Freedom Struggle
At a New Level

The struggle for Afro-American freedom is at a new level. In an over-all sense the new level is a rebellion against tokenism. While some headway has been made against segregation, conditions of the masses of Afro-Americans, especially conditions in the ghettos, continue to deteriorate. The struggle to overcome particular evils arising from the policy of oppression continues, but increasingly the demand is being made to eliminate the system of oppression in a fundamental way. It is a struggle for jobs, housing, education, but increasingly it is also a demand for the elimination of the system that creates inequality in jobs, housing and other conditions.

This new level of struggle requires the development of a corresponding set of tactics, alliances, political and ideological underpinnings. The relevance of our Party to these struggles will be measured by our contribution to the solution of the problems corresponding to this new level.

The scope of unemployment and the plight of the unemployed in the ghettos rival the depression thirties. The policy of "containing the ghettos" as enclaves of oppression, poverty and slum conditions by police terror has become even more firmly institutionalized. The capitalist corporate structure has not given up the system of special discrimination against Afro-Americans. Basically the racial bars maintained by many trade unions remain. This system of discrimination remains the most critical domestic issue facing our country.

I want to speak about winning white America's participation in the struggle for equality, but first a few words on present nationalist trends. It is clear that it is important for us to be sensitive to nationalist currents and developments. We must also agree in which direction we would like these trends to develop. We must know and sense the progressive elements within these trends. But not to determine in what direction we want to influence these currents would make us passive observers, relying on spontaneity.

We have to agree on direction in order to determine our position on such questions as alliances. We must clearly answer such questions as: Do we think nationalist currents should move in a go-it-alone direction, or should we help them to find a different path? Do we think these currents should move toward alliances with the middle classes, or should we try to find a path of struggle that leads to alliances with the working class and with the working poor?

Alliances presuppose independent and separate struggles by various components and movements. Alliances do not replace such separate movements, but give new strength to each component. They attack the common obstacles to the progress of all sectors with greater force. Alliances should stimulate the struggles of separate sectors to new heights. An advanced level of struggle by one group can stimulate struggles of other sectors which are not so advanced.

I want to direct attention to a central weakness afflicting these struggles. Its correction is key to victory. This central problem, the main challenge for us, is the task of winning greater numbers of white Americans to the struggle for Afro-American freedom, the task of burning out the influence of racism among white Americans. Winning this struggle is key to Black-white unity. We can achieve unity to the extent that we accomplish this task.

Our Party has made important contributions to this

throughout its history, including this last period. But we have to say that we have too few "experts," too few "professionals," on this aspect of the struggle. While I don't want to criticize white Communists who study and seek to understand all phases of the Black people's movement, the fact is that to do so and yet fail to be an expert on winning white Americans for the struggle for equality is a serious weakness. Communists who are white must be experts on this above all.

Not only do we have too few experts, but we also have little literature in this area, the most difficult of all phases of the struggle.

The influence of white chauvinism in our own ranks must be measured by how effective we are in the struggle against racism in the ranks of white America. These are not two separate questions; they are two sides of one ideological problem. In our Party it is not enough merely to condemn racism. That can not be the yardstick of our understanding of this question, no matter how fierce or correct our condemnation. Ideological concepts are best molded in the heat of struggle. The test of our ideological firmness lies in how we back up our ideology in practical activity.

There are white individuals who argue that it is not necessary to win white Americans for the struggle for Black equality. Instead they call for armed uprisings in the ghettos. This is not radicalism. It is only a radical-sounding cover for not fighting against the influence of racism.

There are those who maintain that the task is hopeless, that you can't win white Americans for the struggle for Black freedom. This idea, which we must firmly reject, also has some reflections in our Party. And there are reasons for it. There is the fact that racism has such a long history in America. There is the view of ideology as some kind of abstraction, unrelated to real problems. Hence, "once a racist, always a racist"; it's there and nothing can be done about it. This view does not take into account how struggles and developments of life have an effect on racism. Such hopelessness reflects a weakness in understanding ideological struggle in general and a defeatist attitude toward the struggle against American capitalist ideology in particular.

In our approach to this question, we have to ask whether it is possible to win the struggle against the influence of racism among broad sections of the American people simply on the grounds that it is wrong, that it is "sinful," that it is antidemocratic, that it is contrary to religious principles and concepts of brotherhood. Can we win the ideological struggle on this level? To be sure, such arguments are helpful. But they are not enough. They are an inadequate basis for the struggle against racism because our capitalist society has not reached the level of civilization where such moral and ethical standards are daily guides to mass behavior. Many bow to such standards on Sundays, but practice racism on the other six days of the week. These arguments influence behavior, but do not determine it, and therefore they are not enough. Certainly they should be used. But more is needed.

It is necessary to explain the class roots of ideology. In the U.S., racism influences many. It is propagated by people of all classes, but its roots are in capitalism. It is an instrument of exploitation, of class rule. It is an instrument for the exploitation of all workers. This understanding of the roots of racism is a cardinal element in the development of class consciousness among our workers.

The mutual and parallel interests of Black and white constitute the key lever in the struggle against racism, a pillar in the struggle for social progress. We can play our role as a Party and as individuals only if we become experts in its use. We need to make use of this lever in such areas as the struggle for democracy or the struggle for peace. One does not have to argue very long to show that racism is the wedge for antidemocratic forces. This was obviously the case with Hitler and anti-Semitism; it is likewise the case with the ultra-Right today. It is George Wallace's[14] main stock-in-trade. It is our responsibility as

Communists to be experts at showing the American people that we can not win the struggle for democracy unless white Americans see the need to struggle for Black freedom.

Let us take another example in the field of economic struggle. How should Communists have worked in the Ford strike to win white workers for specific demands arising from Ford's policy of racial discrimination?

The workers in the foundry, a very big department at Ford, are mainly (90 per cent) Black and a large section of the assembly line workers are also Black. These departments have in common that they are dead ends. In these departments, because of silicosis, fumes from the motors running on the assembly line and other health problems, the time of retirement is the time of death. The union raised this question in the contract negotiations. Is it not obvious that white Communist workers at Ford should be the experts, should take the lead in this union to promote struggles to put an end to such conditions? Should they not work to convince white workers in Ford that they can not fully win other demands unless the union stays united, and that to stay united the union must fight the deadly conditions in these two departments? For workers at Ford this is the test in the struggle against racism, against chauvinism.

Consider the struggle for peace and against U.S. imperialism. Here we should become experts at convincing white peace activists that to win the struggle against the war policy they must become active in the struggle for Afro-American freedom. We should become expert at making clear to them the relationship of the two. Life has united these issues, and the struggle should reflect this unity.

When we raise the question of mutual and parallel interests, does this imply telling Black people to fit their actions into the schedule and readiness to struggle of white people and white workers? I don't think so. The assertion of militant, advanced pressure by a united, fighting Afro-American people does not contradict seeking out areas that will enhance the struggle on the basis of mutual and parallel interests with white workers. I believe there is a dialectical relationship between the two.

Once more, take the Ford strike. There is no contradiction between white Communists mobilizing the union in the struggle against the specific conditions in the foundry and assembly departments and a caucus of Black union members militantly raising the same question in the union. On the contrary, there is a dialectical process here that everybody should be able to understand. As long as Black workers at Ford suffer from discrimination special forms of struggle will be needed. And as long as division by race exists among the workers the union will not be able to use its full power on any question.

When we speak of becoming experts, do we start from the premise that our white comrades who take up the struggle for freedom will of necessity become isolated in broad movements? Some think along these lines, but I think that misreads the present moment. Such thoughts are part of that same hopelessness of which I spoke. That has not been our experience. White Communists in Ford will not become isolated if they raise this question in the union, because it is in the interest of the union, the Black workers and the white workers. It will lead not to isolation but rather to class unity. Yes, it is a struggle; yes, a difficult struggle. But it will not necessarily lead to isolation. In fact, I am convinced from experience that if the struggle is conducted properly, it is the racists who will be isolated, not the Communists.

We have to be experts in exposing the class roots of racism. Working-class consciousness is the most solid base for the struggle against racism. White workers will understand racism if we show that it is a weapon of the ruling class.

The final result, and, in fact the goal, of the many-sided system of discrimination is inequality of economic status for Black Americans. This is the class base, the profit base of the system. Thus, the elimination of this inequality is the rock bottom test for all struggles for freedom. Struggles must all in some way contribute to eliminating this gap.

The extent of support of white Americans for wiping out economic inequality in every area—rent, taxes, prices, wages and so on—is also the test of how successful we are in winning the support of white Americans for real equality. Again, it can best be done by revealing the class roots of oppression. Communists in shops, in local unions, in communities, must become experts in leading struggles that will wipe out every vestige of inequality.   □

[Report to National Committee, 1968]

The Revolutionary Process

The rise of Black caucuses in shops and unions is a militant response to racist practices of employers and influences of racism in trade unions. Black caucuses are an important, special form of class struggle and add a new dimension to it. We are for class unity; we are for trade union unity. But these can not become realities on the basis of accommodation to racism. Black caucuses are a vitally necessary form of struggle against such accommodation in the trade union movement.

The struggle for unity of Black and white in the labor movement is on a new level. Don't-rock-the-boat unity is out. Unity based on full equality and representation is in. The high-level activity of Black caucuses is in the interest of the whole class. Their struggles against speedup and poor working conditions raise job standards for all workers.

Black participation at all levels of trade union leadership is fundamental to the struggle against racism. There are two million Black workers in the AFL-CIO, but only one retired Black official on its Executive Council. There must be a fight to change the system of electing the top leadership of the AFL-CIO and to multiply the number of active Black trade-union leaders. Putting an end to discrimination against Black workers in union leadership is going to rock the boat. It means extensive changes, both in personnel and structure.

Collaborationist leaders accuse Black caucuses of "dual unionism." This old chestnut has been dredged up from the fight for industrial unionism a generation ago. Black caucuses are not "dual unions." They are attempts to substitute class-struggle unionism for do-nothing unionism; equality unionism for racist unionism.

Let the unions have fully integrated leadership. Let Black workers have full equality in practice in every respect. Let unions become class-struggle bodies, with rank-and-file democracy. Then the need for Black caucuses will disappear. They will merge into higher-level, Black and white, rank-and-file movements.

Black and white class unity has been a basic concept of the Communist Party from its earliest history. We strive for this unity in the labor movement. But when doors of established unions remain obdurately closed to Black workers, in spite of every possible effort to force them open, we support the organization of separate Black unions as a form of struggle to end racial bars. This form of organization can lead to a higher level of unity.

At the same time, we continue to struggle to end all restrictive admission practices in the craft unions and to support the demand that they be opened to all workers, Black and white, able and willing to do the job. We condemn and demand the elimination of those examinations for apprenticeship training—most of which are nothing more than instruments to block admission of Black and other minority people.

The Negro American Labor Council[15] was an important early expression of the Black caucus movement. While this organization may not have come up to its hoped-for potential, it has initiated a number of important struggles and continues to be an important factor in the fight against racism and for the strengthening of the alliance between the labor and freedom movements.

As the struggle goes on, there will be new forms of expression of the present upsurge. One very important expression is the Fight Back Conference recently held in New York, which adds a new aspect to the developing rank-and-file movement. It is a militant expression, a movement of Black and white, concerned mainly with the struggle against racism.

These different forms need not compete with one another. Our task is to seek areas in which they can complement and strengthen one another and thereby strengthen the overall struggle against racism.

A major aspect of the ruling class drive to split the working class through the use of racism is the attempt to convince white workers that they have a stake in white supremacy. While Black and other minority workers are the first victims of racism, the disunity it creates weakens the fighting capacity of the whole class, permitting intensified exploitation of both Black and white. Wherever capitalism has been able to split the working class, as in the South, there has been a general deterioration of living standards. Up to now the ruling class has used racism to restrict trade union organization in the South and has used the resulting lower wages as a threat against workers in all parts of the country. It has maintained the South as a base for the nation's most racist, antilabor and reactionary political forces.

We condemn, as racist inspired and unfounded, the current propaganda campaign among white workers that "the Blacks are after your jobs." Millions more jobs are required to meet even the minimum needs of the American people for homes, schools, hospitals and other necessities. In the fight for these jobs we support preferential job training and hiring of Black and other minority workers, and the strengthening of class unity.

Racism is not inherent in white workers; it emanates from capitalism as a foul instrument to divide and weaken the working class. The Communist Party must constantly expose white supremacy, anti-Semitism and other capitalist ideologies as a threat to all workers. We must make the working-class slogan, "An injury to one is an injury to all," truly embrace both Black and white. We must aim to direct the struggle against the real enemy.

Our Party must build up confidence that the fight against racism can be won, toward this end publicizing the frequent manifestations of Black and white working-class unity.

The historic struggle of 25 million Afro-Americans for freedom and equality continues on a very high level. But it is confronted with many new problems reflecting new factors on the American scene of battle.

After years of militant and heroic struggles, and even though some important victories have been won, the system of special oppression remains intact—the discrimination and inequality, segregation and ghettos, degradation and misery. Black income is one-half the national level, the unemployment rate three times higher, the death rate double; slum housing and hunger are chronic; the majority are denied equal education and forced to work at the lowest-paid and most dangerous jobs, at the bottom of the seniority lists. Despite 350 years of heroic struggles, this system remains essentially intact.

After the passage of many laws and the delivery of many fine speeches, racism still stalks the land. This fact should not blind us to the victories, but the victories should not hide the basic ugly fact.

The Nixon-Agnew Administration aims to halt any further steps to guarantee civil rights. There is an open cessation of federal pressure or influence for civil rights. This policy is not "spotty," as some say; it is on the side of racism. It is racism.

The heartless cancellation of the Job Corps[16] reflects pressures of open racists in and around the Administration. It wiped out this very minimal effort to relieve the plight of ghetto youth. The cuts in housing, education, health care and the Headstart program[17] affect the poor generally, but they are a blow against the ghetto poor in the first place. All this presents some new problems in the freedom struggle.

Side by side with these problems, police attacks on the militant section of the liberation movement are escalating. The poison gas, mace, now in every cop's pocket, is symbolic of this escalation of terror. This attack is coordinated. It takes place from the outside and from within the movement, and this also creates new problems for the struggle.

This takes on added significance because at the same time there is a slowing down of expressions of protest against the attacks, and of support for the movement, from broader white sectors that were active in the past. Church groups are disturbingly quiet. They have turned to questions of celibacy, the Middle East or abortion laws.

There have been very few protests against the attacks on the Black Panthers or other militant groups, against the conviction of Bobby Seale or on behalf of such victims as the Plainfield Seven.[18]

We must draw lessons from the fact that in New York the forces of reaction and racism were able to mobilize support against community control of schools. These forces included sections of the teachers' and other unions. White support for this basic democratic struggle was weak and spotty.

The issue is clear. Its sharpest expression is in the ghettos, but it is not limited to Harlem and Bedford-Stuyvesant. It is a matter of democratic control of education in all neighborhoods, for all groups. Taking decisions on education out of the hands of the elite and placing them in the hands of the people is an important working-class issue.

The forces of reaction used racism—including the blatant racism of the social-democrat Shanker[19]—to blind many white people to the real nature of the issue. The racists raised the fake issue of "Black anti-Semitism" behind which to hide their racism. And we must face the fact that this tactic confused even some in the Left and progressive sectors.

These are real danger signals.

Exceptions to these trends are the electoral coalitions that have emerged in the South and in Cleveland, Gary and Los Angeles, and in some college struggles. There may be other exceptions, but we have to see the basic trends. We have to blow the whistle.

What I have described is a consequence of the racist drive that endlessly repeats, "The Negroes are going too fast and too far." We have to combat this drive, to accept the challenge of revitalizing this aspect of the struggle among white Americans. It is a test of how effective we are in the struggle against racism. We have the task of convincingly explaining to white Americans the nature of oppression, of the freedom movement, the meaning of Black power, the class roots of white racism. We have to accumulate a body of experience in the struggle against racism. White Communists must become experts in this struggle.

The theoretical aspect of Black liberation has been one of the central questions in our preconvention discussion. This is understandable, because it is an area where there is great mass motion and struggle. It is a difficult and many-sided phenomenon, and it is in the midst of serious ideological probing. It does not lend itself to sloganized solutions.

Our Party's National Black Liberation Commission and many of our leading Black comrades have done a lot of creative and deep thinking about these developments and their meaning for many years. Our Party has produced an important body of Marxist thought on the question. My remarks reflect these projections and conclusions.

The basic questions about the nature of the oppression are, of course, not academic. It is necessary to deal with them to understand the nature of day-to-day struggles. This is the key to developing strategic concepts and formulating correct policies and tactics.

As in all questions of struggle for progress, there are

some Marxist-Leninist guidelines based on years of world-wide experience. They are matters of principle—basic points of reference for us.

I am sure they are not new to most of you, but let me point out some of them briefly.

For us, the struggle against racism and white chauvinism is a matter of the highest principle. We can not compromise on this. This principle flows from our class viewpoint on all matters.

For us, internationalism is also a basic principle. This too flows from our class point of reference. For us, it is a weapon of struggle and a way of life, a direction for the future of mankind.

And for us the right of oppressed nations to freely determine their destinies is a matter of principle.

These are more than abstract principles; they contain the essence, the democratic spirit, the living content and philosophy of Marxism-Leninism. This is the spirit and essence of a Leninist approach to all questions of freedom from oppression for nations, national minorities and groups. These principles are expressed in practice in a variety of ways.

We are for an end to oppression; we are for the right of the oppressed to decide what constitutes their freedom. Only they will determine what is free and equal. That is Leninism—that is our Party's basic position.

The struggle for Black liberation is proceeding through many channels, on many levels. It will express itself in many forms and will be influenced by many factors.

The struggle of the Black people to determine their own destiny is and will be expressed through Afro-American organizations, trade-union caucuses, community control of schools, police, hospitals and other institutions. It is expressed in the struggle for power through majority control of cities, counties and states. In other areas it will be expressed for full rights as a minority. Our task is to make these expressions a reality.

The struggle takes place in the context of a class society. Its background is the class struggle. It takes place within the context that the great majority of the Afro-American community are workers deeply involved in the class struggle, in the affairs of their class. They are a militant section of the U.S. working class.

There has been a process of radicalization at work among the whole working class. But the greatest radicalization has been among Black workers. They have become the most active sector of both their class and their people. More and more, this will determine the direction of the Black liberation movement.

This calls for some profound thought, for the application of Marxist-Leninist science to the task of anticipating the direction of the class struggle and the Black liberation movement as both enter this new, more dynamic and fundamental phase. It calls for our participation at the cutting edge of this struggle, in the basic industrial shops. It calls for Communist leadership to help guide this struggle into the course of unity of the whole Afro-American people and the whole working class against monopoly capitalism.

Let me emphasize—we do not have all the answers. Far from it. But we must and will find answers, and through them begin to solve the problem of winning unity of the basic antimonopoly forces of the country.

Any realistic assessment of the brutal oppression of 25 million of our Afro-American citizens must start from the threefold character of the oppression: It is racial oppression; it is class oppression; it is the oppression of a national minority. The Black freedom movement is a struggle against all these forms of oppression.

It is a rebellion against 350 years of racist practices, slander and vilification. It is expressed in a new racial pride, cultural identification with peoples of Africa, slogans like "Black is beautiful," study of and pride in the achievements and contributions of Black peoples. It is expressed in the college struggles for Black studies departments and for an end to racist barriers to enrollment.

The rebellion is against oppression as a national minority. This is expressed in such slogans and concepts as "Black power." It is expressed in the growth of electoral activism and election of increasing numbers of Afro-Americans to public office. It is expressed in such political formations as the Black Panthers. It is expressed in voter registration drives. It is a struggle for a political base from which to fight oppression. It is expressed in the fight for community control of schools, housing, police, medical care.

There is a rebellion against class oppression. Both within and outside the production process the Black worker is exploited and oppressed as a worker who is also a victim of racial and national oppression. The racial oppression follows him into the shops and mills, where he is at the same time the victim of class exploitation.

Black caucuses reflect this. They are organizations of Black workers, but they stimulate the whole class, Black and white, to act. They are shop organizations, but they galvanize the whole Afro-American community to act. They stimulate the building of an Afro-American/working class alliance.

These are three aspects of a single mechanism of oppression rooted in the capitalist system. The rebellion focuses on specific expressions of oppression. The focus may change but the rebellion goes on. Because we have not clearly seen the threefold nature of the oppression, we have not always been able to clearly understand the significance of some forms of struggle. This is especially true in relation to movements and struggles that are a reaction to racial and national oppression. In these areas the Party has tended to tail. We did not see the struggle these expressions would stimulate in the whole freedom movement.

As the struggle develops, the movements and battles will take on many new forms and will develop many new slogans. Not all of the efforts or slogans will necessarily be equally effective or even correct. There will be diversions from the main line of battle, concepts of Black capitalism and new versions of the Garvey movement.[20] But the overall line of march is militant, creative, realistic. The mass line of march stubbornly asserts itself. This is what will break the back of the system of oppression.

Nations are historically molded formations. Marxist-Leninist criteria of what constitutes a nation are not standards to be met before a people can be accepted as an oppressed group. Imperialism oppresses peoples whether they are nations or not. Whether one considers the Afro-American community a separate nation or a racially oppressed national minority does not reflect on the right of this oppressed people to determine their own destiny.

The criteria for what constitutes a nation have a very practical side, that is, whether a particular community has or can have an economic structure of its own; whether it has a means of self-expression in a language of its own. These are important, very practical, considerations. Nations are molded by such practical necessities, which determine whether nationhood is a realistic possibility. National pride and sense of national identity, important as they are, do not themselves determine whether a given people can become a nation or not.

Under the present circumstances, it seems to me the Afro-American community has not responded to the idea of setting up a separate Black government representing a separate nation. I think the reason for this is that they do not see this as a realistic form of struggle or a realistic solution. Many say it is a diversion. This is itself a form of determining one's destiny. We must respect this attitude.

When concepts do not accurately reflect historical reality they do not develop mass support; they do not become social powers. In this context, the slogan of self-determination, as used in Marxist literature, does not apply to the Afro-American community today.

For us in the United States there is one other question of principle. That is our basic class position of fighting for Black-white unity. This is in line both with our basic class approach and with our concept of the right of people to determine their own destiny. There is an underlying unity in these concepts.

The Afro-American community must and will develop forms of organization and programs that give it the leverage necessary to achieve freedom and equality. We start from the premise that the obstacle to Black-white unity is white supremacist racism. Thus, unless the concept of unity of Black and white is backed up by daily, principled struggle against racism, it is a meaningless phrase.

For us the struggle against racism and chauvinism does not stop with moral indignation, but is related to and is a feature of, the class struggle. We must see racism in its deeper sense, as the most formidable ideological obstacle to working-class unity and class and socialist consciousness. We must convince all who seek social progress that racism is an obstacle to achieving it.

To the extent that white chauvinism is an influence in our own ranks, we can not be an effective force against racism. We can only be effective in convincing others of the centrality of the fight against racism to the degree we ourselves understand it. How we struggle against chauvinism in our own ranks therefore influences how successful we are in every struggle.

Black America is deciding its destiny—not in a vacuum but within the realities of American life. We are not neutral, but an active force shaping those realities. What we do to combat racism will in large measure mold the framework within which that determination of destiny takes place.

The special oppression of 40 million Americans within the boundaries of the United States is a manifestation of the brutal and inhuman character of U.S. capitalism. It gives the class struggle another dimension, requiring special attention to the oppressed peoples, to their unity and to their alliance with the working class, of which most of them are a part.   □

[Report to 19th Convention, CPUSA, April-May 1979]

We Can Win
Angela Davis' Freedom

Angela Davis is a very popular personality. It would be possible to build a strong movement in her defense on that basis alone.[21] But we would make a fundamental error of assessment if we did not see that the mass response is to the defense of Angela Davis as a militant Black woman, a member of the Communist Party. This gives the response special significance. This unprecedented reaction is a yardstick of the deep new patterns of political thought in broad sections of the Black community, especially among Black youth.

The defense of Comrade Angela Davis is our most urgent task and is of key importance. There is no question that the defense of Angela Davis has triggered a movement that will not only free her but will develop into a movement against repression, against racism, and for the democratic rights of all Americans without precedent in our memory. The initial reactions are already evidence of this. The reaction to her arrest has been explosive. There has never been such a response from the world Communist movement. Overnight her defense has become a world movement of great significance.

To millions of people the frameup case against Angela Davis has become symbolic of the continued racist frameup of 25,000,000 Black Americans. Her imprisonment is symbolic of the racist ghetto imprisonment of 25,000,000 Black Americans.

The frustrations of Angela Davis, even after winning her degree in philosophy, and despite her academic brilliance, are symbolic of the frustrations of millions of youth—especially Black youth.

To tens of thousands of youth, her probing and seeking solutions to the evils of capitalism are symbolic of their own probing. They identify with her militancy and dedication.

Angela Davis' probing and her experiences led her to join the Communist Party. What the ruling class most worries about and is trying most desperately to avoid is that her joining the Communist Party may also become symbolic for thousands of others. And they are right to worry. Thousands are saying and tens of thousands are thinking: "If Angela Davis is a Communist maybe I should also join."

Angela Davis has become known to millions through her struggles against racism, against imperialist wars of aggression, against injustice, and especially through her struggle for the right to teach and to do so as a Communist. Angela Davis has made her mark in the struggle for progress. She has earned the hatred of the capitalist class.

Angela Davis is also identified with the movement for the rights of prisoners. This movement has grown, especially against the barbarism and brutalities practiced against Black, Puerto Rican and Chicano youth in prisons. Racism in prison is genocide at its worst. For us and the world Comrade Henry Winston's blindness is an ever-present reminder of the nature of racism in our prison system. In prison racism has its victims in chains, beyond the protection of the law or the public.

Thousands identify with the struggle against the social conditions—racism, hunger, slums—which result in young men and women being thrown into prison. Countless numbers—many thousands—who are serving long prison terms are also victims of police frameups. They are guilty of nothing more than being poor, being Black, Puerto Rican or Chicano. This is also a feature of racism. Thousands identify with the struggle against the unjust conditions and against the brutalities, frameups and the racist system of justice, even while correctly not condoning or identifying with many of the specific acts that result in prison sentences. Individual acts are not the way to fight the evils of a social system.

Thousands identify with the struggle against prison brutality. The Soledad Brothers'[22] struggle is part of this struggle. They are victims of this endless vicious cycle of longer and longer prison sentences.

Young Jonathan Jackson[23] was a participant in this struggle and a victim of the brutal system. Thousands identify with the motives of young Jackson in his desperate attempt to do something about the endless imprisonment of Black youth. For Jonathan Jackson prison brutality was a personal matter. For most of his life, his older brother had been in prison, victim of a police frameup.

But while identifying with such motives and self-sacrificing heroism, most people correctly see the events in San Rafael as ill-considered acts of desperation that could lead only to tragedy. Thousands correctly admire the personal heroism of 17-year-old Jackson, but see that the events in San Rafael did not advance the very cause he so desperately wanted to serve. The lesson of history, of the class struggle, of all struggle against reaction and racism—the lesson of San Rafael—is that the only path that will keep people from being sent to prison or free people from prison or put an end to the barbarism of the prison system is the path of mass struggle.

Jonathan Jackson, in his 17 short years, personally lived and learned about the brutalities of the system of racism in and out of prison. He emerged for only a few brief moments into the movement to end the racist brutality of our social system. It is understandable that he had not yet had time to learn that in the struggle against oppression there are detours but there are no shortcuts. It is not necessary to criticize young Jackson. It is only necessary to know the lessons of struggle.

Despite all the talk in the mass media about guns and gunplay at San Rafael, we must never lose sight of the incontestable fact that the only guns fired were those of the prison guards. We should bear in mind the words of the District Attorney who stated, "I killed them."

In memory of many young Jonathan Jacksons of the past and for the benefit of thousands joining the battle, we can not and we must not play hide and seek with what is right and what is wrong in tactics. We must be forthright about correct and mistaken concepts of struggle. Attempting to free prisoners by force of guns, in the context of our struggles, is not "tactical diversity." We can not accept such concepts of struggle, even if they are not the "primary" or "sole" tactic, as some have proposed. Once this door is opened, it follows, as one person said, that "The final significance of Jonathan's revolt was its clear connection with the mass movement—certainly a revolutionary act." No, the motive was revolutionary—the act was not. An act that does not advance the revolutionary cause is not revolutionary. On the contrary, it was an act of heroic desperation, unrelated to the movement and its needs at this moment. It was an act leading to withdrawal from the mass movement.

We must speak about the tactic because some on the Left now proclaim that it is the way to free prisoners. They reject the concept of a militant, united mass struggle. Silence on our part would be opportunism.

The racist enemy works very hard to link individual acts of terror to the mass movements which they are trying to suppress. This is the meaning of the frameup of Angela Davis. We do not play this game. Any concept of "tactical diversity" opens the doors to police agents. Let us not in any way open those doors.

We Communists must have the deepest understanding, the closest identity with the hopes, desires and frustrations of the thousands of young Jonathan Jacksons—victims of capitalist and racist oppression who are moving into struggle. The youth who are probing and seeking solutions are joining and will join the YWLL and the Communist Party in greater and greater numbers. They will join the Communist movement on many levels of development. As new forces always do, they will bring the conclusions of good experiences, as well as some not-so-good experience. They will have to acquire the science of revolution, as all must, through further learning and experience.

Our Party has high standards, but it also reflects this process. Our Party is an organization of struggle, but is also a school for the working class. In our Party every member undergoes daily on-the-job training. We must not, by applying mechanical standards, close the doors to our Party to thousands who are in struggle, who are drawn to the revolutionary process, who identify with the defense of Angela Davis. In the experiences of struggle they will become Marxist-Leninists. We must have a deep understanding of people's motivation and development. But we can not fulfill our responsibility by compromising with mistaken ideas. We must always put our position forward honestly, in a straightforward manner. We can not win people to the Marxist-Leninist position or to the Party in any other way.

I am now more confident than ever that we can win Angela Davis' freedom. We can do so by building a mass defense movement without precedent in our country's history. We can do it by building a movement that will go a long way toward freeing all victims of racism. In this epic struggle millions will learn about the evils of capitalism. In arresting and indicting Comrade Angela Davis the ruling class has made a historic miscalculation.   □

[Report to National Committee, November 1970]

Freedom
For Angela Davis!

In order to achieve greater integration of different areas of movement and struggle, it is necessary to speak of the Black liberation movement as it is in life—an important segment of the general movement, an important segment of the working class, the peace movement, the youth movement, electoral struggles, etc. But it is necessary to single out certain special features of this movement.

In the movement for Black liberation the forms of struggle have changed but the process of radicalization continues. This is reflected in the role of Black workers' caucuses, which continue to inject a sense of militancy into the working class as a whole. In many industries caucuses of Black workers remain the pivotal force.

Mass radicalization is reflected also in the work and program of the Congressional Black Caucus. It is reflected in the unprecedented number of electoral campaigns and victories of Black candidates for public office. It is reflected in new voter registration campaigns in the South. It is reflected in the militant role of Black veterans in the movement of Vietnam veterans for peace. This militancy and radicalization is evident in the leadership role of Black workers in the rising movement of the people who are forced to go on welfare.

This radicalization is evident in the unusual numbers of

Black youth who are studying Marxism-Leninism in organized groups. It is evident in the growing numbers of Black youth who are now joining our Party. But possibly in its most dramatic fashion this process of radicalization has surfaced in the reactions of Black communities to the movement to free our comrade, Angela Davis.[24]community has brushed aside all of the Establishment's political and ideological garbage. This includes the most slanderous redbaiting filth spread by people from Eldridge Cleaver to George Wallace.[25] Of course, it includes rejection of the frameup charges of murder and kidnapping against Angela Davis.

The organized movement in the Black community for the freedom of Angela Davis does not even begin to touch the breadth of the mass sentiment. The Black community correctly sees this struggle as an important struggle against racism.

The continuing radicalization is a reflection of the fact that basic conditions in the Black communities have not changed. In fact, the policies of the Nixon Administration and the effects of the economic crisis have resulted in setbacks on many fronts. In the ghettos economic crisis has become a permanent feature of life under capitalism. The Nixon-Rockefeller-Reagan onslaught against the poor is in the first place a war against the residents of the ghettos.

There is renewed activity in the electoral field. The sentiment for political independence has grown significantly in the Black liberation movement. This has resulted in the election of new Black congressmen and congresswomen, Black mayors, state representatives and judges. The electoral vehicle in most cases is the Democratic Party, but the political movements have been independent. This pattern is now national in scope. The independent forms are the only avenues through which the Black political movements can build alliances with other sectors, with the rank and file of labor, with peace forces, with radical groups.

This can not be done within the two old parties. The two old party machines remain racist. The development of independent forms has become an indispensable aspect of the struggle for Black representation.

This is the main lesson from Carl Stokes' experience in Cleveland.[26] The same lesson is emerging in Newark and Gary.

In general, the situation is ripe for a qualitative advance in the struggle for Black representation on all levels. For this independent forms are a must. So far the independent forms are largely top committees. The realization of a qualitative advance in Black representation requires a movement of independent political action—a grassroots movement of committees in wards and communities.

A qualitative advance in Black representation can be a qualitative advance in working-class, radical and peoples' representation. A qualitative advance in Black representation is a necessary feature of an overall political realignment. It is an indispensable part of an antimonopoly coalition of forces.

The ideological struggle is especially sharp in the Black liberation movement. The National Chairman of our Party, Comrade Henry Winston, has written a number of very important pieces on this. They must become a part of our preconvention discussion. They give a clear lead.

As in other movements, in the Black liberation movement there is continuing struggle against petty bourgeois radical currents. As in other areas, these currents have suffered serious defeats. As in other movements, these currents reject basic concepts of class struggle and the class nature of capitalism.

As in other movements, in the Black liberation movement there is a struggle against reformism, against social democratic concepts and against liberalism. The concepts and the struggle are the same, but they operate in the context of a movement fighting against special racial and national oppression. The concepts and the struggles against them are the same, but they operate in the context of a people fighting against 300 years of racist oppression.

Our Party's special contribution in the working-class movement is to explain the need to fight against racism in the ranks of the working class in order to be able to fight for working-class unity.

Our special contribution has always been to fight white chauvinism as a precondition for a struggle for Black-white unity.

The enemy never gives up. It shifts its tactics to meet each new situation. Wherever there is an upsurge, the class enemy is there. Because of increased movement in the ranks of Black workers, there are also new activities by the enemy in the ranks of the working class. The racists in the ranks of white workers work the racist side of the street. This has not diminished. Their main aim is to block class unity.

In the present stage there is a need for Black caucuses within shops and unions. Without such forms the racist barriers can not be broken down, either in industry or in the unions. They are necessary instruments in the class struggle. But the enemy knows this also, so they have agents working that side of the street as well. Their aim is to use the legitimate grievances of Black workers against the racist practices in the trade unions to build movements that lead to splits, that lead to antiunion positions.

Black workers, by and large, have not followed either the revolutionary caucus movement, such as has sprung up in some auto locals, nor those who have an outlook of setting up separate Black unions. The Black caucuses with the greatest staying power are those which view the struggle against racism in industry and in the trade unions in the context of the class struggle. In place after place, Black workers have rejected policies that move away from this class approach.

We will be leaving the door open for enemy agents unless and until we find more effective forms for combatting them, until we show greater initiative in giving the right lead, a lead that moves towards elimination of racism in the ranks of white workers within the trade union organizations and toward class unity. The way to fight enemy agents is to improve our leadership in the struggle against racism on all fronts.

In the Black liberation field we are not giving a lead to working-class concentration.

This is because we underestimate the role of Black workers, both as members of the working class and as members of the Black community. This is a weakness we have not yet corrected.

Since our last convention, the struggle has continued to escalate among all sections of the people who are victims of special national and racial oppression.

The Chicano movement has moved forward on its working-class base. The victories of the agricultural workers, the growth of their union, is a historic development. This has given the Chicano movement a solid working-class base. The Chicano movement has developed a deep sense of political independence. It is a strong factor in the antiwar movement and the welfare rights movement. The Chicano movement is a significant factor in the militant sector of every mass movement.

As in other movements, the enemy is also busy in the Chicano movement. It works on many fronts. It creates provocations. It tries to direct the attention of the movement away from concrete issues. It opposes alliances with other oppressed groups. It uses all of its ideological weapons—chauvinism and nationalism.

The central fact of the Chicano movement that stands out is its growth, its militancy, its working-class base and its politically independent orientation.

Since our last convention, the movement for Native American Indian equality has also advanced. The struggles in Washington, Chicago and Alcatraz are symbolic of the rise of the movement.

The election of Congressman Herman Badillo is a reflection of the quality of the movement in the Puerto Rican community. The Puerto Rican movement is influenced both by the policies of discrimination in the United States and by the colonial policy of U.S. imperialism in Puerto Rico. The rising movement for independence in Puerto Rico directly influences the movement in the U.S.

This is not an attempt to assess or go into the various developments and problems in each of these movements. Special theses are being prepared in each of the areas. They will be ready for preconvention discussion. I refer to these movements because we have to take up an overall question affecting all these groups.

The enemy has increased its efforts to drive a wedge between the Black liberation movement and the Chicano movement, between the Puerto Rican movement and the Black movement, between the Indian movement and the other movements. This is done in the framework of driving a wedge between all these movements and the working class. The weapons of the enemy are manifold. They use chauvinism and nationalism. They use real and imaginary differences. They use redbaiting. They counterpose group interests.

We must be clear about some basic questions. Black Americans, Chicanos, Puerto Ricans, Native American Indians as well as other groups are all victims, to one degree or another, of special systems of oppression. But these are not the same. The basic system of special oppression, the root of all other special forms of oppression, is the 300-year-old system of racial and national oppression of 25 million Black Americans.

Racism is geared to perpetuate this system. To destroy all systems of oppression, all practices of discrimination against national groups, this system must be destroyed. To destroy all forms of chauvinism, anti-Black prejudice must be destroyed, including its influence in the ranks of groups who themselves suffer from oppression.

When this relationship is understood, one will not counterpose the interest of one group to that of another.

It is necessary that we understand these connections if we are to be a factor in molding unity among all the victims of racial and national oppression.

This is our understanding when we speak about class unity. This is our understanding when we speak about Black-white unity. The struggle against racism, against white chauvinism, must be the basis for the unity of all workers, Black, Chicano, Puerto Rican, Native American Indian and white. The struggle against white chauvinism is a solid basis for the struggle against all forms of chauvinism against all oppressed groups.

The struggle for Black-white unity is a basis for the unity of all people.

We must deepen our understanding of all these relationships as they are linked to the class question. Not only must we adopt a class approach to all problems; we must impart that approach to broader mass movements.

I must say a few words on the movement for the defense of Comrade Angela Davis. Life has proven the correctness of our original assessment of how great the possibilities of such a movement are. It has created a sentiment in defense of a victim of a political frameup without precedent. But we must also honestly say it has exposed some serious weaknesses. There are hundreds of defense committees throughout the country. But after eight months of talking and planning, there is only a framework of a national defense committee. We must all be self-critical—but the comrades who have been given the full-time, direct responsibility for leadership in this field must, in the first place, self-critically examine their work. In some areas and in the national effort the most serious obstacles which have emerged are a deepseated sectarianism and organizational ineptness. We have relied too much on spontaneity. Illusions about the nature of the case, illusions about the courts, illusions about the viciousness of the frameup are all obstacles to total mobilization and a higher degree of organization.

To win Comrade Davis's freedom is going to take more than rhetoric. It is going to take solid organization and campaigning.

These remarks should not give the impression that good work has not been done. Some local committees have done outstanding work. We should not underestimate the fact that the Angela Davis case is now the focal point of the struggle against repression and racism. We should not lightly dismiss the contribution we have made to this. But it is not enough.

We must decide now that Comrade Angela Davis is going to be present at our 20th Party Convention!

Racism remains a major ideological weapon of U.S. capitalism. The passage of civil rights laws has not ended the influence of racism. On the other hand, there are areas where the influence of racism is receding. The examples are mainly in working-class areas. It shows up in local union elections. Struggle and the objective need for class unity set the stage for this development. The examples are proof that, with struggle, racism can be defeated.

At the last meeting of the National Committee we undertook a major campaign to burn out the influences of racism and chauvinism in the ranks of the working class, the Left movement and in our Party. I don't want to repeat what we said then; since then we have made some headway—but events since then also prove how deep the roots of chauvinism are.

The discussion in the Party has not been self-critical enough. Comrades are mostly looking for chauvinism someplace else, in the work of some other comrades. The discussions of the National Committee must continue to press this fight. It is a struggle we can never give up—it will be with us as long as capitalism is with us. The report to the National Committee on this question must become an integral part of the preconvention discussion.   □

[Report to National Committee, July 1971]

1972

Imperialism
And Racism

The voices of imperialism never proclaim, "We oppress and exploit the peoples of other nations for our private profit." Each imperialism has developed a special line of deception to cover up its profit motive. Earlier they were in the "humanitarian" business of "bringing religion and civilization to backward peoples." This line of deception became the foundation for the ideology of great power chauvinism. When this line wore thin, they added a new line. Now they are "exporting democracy" and "the benefits of modern industry."

Because most of the imperialist countries are populated by people having white skins, while most of the peoples in the countries oppressed by imperialism have darker skins, racism has always been an ideological tool of imperialism. Racism has become the main ingredient of great power chauvinism. Indeed, the main pillar of imperialist ideology is racist great power chauvinism. Because U.S. imperialism is the center of world imperialism, it is the fountainhead of racist great power chauvinism.

But there is another reason for the deep roots of racist ideology in the United States. Racism was an ideological pillar of U.S. capitalism long before it became an imperialist power. Racism was the poisonous fog covering the hijacking of African people into slavery in the United States.

Racism was the ideological foundation for the system of slave plantations in the South. From the very beginning of U.S. capitalist development, racism was the basis for the system of discrimination against Black Americans in industry. It is the basis for segregation in housing, schools, business, churches and trade unions. The weapon of chauvinism is also used against Mexican-Americans, Puerto Ricans and Indian Americans. Anti-Semitism, too, has deep roots in the United States.

The propagation of great power chauvinism by U.S. imperialism is an extension and enlargement of its domestically-developed racist ideology. Because of its history, the essence of the ideology of U.S. imperialism is racist great power chauvinism. In most parts of the imperialist world, but especially in the United States, this ideology surfaces as white chauvinism—the concept of white supremacy. It is the most persistent and penetrating of all imperialist ideological concepts. It is the moving force behind all forms of prejudice, from sickening paternalism to the actions of a lynch mob. The struggle against racist great power chauvinism is a special responsibility for us in the United States because it is a tool of both domestic and foreign policy.

The system of special oppression in the United States is without precedent. It is institutionalized in government, industry, and all areas of social, cultural and political affairs. There is a relationship among the forms of special oppression of different groups. But the system of oppression and racism that fuels the others is directed against Black Americans.

The special system of racist oppression of some 25 million Black Americans, 5 million Chicanos, 2 million Puerto Ricans and 2 million Native American Indian people is a source of special profit for the capitalist class. Because profits, from whatever source, go into the same corporation bank accounts, it is difficult to separate them by source. However, the basic economics of racism are clear from the following facts, reported by the U.S. government:

Median income of white households ($)	$8,756
Median income of Black households ($)	$5,291
Difference between the two	$3,465
Number of Black households (thousands)	6,053
Profits from superexploitation of Black people ($billion)	21

On the same basis of calculation, extra profits from the superexploitation of Chicano, Puerto Rican and Indian people amount to $7 billion, for a total of $28 billion. Calculations based on racial wage differentials among employed workers yield similar results.

Even these figures do not give the full story. Racist ideology is geared to divide the oppressed. Capitalism uses these divisions to cut the incomes of white workers. White workers pay for racism through lower wages. These are also extra profits for capitalism.

The purpose of racist great power chauvinism, white chauvinism, is to uphold special exploitation, to justify the system that results in these extra profits.

Although colonial oppression and the system of segregation and discrimination within the Unites States seem distinct, the links between them are many. Both serve the cause of extra profits. Both continue under protection of a fog of racist ideology.

It is important to see the relationship between the two forms of oppression. But it is wrong and a disservice to the cause of progress to say they are the same. To view the Afro-American community as a colony leads to tactics that are self-defeating. Afro-Americans by and large consider such concepts unrealistic.

The struggle against world imperialism complements the struggle against racist oppression in the United States. The struggle against racist oppression at home is an important contribution to the struggle against U.S. imperialism in the world. The enemy is the same.

Winds of social change that have gathered tremendous

momentum are battering at the centuries-old walls of racist oppression. The high level of political and social consciousness of Black Americans has generated wave upon wave of militant mass protest. The struggle has torn open the carefully woven curtain of promises and platitudes that has endured for generations. Exposed for the whole world to see, in the heart of the land that boasts of "equality for all," is the most inhuman kind of oppression. If many in the nation always knew it was there, many more had closed their eyes to it.

U.S. capitalism has refined and adapted the system, the practice and the mentality of racial discrimination—the special exploitation of a minority within the system of class exploitation. More than 100 years after the Emancipation Proclamation, racism can not be described as the aftermath of slavery, but more accurately as a strategy for corporate superprofits.

In the 1950s and 1960s the United States found itself facing a serious political and social crisis. This was not a crisis of Black America, but a national crisis, a challenge to our vaunted democracy and morality. Large sections of white Americans, especially youth, responded to this moment in history.

The civil rights movement took on mass proportions and turned into a potent struggle for liberation. It revealed the harsh fact of servitude existing within our nation, awakening a new political consciousness among millions of our people.

Since the Montgomery bus boycott,[27] the struggle has secured many important victories. These can be viewed in two ways. If they are seen as substantive solutions, their significance is grievously limited. Like the assassins in Mississippi waiting to ambush freedom fighters, racism and reaction are always waiting for an opportune moment to counterattack. Seen as initial steps preparing the way for decisive change, their implications are truly revolutionary.

Racism has always been one of the most deadly weapons of imperialist ideology. Skin color has been the pretext for instances of man's inhumanity to man on a scale to equal almost any atrocity in history. Imperialism has cultivated race prejudice and given it a global character. Its influence has been the most serious obstacle to the development of class consciousness in the ranks of workers and to anti-imperialist struggles.

U.S. imperialism is an extension abroad of the system of exploitation at home. It directly exploits millions of wage workers around the world, extracting tens of billions in profits each year. U.S. capitalism derives additional tens of billions in superprofits from the racial and national oppression of millions of its citizens. These policies and practices can continue only because so many Americans, brainwashed by racism, permit it.

Nothing packs such dynamite as a question that history has placed on the agenda. Its resolution can no more be prevented than the rising of the sun.

In 1776, independence for the colonies was such an issue. And independence was won. In 1860, it was freedom for the slaves. And slavery was abolished. Victory in each of these momentous conflicts was assured by the fact that great numbers of Americans, though not fully grasping the significance of the issue, were nevertheless compelled by self-interest to join in the battle.

In our day, ending imperialist oppression of peoples and nations is such an issue. And the world system of colonialism is well on its way out. In our country, a key issue is eradication of the system of segregation and discrimination. Just as the people of our land could not have moved forward without achieving national independence two centuries ago, so we can not move ahead today without putting an end to a system that keeps millions of our citizens half slave and half free.

Destruction of this system is of crucial significance for the majority of our people: to the preservation and extension of democracy and to the economic struggles of the working class. It is a question that decisively influences relations between the United States with the rest of the world. The national character is at issue, for no nation can tolerate the oppression of a large section of its citizens without weakening and corrupting its moral fiber.

Since the Supreme Court declared school segregation unconstitutional,[28] millions of Black Americans and many whites, including tens of thousands of clergy and hundreds of thousands of youth, have marched, sat in, demonstrated and picketed, gone to jail, suffered beatings and the thrust of cattle prods in the struggle for human decency and equality. Men, women and children have died as heroes and victims in this campaign.

After all the militant actions, how do we evaluate the results? There have been gains. Not to see this would be a disservice to the struggle. Some of the solid walls of segregation and discrimination have been broken down. There has been some progress in every area. But it has been painfully slow and limited. To fail to see how stubbornly the Establishment resists full equality would also be a disservice. Disproportionate joblessness, wretched housing and a degrading ghetto existence are still the fate of the great majority of Black people, as they are, in one degree or another, of the Puerto Rican and Chicano people.

Therefore, the people of the United States must ask again and again, what forces so stubbornly resist and obstruct the nonviolent elimination of this shameful heritage? What are the roots of its persistence? Who are the main perpetrators?

The affliction is imbedded in the very fabric of U.S. capitalism. Racism has been and is still the policy of every major corporation in America. Racism is inherent in Big Business.

It is a method of squeezing maximum profits from the labor of all who toil. It is an instrument for maintaining, in the halls of Congress and in state and city legislative bodies, reactionary blocs of antidemocratic, antilabor and anti-Black politicans. It is an effective device for keeping the working class divided. White supremacy is a central pillar in the ideology of U.S. imperialism.

It is this that explains the stubborn persistence of racism and bigotry.

At stake in the civil rights issue are all past gains of our people. The stubborn resistance by the forces of reaction unifies and strengthens the ultra-Right coalition. The nuclear war maniacs, the rabid antilabor crowd, the anti-democratic, profascist gangs, the professional anti-Semites, the anti-Communist racketeers—all now gravitate toward unity with the Southern racists, the KKK and similar groups. This is indeed a crystallization of reaction, an alliance that can open the gates to fascism. And open racism flows through all their veins.

They emerged as the organizers and the shock troops of the presidential campaign of Alabama's Governor Wallace. Most of the Wallace-appointed electors were members of the Birch Society. Antilabor corporations financed the campaign. Nazi groups financed the goon squads. Wallace furnished unsurpassed demagogy. Each group made its special contribution to the evil alliance whose ultimate aim is the destruction of democracy in our country and the use of nuclear weapons in the crusade to plant the iron heel of U.S. imperialism on all mankind.

The Big Business ideology of bigotry is like a poison gas designed to incapacitate the people, distort their perception of reality and bring on a state of mass delusion. We read stories of witchcraft in New England in an early period in our history. But is not the witchcraft of racism more fantastic, taking possession of the minds of millions of otherwise sane Americans?

U.S. capitalism took over the ideology of white supremacy from the slavemasters. Corporate capitalism has further developed it, disseminated it to every corner of American life. In order to imbue the masses of white Americans with the illusion of superiority, it is necessary to deprive Blacks of equal educational, social and economic opportunities. The aim is to make millions of white people unwitting instruments of the oppression of their brothers and sisters.

Under the influence of the deadly virus of racism, their own lives of toil, debt and hardship are transformed, in comparison with the lot of their Black neighbors, into a superior existence. While they rant against Black, Puerto Rican and Chicano people, they temporarily forget their own empty cupboards and insecurity. It becomes more and more difficult for them to focus on their real oppressor—Big Business—which exploits both Black and white.

If the roots of the system of discrimination and segregation are deep within the profit system, is it possible to eliminate it before capitalism is discarded as the outmoded system it is? As militant resistance to this evil increases, this question is asked more and more often.

It seems obvious that it will not be possible to dig out all of the poisonous shoots while the present system exists. Capitalism, by its very nature, constantly revives and regenerates racist practices. But it is possible to sever many of the roots and destroy many branches even while capitalism still stands.

Victories in the fight for freedom are on the agenda now, and many are being won. The struggle for Black freedom has moved into the realm of economic and political equality—jobs, promotions, access to professions and business. In the political arena it means extension of registration and voting opportunities to all and election of Black public officials on every level.

The demands now go into areas that Big Business considers its private preserve, on which the monopolists have placed a "No Trespassing" sign. They are infringing on the prerogative of making a profit. As the struggle develops in these areas, its nature changes. There are new alliances, new support as well as more insidious and subtle resistance. It is law of capitalism that Big Business never relinquishes one cent of its profits or one ounce of its political power until it is compelled to by an irresistible force.

At this stage, the civil rights movement comes up against the workings of the state-monopoly conspiracy. In some cases, the government runs interference for the monopolists; in others, it silently condones abuses.

In the South, the conspiracy more frequently comes out into the open. The government condones terror and vigilante movements. It grants immunity for murder. Militant leaders of the Black people are harassed, jailed and murdered in other parts of the country as well.

The path to victory for civil rights and peace—and they have become increasingly interdependent—lies in the working class, Black and white together, confronting the same foe, coordinating economic and political struggles.

A labor/Afro-American alliance is not a new concept, but it has a new urgency today. The state-monopoly conspiracy and problems arising from automation are pressing hard against all working men and women. Corresponding relationships and alliances must be molded to meet these realities. These must be based on a new political consciousness.

To the indignation of the press and certain elements among our fellow citizens, Black leaders have been calling for a buildup of political power, based in localities where Black voters constitute a majority or at least a sizable bloc. People (some erstwhile liberal or labor supporters of the freedom movement who never had difficulty accommodating to the ancient practice of white domination and exclusiveness) profess shock and alarm when Black leaders assert that the time has come to secure majority rule in the counties, cities, towns, congressional, senatorial and state assembly districts where Blacks are the majority. Why is majority rule democratic only when the majority is white?

Speaking directly to those white Americans who are raising the "specter" of Black political power in the most alarmist manner, we say that Black people must be allowed to secure full particiaption in government and community bodies, reflecting a just and equal role in public office and leadership.

A further word about integration may be in order: Formal integration does not necessarily mean equality. It can, in fact, substitute tokenism for real equality. The new stage of struggle is not so much concerned with the appearance of change as with its substance.

For example, the continuing terror in the South shows how constitutionally guaranteed rights may not exist in reality. In the interest of democracy for all, the American people must put pressure on the federal government to enforce the laws. It is quite understandable why some have been compelled to seek protection in self-defense.

The labor/Afro-American alliance will only be as real as the underlying unity of the working class. Such unity must start with the elimination of all bars to Black membership and leadership in labor unions.

The size and importance of other minority groups have grown greatly in the past few decades. There are millions of Chicanos, Puerto Ricans and other Spanish-speaking peoples who suffer the indignities of discrimination, are crowded into the worst slums and given the lowest-paying jobs. Chicanos make up a large part of the most severely exploited section of the working class—agricultural workers. Large numbers of them work in unorganized industries, live in unspeakable slums, and are, like Black people, the object of police brutality.

There is another group of Americans—indeed the original Americans—whose oppression is in some ways the worst of all. These are the Native American Indians. Confined to reservations, denied many rights of U.S. citizens, robbed of their birthright by broken treaties, they have moved onto the stage with strong protests against their exploiters.

The struggle for the rights of all these millions of Americans is essential to the fight for a united working class. A factor of special importance is the organization of unorganized workers. Some breakthroughs have taken place, particularly among the Chicano agricultural workers of California. Class unity, beginning with Black-white unity and extending to embrace all oppressed minorities, starts at the level of self-interest. With the rise of a new political consciousness, it should develop from an alliance of convenience to a true brotherhood of mutual respect and equality.

The history of Afro-American people is one of heroism and sacrifice, struggle and bloodshed, of tremendous obstacles overcome, of survival against heavy odds. The struggles against enslavement by the white rulers of the United States have bequeathed a proud legacy to each succeeding generation to guide its resistance to tyranny.

Working-class unity is essential to achieve a world where class oppression and exploitation and national subjugation and discrimination will be only bad memories, faded relics in the museums of human history. Under socialism all peoples will live in peace and happiness.

Science and technology make the winning of equality for all peoples on the basis of a high level of satisfaction of human needs a realistic possibility. Such a world will also be a world without war, bigotry or prejudice, without oppression of individuals, peoples or nations—a world where man's practice of inhumanity to man has become unthinkable.

This goal is within humanity's grasp. Capitalism is the obstacle to its realization. Big Business, in its greed for maximum profits, is the one great hurdle civilization must scale before it can proceed to the "real history of humanity." One-third of the world's people have adopted the new social order that discards the profit motive. This is a decisive factor in favor of achieving socialism in the rest of the world.   □

[*Imperialism Today*, International Publishers, 1972]

1978

Honor History
By Making History

To celebrate past struggles and honor heroes and heroines while doing nothing about the issues and injustices that gave rise to struggles, heroes and heroines is meaningless lip service to history. Any meaningful observance must serve the purpose of continuing the struggle. The past must serve the present.

February is observed as Black History Month. The observance of Black History Month serves a very positive purpose. In most cases the events are linked to the struggles against racism today. In most cases it is a month of protest against racism. It serves as a month of discussions and assessments of advances, as well as the remaining tasks of removing obstacles on the path of total elimination of racism in all walks of life.

In general, the month's activities serve to raise the level of consciousness and struggle. The events tend to strengthen Black-white unity.

Black History Month helps to correct and fill in the racist deletions of the role of Black Americans in the struggle for democracy and economic security.

But there are forces that would like to take the element of struggle and protest out of the February observances. This is true with many liberals and is especially the case with white liberals.

There was a time when a public recognition of the role of Black people in the history of our country by white Americans was considered a step forward. But it does not even begin to measure the tasks and responsibilities of white Americans in the struggle against racism today.

To observe Black History Month without taking part in the struggle against today's racism becomes, in reality, a screen that hides racism. It becomes a substitute. A Black History Month observance that is not related to and concerned with developing, initiating and supporting struggles for affirmative action turns into an empty ceremony. The very meaning of affirmative action is to get away from hypocritical, empty ceremony and to get into action against both the very real effects of past racism and the concrete manifestations of today's racism.

Not to use the February events to bring pressure on the Supreme Court, the Carter Administration and the Congress on the precedent-setting Bakke case is "to sing psalms for pretense" and a dishonor to the heroes and heroines of Black liberation.

For white Americans, Black History Month must be a time of rededication to burn out the cancer of racism, a time for a deeper understanding of the critical nature of the struggle for democracy and social progres.

Racism affects the lives of Black, Latino, Indian, Asian and Mexican Americans. But it is white Americans who are afflicted by it. We have a special responsibility in the struggle because the crimes of racism are committed in our name. Racism continues because white Americans tolerate it, make excuses for it. To speak about Black-white unity without white initiatives against concrete manifestations of racism in the shops, neighborhoods, schools, is meaningless, empty rhetoric. The fact is that racism remains our country's most dangerous pollutant.

The struggle against racism must take place on many levels—social, economic, political, ideological and moral. It is related to most issues and phases of life. But the struggle against racism can be victorious only if it is related to the struggle against the evils of capitalism. Many liberals would like to observe Black History Month without any reference to racism and corporate profits.

Any idea that what is good for monopoly capitalism will somehow be beneficial for the victims of racism is a dangerous illusion. It is a variant of the old trickle-down theory that if a government passes enough money to the big corporations in the form of gifts, tax cuts, government jobs and price increases, that, somehow, some of this will trickle down to workers in the form of wages or jobs. This has always been a part of class gimcrackery. It is a scheme to convince workers that their class interests are best served by giving Big Business whatever it wants. This is very much the essence of President Carter's proposed federal budget. In fact, most governnment programs and policies of most administrations are based on the trickle-down theory. This has been going on for years and years. But the workers are still waiting for the trickle to begin. The flow of cash into the coffers of Big Business keeps gushing. But the expected trickle remains a dry run.

The roots of racism are imbedded in the system of corporate drive for ever-increasing profits. The increased profits have never resulted in less racism.

For example, besides the record one-half trillion dollar Carter federal budget, of which most is pumped back to the corporations, this past year also broke the profit record. The after-tax profits of Big Business went over the $100 billion mark. In fact, one of the factors that makes it possible for monopoly capital to amass such unconscionable, gluttonous wealth is the extra profits it reaps from the policies and practices of racism. More of the same evil is no solution to the evil.

The roots of racism are in the exploitative system of capitalism. Victories against racism, therefore, are best served by relating struggles against racism to struggles against the evils of capitalism. □

[*Daily World*, February 18, 1978]

4

AGAINST WAR AND REACTION

U.S. Racism
Brought Before the UN

The first case against the United States has been filed with the Director-General of the United Nations Security Council.

The petition asks for relief from oppression, segregation and suppression by the United States. The petition is not filed by a foreign power, but by a section of the population of the United States. They ask the world body to make an investigation and help them in their plight.

In a convention of the National Negro Congress,[1] one thousand delegates, speaking for the Negro citizens of the United States, sent their plea to the United Nations body. The petition reads, in part:

> It is with an expression of profound regret that we, a section of the Negro people, having failed to find relief from oppression through Constitutional appeal, find ourselves forced to bring this vital issue—which we have sought for almost a century since emancipation to solve within the boundary of our country—to the attention of this historic body; and to request you, as Director-General, to place it for consideration before the Economic and Social Council, or that body to which, in your understanding, it may belong.

The announcement of this move by the National Negro Congress made headlines in most parts of the world. Here in the United States it seems the press is trying hard to make believe it never happened, that the situation the petition deplores does not even exist. The newspapers simply refuse to print anything about it. And the radio commentators are silent.

If anything proves the correctness of the accusations, it is precisely this silence. For who can honestly deny the ugly facts of segregation and discrimination against the Negro people? Who can deny the criminal lynching, both legal and illegal, of the Negro citizens in the South? It is difficult to deny them when they are everyday practices. It is impossible to hide them when not only are these everyday events, but this system is praised and boasted about in the halls of the U.S. Congress by congressmen such as Rankin and Bilbo.

The complaint of oppression by the National Negro Congress is well-documented by the case that is now being tried in the court of Columbia, Tennessee. This case started with the attempt of Ku Klux Klan elements to lynch Jimmy Stephenson, a 19-year-old Negro veteran, who defended his mother from a beating.

The Tennessee state militia moved in and for days made the section of the city where Negroes live into a concentration camp. The KKK thugs went free. And now, instead, the state is prosecuting 31 Negroes on charges of attempted murder.

This case has turned into a trial of the whole system of trial by a white jury. The defense has already produced and put on the stand almost 400 citizens who testified to the fact that a Negro has never served on any jury in that county. While such discrimination in selecting juries is contrary to the Constitution, there is no denying that it is an old Southern custom. I believe there is room for investigation of this same practice in most Northern cities.

The petition of the National Negro Congress of course does not limit itself to just this type of discrimination. It raises the whole gamut of discrimination in fields such as jobs, education and housing.

The trial in Columbia, Tennessee, is not the first of this type of case. Among such trials was the famous Scottsboro case. The famous Dr. Sweet case, tried and won by Clarence Darrow in Detroit before Judge Frank Murphy in the late 1920's, is a precedent for the trial in Tennessee.

Dr. Sweet, a Negro, and eleven other defendants were freed after they were charged with murder because a man was shot and killed when a mob threatened the Sweet home. In Tennessee, 31 Negroes are accused of attempted murder. Like Sweet and his friends, they are accused of firing shots at a mob bent on lynching—in this case lynching a Negro veteran and his mother.

The immediate result of this trial must be the liberation and vindication of the 31 Negro citizens. This must be followed by the arrest and conviction of the Tennessee officials who permitted and helped organize the attack on the Negro citizens and by the arrest and conviction of the leaders of the lynch mob.

This case must serve notice in Ohio, as in every place else, that this unAmerican, undemocratic lynch mob terror must come to an end.

We urge all of you to protest to Governor James McCord, Nashville, Tennessee and to the trial judge, Joseph Ingram, Columbia, Tennessee.   □

[Speech on WHK radio, Cleveland, June 1946]

1946

Stop
Racist Violence

The murderous mob that fired 60 shots from rifles, shotguns and pistols into the bodies of two defenseless Negro couples a week ago in Monroe, Georgia, remains at large.

The world was shocked and outraged by this brutal murder of two ex-servicemen and their wives, for no apparent reason.

This attack took place just a week after Eugene Talmadge was elected Governor of Georgia by a minority vote. He ran on the promise "to return Georgia to normalcy." "Normalcy" in Georgia is a racist atmosphere of lawlessness, which looks the other way when the victims are Negro.

Cleveland has responded with anger and disgust at this wave of terror in the Southern states. All of labor has sent telegrams demanding federal action. In a resolution, the executive board of the Ohio CIO condemned these fascist-like gangsters. The state convention of the Ohio Federation of Labor joined in the movement demanding the government act against this "white supremacy" gang. The state meetings of the Painters Union called for death sentences for the murderers.

The Communist Party of Cleveland held a series of neighborhood meetings and sent hundreds of telegrams to President Truman and Attorney General Clark asking them to send federal troops to Georgia to put an end to the lawlessness.

All the labor gatherings have called for unity of the people in Cleveland and for positive steps to wipe out discrimination and violence against citizens of our city and state.

The National Maritime Union, CIO, has offered a $5,000 reward for the apprehension and conviction of the Georgia lynch mob.

In a telegram to President Truman the union charged: "This stormtrooper butchery is designed to hamper effective efforts by labor to organize the South, because fascist elements feel that strong trade union organization will successfully combat lynch terror."

The world has watched with anger and horror the recent developments in our country. Our correspondents abroad have heard on numerous occasions that we should put our own house in order before we tell others how to behave.

For instance, what can be the thoughts of the Polish workers who read on one page that the U.S. State Department has cut off the loan to Poland because the Polish government has placed certain restrictions on the voting rights of past supporters of Hitler, and on the next page read that only one Negro in Taylor County, Georgia, voted in the last elections, and that the next day this citizen was found shot dead on the roadside?

What does the Korean ex-serviceman think when reading that the U.S. authorities are objecting to the "mistreatment" of Japanese prisoners of war by the Soviet Union, and then turns the page to read that on February 13, in Aiken, South Carolina, Isaac Woodward, discharged from the Army just three hours, on his way home gets into a minor argument with a bus driver and is arrested and jailed; that when he regained consciousness in jail he was in total darkness, for life, his eyes beaten to a pulp. Or, that in January 1946, in Birmingham, Alabama, four Negro citizens were ambushed and killed for no known reason?

What can a Yugoslav farmer conclude when he reads on the front page of his newspaper our pronouncements about conquering fear itself, of freedom from fear as our policy for the world. Then he turns on his radio and hears that in Monroe, Georgia, a few days following the murder of the two young Negro couples, most of their relatives, fearing for their lives, did not dare to attend the funeral? And that a big percentage of Negro school teachers did not appear to teach the summer school session, because of fear?

What does the Bulgarian say who, while on the way to the voting booth, reads the text of the U.S. protest against the present Bulgarian government because it does not include representatives of all groups, Left and Right. Then he turns the page and reads that Mr. Tallmadge, candidate for governor, the highest office in the state, campaigned on the slogan, "This state is for whites only. White supremacy is Christianity."

Tallmadge gets many less votes than his opponent, but wins the nomination and election. The week following the election, five Negro citizens of Georgia are ambushed and killed.

What are the people of tiny Albania to think when they listen to our Secretary of State Byrnes on the defense of the rights of small nations and then read the February 25, 1946, news report from Columbia, Tennessee, about how a mob invaded the section of town where Negro people live and destroyed tens of thousands of dollars worth of property and wounded approximately 60 people. Two ex-service-ment died from their wounds.

Now the Albanians can also read that despite this attack not one member of the mob is on trial, but 18 Negro citizens are being tried and charged with attempted murder.

What does the Soviet worker say when he reads about our ideas for projecting our kind of democracy throughout the world, about the American way of life. Then follows news about the daily reign of terror in the South, and about a speech by the Attorney General of the U.S., Thomas Clark, in which he stated:

> The Department of Justice can not protect the individual or mi-
> nority against mob or ruffian activities. While such activities may

amount to deprivation of freedom of speech or other rights guaranteed by the Bill of Rights, these rights are rights protected only against official action, not private action.

What must be the thoughts of the German workers who have started on the road to discarding the Nazi ideology of the "master race," when they read the speeches by "white supremacy" Bilbo? Or when they read about the burning of Ku Klux Klan crosses? Obviously, it must dawn on the German workers that that is how they started on the road to ruin. For the Germans it was Nordic supremacy and the Jews and Communists were the targets.

What can a citizen of Trieste say when he sees our troops keeping law and order in Trieste, but not in the state of Georgia?

All these people have a right to say: "Brother, before you come over here and tell us what to do, how about starting to practice what you preach? We appreciate your help in driving the fascists out of our house, but now you must clean them out of your own front yard." ☐

[Speech on WHK radio, Cleveland, August 1946]

1966

Toward
A Peace Ticket

In the trade union movement, the leadership's support for President Johnson's war policies in Vietnam created a dilemma in the 1966 elections. It drastically cut the effectiveness of the trade unions. Labor simply could not utilize other issues effectively as long as it was weighed down by its position on the war issue. It was a contradiction to support Johnson's war policy while opposing war-induced inflation, higher taxes, wage restrictions and the Johnson-instigated antistrike legislation. The trade unions were able to overcome this contradiction only where they took a stand against the war policy.

A very important lesson emerges from the contrast of this experience with the victories of Black candidates. The most successful Black candidates were those who united opposition to the war with the struggle for civil rights. This is the meaning of Julian Bond's history-making third election to the Georgia legislature, Edward Brooke's election to the U.S. Senate from Massachusetts, the election of Adam Clayton Powell to Congress from New York. Congressman John Conyers of Michigan stands out in this regard. During the campaign he said, "The peace movement is clearly the advance wing of progressive America. . . . The only way we can achieve a really strong liberal coalition is for the members of the peace movement and the predominantly Black civil rights movement to join together to seek progressive legislation and policies."

What is the lesson? That if not for the dilemma created by its contradictory policies, labor could have had a much greater influence on many campaigns. This is the answer to the question of the president of the AFL-CIO, George Meany, as to why labor's money and efforts did not pay off. They did not pay off because the union membership did not follow Meany in backing pro-war candidates. They did not pay off because it is impossible to ride two horses at the same time, especially when they are going in opposite directions.

The second-most-discussed issue in the "battle of interpretation" of the election results is the effectiveness of the appeal to racism. That racist appeals were a factor in the electoral picture is serious enough. That they influenced the outcome of elections in the North and West adds to the seriousness. The widespread use of racism adds a new dimension to the danger posed by the ultra-Right. In this election we witnessed a coming together of ultra-Right forces whose starting point is racism and those who start from other reactionary positions.

The effects of the racist appeal are not easy to assess, especially in cases where it was used indirectly, in underground fashion. However, it did affect the outcome of the California and Illinois races as well as congressional races in many states. It was a factor in the defeat of the initiative to establish a Civilian Review Board to hear complaints of police abuses in New York. Its appeal is reflected in the setbacks suffered by many moderates in primaries throughout the South. However, my guess is that these are only setbacks, and not a reversal of a trend that has slowly emerged in the South.

This is one side of the picture. The other side is that racism did not turn into the weapon of mass hysteria many of the ultra-Rightists and reactionaries had hoped for.

Against the negative aspects, one must balance the following facts:

1. The election of Brooke broke through the "for whites only" walls around the U.S. Senate. This is a historic victory in many ways. It helps to destroy the fiction that Afro-Americans can be elected only where they are the majority. And while Brooke's opponent apparently did not openly appeal to racism (which is itself an important commentary), racism was used against Brooke in Massachusetts. This was Brooke's third election to statewide office.

2. *Newsweek* estimates that of 37 congressional candidates who made race their big issue, 22 were defeated. In addition, the defeat of the racist Mahoney for governor in Maryland was an especially important victory. One must also view the defeat of Johnson in the gubernatorial race in Arkansas as a victory over extreme racism. Incumbents won reelection in most congressional districts where their pro-civil rights positions were under attack.

What conclusions can be drawn from this?

Racism is an insidious ideological factor with deep roots that can be exploited by reactionary forces. Its influence must be continuously fought. But this struggle can be won. The fight to eliminate racist ideology will be long-range, but it can be curbed, prevented from spreading, reduced in effectiveness, now. We can not defeat the war policy without winning this struggle. We can not unite the working class without winning this struggle. This struggle is the very essence of the struggle for Black-white unity, for the labor-Black alliance.

The coming together of different ultra-Right groups and their increased use of racism increases the danger from both the ultra-Right and racism. It also adds a new dimension to the use of anti-Semitism by reaction. It points to the inherent unity of the struggles for civil rights and civil liberties; against the ultra-Right, racism and anti-Semitism; and highlights the key role of these struggles in the overall battle for democracy.

In this context, we must reject the concept of "white backlash." This concept is a weapon of reaction and of the racists. It justifies racism as being only a reaction to the so-called extremes of the civil rights movement. It is a cover for all kinds of crimes. The backlash idea is a method of political extortion. "If you demand your just rights it will result in a backlash. Therefore, you must accept tokenism—accept the status of second-class citizenship for another 300 years."

Racism is most effective among poor whites in the South. Many poor Southern whites have been left to eke out a living, originally from the remnants of feudalism and more recently in the polluted backwaters of capitalism. They are among the poorest of the poor, with a high proportion of illiteracy. The struggles of working people for democracy and a higher living standard have largely passed them by. Considerable numbers of them have moved to the cities of both the North and the South. While they work in industry, one can not yet classify them as working-class ideologically. They bring their fears and prejudices with them. This gives a new dimension to the ideological problem of racism in many industrial centers.

We must take the task of countering the effects of the ultra-Right's concentration on white workers more seriously. This is a new drive by capital to divide the ranks of the working class, to halt the process of development of class unity and the labor-Black alliance.

Racism is also a prominent factor among homeowners. Real estate operators create and use the weapon of blockbusting in areas where individual homeownership prevails.

Racist ideology is as old as U.S. capitalism. It has deep roots in the ranks of white America. Yet it is a fact that much headway has been made in the struggle against it. We must intensify this struggle.

While the election results do not signal a reversal of the overall trend, this should not lull us to slumber or lead us to overlook the fact that in some areas the struggle has become sharper.

One of the encouraging signs is the role of the trade unions. The *American Federationist*, organ of the AFL-

CIO, devoted an entire issue to the fight against racism. The United Steelworkers sent out a special letter on this subject to its million members. The United Auto Workers devoted a special issue of its monthly, *Solidarity*, to it. *Labor Today* reprinted a number of statements by leading civil rights figures and trade unionists as a folder for mass distribution. The trade unions of Maryland made the defeat of Mahoney their main task. In Georgia, the trade unions were the main force behind the write-in campaign against Lester Maddox. COPE (Committee on Political Education), electoral arm of the AFL-CIO, put out very good material on the issue of racism and labor.

One of the positive features of this election is a modest but important increase in the number of winning Black candidates. A total of 139 Black candidates were elected to state offices. However, there was no breakthrough in the lower house of the U.S. Congress.

The victories in 1966 should become the basis for a fresh look at this question. For a breakthrough in Black congressional representation, early initiatives are needed. It will not happen if progressives continue with the old song, "Let it go this time, we will do it in the next election." The election of Black congressmen is a task in every state—now. The election of Edward Brooke to the U.S. Senate shows this to be all the more necessary and possible.   ☐

[Report to National Committee, December 1966]

Against the Nixon-Agnew Road to Disaster

The struggle for Black liberation continues in diverse forms at a very high level, even though in the last few years it has not resulted in mass explosions.

As in the case of class confrontation, murder and terror mark the path of sharper struggles. The systematic, planned extermination of the leaders of the Black Panther Party[2] is stark evidence of the nature of the current ultra-Right offensive. The gunmen feel they have official, legal and public license to murder militant Black leaders. Police departments are without moral compunction and feel immune from legalities. This is the path to fascism. If not stopped, the undeclared license will become a declared license. If not stopped, an ever-expanding circle of people in political groupings will become fair game under the license established by precedent. This is the nature of the "law and order" of the new administration.

In a speech at Harvard University, Comrade William L. Patterson[3] placed this question profoundly when he said:

Where racism abounds "law and order" are turned into their opposite. Unless there is equality of opportunity and rights for all alike, "law and order" becomes tyranny, the protest actions of those denied their rights are called "lawlessness" and their suppression becomes the order of the tyrant. The Constitutional basis for a legal struggle for a redress of grievances is destroyed and the ghettos into which the exploited and oppressed Black nationals have been herded become occupied territory on which every known vice can be superimposed. The government stands ready with its storm troopers to enforce the racist policy it has made the basis of its relations with Black citizens.

The question of the fight against racism is logically being linked with the fight for peace and against the inhuman war in Vietnam.

The Nixon Administration adds a new component to the struggle for Black liberation.

It, more than any other force, has created the atmosphere for racist terror. It, more than any other force, issues the license to murder.

It scuttled the Voting Rights Law.[4] This gives the racists in the South license to close voter registries to Black people.

It has taken every possible step to block school integration. Its appointed Chief Justice of the Supreme Court now leads the maneuvering to undo past Supreme Court decisions favoring school desegregation. So far the majority of the Supreme Court has not bowed to the pressures to end school desegregation.

The Nixon Administration's economic steps—especially those related to inflation—have a special effect on Black, Chicano and Puerto Rican workers. The advent of a new recession means we are again entering the last-to-be-hired and first-to-be-fired phase of the cycle; with the layoffs, those with least seniority, those who can least afford it, will now be laid off.

The Nixon Administration is motivated, in addition to its class-based racism, by Republican Party electoral strategy. It would be a mistake to view the so-called Southern strategy as simply a vote-getting gimmick. In essence, it is a plan to unite the most reactionary and racist elements of North and South as a reactionary electoral base. This is more than just an electoral policy. It is a foundation for the establishment of political power by the most reactionary sections of monopoly capital.

This policy seeks to unite the most reactionary trends in the political spectrum. It is based on the acceptance of racism. Its "law and order" theme is to accept racist order as law. This was the long-range significance of the Haynsworth[5] nomination. Incidentally, the coalescence of labor, Black and liberal forces in opposition to that nomination has great significance for the developing political confrontation.

A prominent feature of the Nixon Southern strategy is the creation of an active ultra-Right minority force to terrorize and create a conforming silenced majority; to make the reactionary, racist bloc the dominant political force in the country. It is an attempt to create a mass base for the political operation of the ultra-Right forces. In the South, the aim of the Southern strategy is to crystallize an open ultra-Right force around the Republican Party. At the same time, the growing number of Black voters being registered under the Voting Rights Act is a threat to the Nixon-Thurmond[6] axis. Thus the Southern strategy of the Nixon Administration presents a major challenge to all democratic forces. It is a feature of the new fascist danger.

As the Nixon Administration unfolds its racist policies, democratic forces generally, and the forces of Black liberation particularly, will be forced to take a new look at questions of unity and alliances. They will have to take a new look at issues of mutual self-interest.

The elections in Cleveland, Detroit and Atlanta make good case studies for the struggles ahead. In each of these campaigns the crucial questions related to unity between the working class and the Black community. More and more this becomes the critical question in all areas of struggle. It is an area in which we Communists can make the greatest contribution. It is one of the most difficult but also most decisive matters. I do not think we have approached this question with sufficient diligence, firmness and imagination.

The struggle for Black liberation is many-sided. One of its important advances has been in the electoral arena. This advance has been most significantly expressed by Black voters in the South, with the election of 528 Black candidates to public office in eleven Southern states. This includes 31 state legislators, 259 city officials—including Maynard Jackson as vice mayor of Atlanta, 58 county officials, 89 law enforcement officers and 91 school board members. In Mississippi there is 1 state legislator, 33 city officials, 20 county officials, 18 law enforcement officers and 6 school board members. Georgia has 14 Black members of the state legislature. North Carolina has 45 Black city officials and South Carolina, 24. Tennessee has 8 Black members of the state legislature; Texas, 3; Virginia 2. Louisiana has 22 Black law enforcement officers and 22 city officials. In the country as a whole more than 1,200 Black people hold public office. This is an important development, and much more can be achieved.

The election of Black candidates to public office raises the question of acting on time in relation to the 1970 elections, when every congressman and all state legislatures (except Kentucky, Louisiana, Mississippi, New Jersey and Virginia), 35 state governors and 33 U.S. senators are up for election. The recent electoral conferences in the South set realistic breakthrough goals for the 1970 elections.

There is a rising curve of action in the ranks of 40 million oppressed and discriminated-against Americans. For example, the organization of Chicano agricultural workers has created a new base for the trade union and working-class movements of many states.

The reclaiming of Alcatraz Island by Native American Indians is symbolic of their rising movement against inequality and oppression.

The rising struggles of the victims of racism and special oppression continue to be the most consistent base for the sweeping democratic movements of this period.   ☐

[Report to National Committee, January 1970]

1972

A Lame Duck
In Turbulent Waters

Racism was used in a new way in the 1972 elections. Nixon's positions reflect a shift in the position of monopoly capital. On civil rights the shift is away from a policy of concessions to the mass movement, to one of racist attacks. The slogan is: "The Blacks, Chicanos, Puerto Ricans and now the Native American Indians have gone too far." The shift in policy is accompanied by new appeals to the backward fears of whites. George Wallace[7] has a right to boast that Nixon and Agnew have taken up his line. Nixon's appeals are on the same level and the same issues as Wallace's. The transfer of Wallace's support to Nixon creates a new danger and a new base for racism.

A presidential appeal to racism becomes a presidential license for racist violence. The cold-blooded murders at Southern University[8]; the violence at housing project sites; the racist actions in Canarsie and dozens of other areas are not isolated incidents. They are incited by the atmosphere created by the drive led by Nixon. These actions enjoy government sanction.

There is a new "refinement" to the racist appeals. They are geared to take full advantage of the backward fears and concrete concerns of whites. They are geared to take full advantage of real problems people face. They are especially geared to economic issues.

This appeal to racism is especially dangerous because it is influencing new sections of the people. It was an ultra-Right instrument and influence in the elections. It has involved thousands in racist acts—on picket lines, in meetings, in acts of violence. The racist dagger was behind all of the talk about busing, jobs, taxes and "the work ethic."

We must see the significance of the new danger. The use of racism in the 1972 elections serves as a warning of how it can push the country to the Right, how it is related to the danger of fascism in the U.S.

We must draw lessons about how to fight racism. Just as racism is geared to taking advantage of concrete issues, our struggle against racism and our exposure of racist demagogy must be also geared to issues. We must present real solutions to real issues in a way that exposes the corporate interests behind the racist appeals. We must place the class issues and the class solutions. We must convince, organize and move white people on the basis of their own interests to get into the struggle against racism. We must concretely demonstrate that the racists' demagogy is intended to use white masses as dupes.

It is necessary to see the danger within the framework of a lame duck administration. But this need not and must not lead to paralyzing hopelessness. We reject any idea that only prolonged additional experience will create the basis for a struggle against racism. It is important to keep in mind that racism was a reactionary influence in the elections because it was wrapped in a fog of demagogy. Therefore the struggle against it must include the exposure of this new demagogy.

One very clear pattern in the 1972 election was the 87 per cent vote against Nixon by Black voters. This was a very conscious vote against reaction. It was a vote against racism, but it also reflected a deep concern about the overall reactionary direction of Nixon's policies. The Black delegates at the Democratic Party Convention were an important force for political independence. And this is the case in each area of movement.

In light of the elections, we should take a new look at the question of political independence. These experiences point to the need for political independence to have a grassroots base. Emphasis on such a base should not be counterposed to the electoral victories of Black candidates. As long as such a base does not exist, candidates will go on making political deals with the old machines. They almost have to be re-elected. At the same time, the large attendance at the Gary conference,[9] the role of the Black Congressional Caucus and the Black Labor Conference are all moves toward political independence. How such developments can be related to work on the grassroots level is a very important question. Without political independence it is difficult to build grassroots movements, and without grassroots movements it is difficult to build political independence. The 87 per cent vote against Nixon in the Black community is a solid base for such movements.

The number of Black members elected to the U.S. Congress has increased from 4 in 1962 to 13 representatives and 1 senator in 1970, and now to 16 representatives and 1 senator. Three representatives are Black women—Shirley Chisholm of New York, Barbara Jordan of Texas and Yvonne Burke of California. The election of Andrew Young from Atlanta also has special significance, as does the re-election of Ronald Dellums of California. There were Black candidates in 44 congressional districts.

The number of Black public officials continues on an upward swing. It is estimated that there are 1,000 Black elected public officials in the South—an increase of 25 per cent from 1970. There are 227 Black state legislators in 38 states, compared to 206 in 37 states in 1970. And there are 43 Black state senators in 26 states compared to 37 in 21 states in 1970.

The increase of Black public officials is not only in numbers; it adds a new quality to the legislative and democratic process. It provides a challenge and a base for greater independence and participation by labor, women, youth and other forces which form the base for a people's party and for independent formations outside the two-party prison.

We still do not have all the facts about the vote in the Chicano community. According to some estimates, 67 per cent voted against Nixon. All indications are that the trend toward political independence continued in the Chicano community. In the policy of La Raza Unida Party,[10] this was reflected in advocacy of abstaining from voting on the presidential level. We need to hear more from comrades about this policy. Did it in practice become a policy of neutrality? What was the reaction of broader forces to this policy? How did it reflect the relationship with other forces? What was the policy towards candidates for other offices? What were the results insofar as Chicano representation in the various states was concerned?

It is obvious that policies of the Party must be carried out thoughtfully and with common sense. That is always a characteristic of a mature Party. Let me give a couple of examples in the electoral field to make this point. For example, we must not do what the Trotskyites have been doing for some time. Their policy is to pick campaigns such as those of Stokes, Abzug and others, of Black, liberal and working-class candidates, and especially campaigns of Black candidates, and run Trotskyite candidates against them. This has long been a very conscious policy of the Trotskyites. There is no question that such a policy is irresponsible. The concentration against Black candidates is a reflection of their racism. Of course, that is not our policy.

In such elections we must work with the progressive forces, but we do so from a position of independence.

It is necessary to identify the new elements of racism, the sophistication and adjustment of racist ideology. The same kind of shift also is occurring in the chauvinism against Chicanos and Puerto Ricans. It is expressed in attacks against the farm workers; Proposition 22[11] has mass appeal. It is related demagogically to concrete issues.

That racism has been "refined," adjusted and geared to concrete issues is an important development. It is covered with demagogy, but because of its camouflage it is also more aggressive. These tactics make it possible for people to be on picket lines which everybody knows are racist picket lines and yet demagogically say, "We are not racists." And it is on this level, in terms of this new element, that we must develop concreteness in fighting against racism.   ☐

[Report to National Committee, December 1972]

1973

THE SAKHAROV
FRAUD

Let us look at a "basic" in the Sakharov[12] thesis. In speaking about racial discrimination against Black Americans, Sakharov states: "Our propaganda materials [i.e., Soviet reporting—G.H.] usually assert that there is crying inequality in the United States while the Soviet Union has something entirely just, entirely in the interests of the working people. . . . I have no intentions of minimizing the aspect of poverty and lack of rights, but we must clearly understand that this problem is not primarily a class problem, but a racial problem, involving the racism and egotism of white workers, and that the ruling group [notice he does not want to say 'ruling class'—G.H.] in the United States is interested in solving this problem."

As if this were not enough, Sakharov adds, "It seems to me that the socialist camp should be interested in letting the ruling group in the United States settle the Negro problem without aggravating the situation in the country." Let the ruling class in the United States settle the "Negro problem"! That idea is not new or unique, but to see such blatant racism in print is digusting and shocking. It is a cowardly act of surrender to the racist oppressors.

There were many, including in the United States, who said, "Let Hitler and the German ruling class settle the 'Jewish problem.' " Voices are also heard saying: "Let

Portugal settle the Angolan and other colonial problems."
Or, "Let the British settle the 'Irish problem.' " Or, "Let
the Chilean junta settle the fate of political exiles and the
Chilean people—in blood!" To add more fuel to the fire,
Sakharov excuses the inaction of government bodies because, as he states, action would possibly result in "acti-
vating extreme leftist and extreme rightist parties." Such
statements are more outright racism! They are unabash-
ed coverups for racism.

White workers and white people generally are influenced by racism. This is one of the most serious problems in the United States. It is a serious obstacle to uniting
the working class. It is an obstacle to building an anti-monopoly movement. There is movement and struggle
against racism in the United States, but it is a movement
against, not by, the ruling class.

Sakharov tries to cover up the fact that the roots of racism are in the very bowels of the monopoly capitalist system that he defends. It is intertwined with the system of
class exploitation. To say that the "ruling class is interested in solving this problem" is as big a falsehood as it is
possible to say about the United States scene. There is not
one iota of evidence in our more than 350-year history that
would in any way give credence to such idiocy. Have the
slavemasters anywhere in the world ever been "interested" in freeing the slaves?

To add to the criminal nature of Sakharov's thesis, he
implies that those who speak out against racism are responsible for "aggravating the situation." The ruling class
has used this phony argument throughout history—that the
victims of oppression make their oppression worse by
fighting against it. The logic of such advice is for the oppressed to suffer indignities, to starve and suffer in silence, to be kicked and humiliated, but to say "thank you"
because to do otherwise would "aggravate the situation."
This thesis in all its ugly aspects is an apology for the actions of monopoly capital. Silence about an evil, especially
the evil of racism, makes one guilty of acquiescence. It

bothers Sakharov that the people of the world speak out against the racism of capitalism. It seems to irritate Sakharov that the Soviet Union takes a forthright stand against racism!

Yes, there is "crying inequality" in every phase of life in the United States. There is a 350-year history of brutal, racist oppression practiced against Black Americans in this country. There is racist oppression of millions of Chicanos, Puerto Ricans, Indian and Asian Americans. And there is a basic "crying inequality" that is the outcome of the system of class exploitation. There is the basic inequality of 90 per cent of the population barely making a living while unprecedented profits go to a handful of ultra-rich. To say that the ruling class "is interested in solving this problem" is like saying that the wolf kills sheep because it is interested in solving the grazing problem. Monopoly corporations are interested only in greater profits and unlimited power. They will never willingly give up either their system of class exploitation or their system of racist exploitation and oppression.

Even the phrase, "We must clearly understand that this problem is not a class problem," is racist. What does it imply? That working-class forces should not be concerned because it is not "a class problem." In Sakharov's thesis there is a benevolent, magnanimous, concerned white capitalist class, "interested in solving this problem" if given only half a chance. But there is not a word about the heroic struggle of the oppressed, not a word about the growing unity of Black and white, not a word about the working-class movement and its struggle. Sakharov has eyes only for the racist ruling class.

Yes, socialism in the USSR is "entirely just," entirely in the interests of the working people. It is working-class power. There are no exploited classes or oppressed nations or peoples in the Soviet Union. That is an undeniable fact. Even Sakharov dares not deny that the Soviet Union has burned out the racist structure that was inherited from czarism, the mixture of cruel capitalism and brutal, backward feudalism that his close friend Solzhenitsyn glorifies in his writings. Even he does not dare deny the historic fact that the Soviet Union was the first country in the world to wipe out a major ideological underbrush when it illegalized anti-Semitism—one of the evils left over from the bigoted czarist past.

Even a Sakharov dares not deny that the Union of Soviet Socialist Republics is a multinational federation building socialism in peace and equality. Sakharov dares not deny this. That slander, that crime, was left for the *New York Times* and Harrison Salisbury to commit. They dug up and rewrote all the filth and falsehoods that have been flowing in antisocialist, anti-working-class sewers throughout the world. This, of course, became part of the "Sakharov textbook."

There is really no limit to the idiocy of Sakharov's "basics." Listen to this: "National egotism gave rise to colonial oppression, nationalism and racism." Today most serious people throughout the world are aware that it is the drive of monopoly corporations for more superprofits that breeds and sustains colonial oppression and its accompanying ideological cover, namely, racism. "Egotism" is not what gives rise to imperialism. Imperialism is a logical, inevitable stage of capitalist development. But of course this is exactly what Sakharov wants to hide.   □

[From the pamphlet, *The Sakharov-Solzhenitsyn Fraud*, 1973]

Mastering the Struggle Against Racism

The purpose of my remarks today is to probe areas concerned not so much with political assessment of the struggle against racism as with our approach to the struggle.

Our approach today should be that we can influence developments. We can take this approach because objective factors make it possible.

This assessment is based on an estimate of objective developments that permit us to have a positive outlook toward finding solutions and influencing broad developments and the direction of movements and struggles.

One of the developing objective factors in the declining stage of capitalism is the growing interrelationship among processes, sectors and struggles. This feature has become more prominent as well as more significant.

The interrelationships are also becoming more obvious to broad masses. That people now recognize these overlapping mutual self-interests is an important new element.

Understanding those interrelationships is a source of great strength. Mastering their use is key to mass struggle. It can mean the difference between just waging a struggle and winning it. It is, in a sense, a new tactical question. We have not as yet mastered this inherent aspect of the art of leadership, but we have made headway in understanding the new elements of unity between the class struggle and the struggle against racism. This higher level of understanding is based on objective developments which bring the struggles closer together. We have been forced to probe the interconnections and interrelationships between these two areas. But we still have some way to go.

We have made some headway in understanding the interconnection between the working class and the Afro-American community, between the working class and the Chicano community, etc. Here again, we still have some way to go.

We have to step up our probing and mastering of the interconnections, the interrelationships, the overlapping mutual self-interests. The interconnections and interrelationships are a concrete part of the reality of the overlapping self-interests of different sectors and movements.

We must also take note of the fact that making use of the interconnections and interrelationships does not in any way replace the need for emphasis on the specific struggles. This, too, has to be clearly understood.

For instance, understanding the interrelationships and overlapping self-interests of the class struggle and the struggle against racism (between the working class and the racially and nationally oppressed peoples) must not in any way lead to a lessening of the specific emphasis on the struggle against racism. Such an interpretation would show a failure to understand the interrelationship.

In fact, this understanding demands greater emphasis on the specific struggle against racism—a clear picture of the mutual self-interests in fighting racism, the knowledge that white workers can not win significant victories without taking an active part in the struggle against racism and discrimination.

Likewise, a recognition of the need for white allies on the part of the racially and nationally oppressed points up the necessity for uniting the struggle against racism with the class struggle. This is a recognition of the dialectical interrelationships and overlapping self-interests.

However, we must not permit the replacement of one by

the other when raising the question of overlapping mutual self-interests. We can not allow the struggle against racism to be submerged in the class struggle. It is a vital struggle in and of itself. The recognition of the interrelationship, however, strengthens the struggle against racism.

Recognition of the need to fight racism and discrimination is central to the class struggle, to winning working-class victories. This is the dialectical process we must be able to convey to the different sectors, movements and struggles. They are interdependent and irreversibly linked as never before. This is the objective process of the growing unity between the class struggle and the struggle against racism.

In addition, we have to keep explaining that an essential feature of building the antimonopoly movement is the struggle against racism and that here, too, there is an interrelationship between the two. Anyone interested and involved in building antimonopoly movements must be helped to understand that the struggle agaist racism is a precondition for the success of such an antimonopoly development.

The new structural crisis resulting in plant closings and giveback wage cuts is further proof that exploitation of the working class and racism in the workplace overlap. The trade union movement must accept and understand this new reality. This overlapping must be reflected in labor-management contracts through the inclusion of affirmative action clauses.

The same can be said of the interrelationship between the struggle against racism and the struggle for democracy in general; or the struggle for world peace and the struggle against racism and for democratic rights in general; or between democracy, the struggle for world peace and the struggle against racism; or between anti-imperialist and antimonopoly struggles and the struggle against racism.

Recognizing, understanding and tactically applying these interrelationships correctly are now preconditions for success.

Racism is related to both domestic and foreign policy. There is an interrelationship between national liberation struggles, the struggle against racism and imperialist foreign and domestic policies.

It is important to recognize that racism is a factor in the ability of monopoly capital to cut real wages and force a reduction in the standard of living. It is our task not only to expose that, but also to use that relationship in the mobilization of the working class against declines in the standard of living, cuts in real wages and the struggle against racism. Correctly understanding the interrelationship will strengthen both the economic struggle and the struggle against racism.

When the interconnections are understood and acted upon, the victories and advances in these areas are considerably greater. The interlinking of these struggles does not downgrade or weaken, but rather strengthens each one; it upgrades the overall level of struggle and adds great strength to the class struggle as a whole.

Another example is the interconnection between the general struggle for reforms and the fight for affirmative action. One can not fight for reforms without bringing forward the demand for affirmative action.

The struggle against racism and for affirmative action with quotas must become an integral part of the struggle for reforms. Otherwise the reform struggles are one-sided and unsuccessful because racism continues to be an obstacle. Therefore, reforms are possible only if affirmative action with teeth becomes a key demand. This link between the two can be utilized to draw strength for both struggles.

When we speak about becoming experts, capable fighters against racism, we are speaking mainly about white Communists and white trade unionists, those who understand the class roots of racism. But it is just as important to understand and to explain clearly the interconnections, the overlapping self-interests. One can not be an expert and a capable fighter without that knowledge.

Winning white workers and white people in general is the most difficult aspect of the struggle against racism. It is an area of the struggle which we still tend to avoid. The task can best be done when the mutual self-interests are thoroughly understood and clearly explained to white workers.

There has been some progress in the struggle against racism, although slow and spotty. The progress achieved is a result, first of all, of the militant struggles of the Afro-American community. This has been the major contributing factor. There are some advances in winning white workers and white people in general. This is a slower process, but it is important to take note of it.

We have to take note of progress if for no other reason than to convince people that it is possible, because there are many who are not convinced that victories over racism and discrimination are possible.

In assessing the progress we have made in this connection we have to throw onto the scale not only those who have been won to active participation in the struggle, but also those who have been neutralized. In struggle, that is a very important factor. To win over sections from a position of being militant racists, or supporters of racist policies, to a position of neutrality is important and can be decisive.

Lenin always placed great emphasis on this process. When he studied a revolutionary situation one of the questions he would ask is: What forces have been won to a position of neutrality? This was always a big factor in making an assessment. He especially focused on the critical importance of winning the middle class and petty bourgeois elements to a position of neutrality.

The struggle against racism is still very much a struggle against tokenism. In spite of progress, it very often remains at that level. For instance, there are only a token number of Afro-Americans who have escaped the economic gap. This is tokenism. Tokenism is still the rule, especially in upgrading and promotion, housing, school integration and total income.

We have not yet mastered the interrelationship between the role of Black workers and the struggles of the Afro-American community. We must study this question seriously. Our weaknesses are mainly in the area of not understanding fully the role of the working class in general, and therefore a lack of understanding of the role of Black workers as a part of the working class and in Black liberation movements. Many Black workers are trade union leaders who bring extensive trade union experience to the community.

We should take note of some changes in the Afro-American community. When you are involved in it you don't see the changes. I was away for about five months and when I returned I was surprised at the number of changes in every area in that short time. Some of them were small but very significant.

The Afro-American community is not politically or ideologically as homogeneous now as it was in the past. Certain changes and shifts have taken place generally in political and ideological positions.

The U.S. ruling class has increased its efforts to create divisions. It hasn't been very successful so far, but it won't give up. It will continue and the efforts will produce some results.

There are enough similarities between the struggles of the Afro-American community and those of the working class and the trade union movement that we can consider some of the same tactics we put forward in the trade union movement.

We can be of the most help to the Afro-American liberation movement by assisting in building movements that are based more on the grassroots and on the rank and file. Sinking deeper roots in communities is an especially urgent task. This is still an unresolved question in most areas, not just in the Black community. Here again, there are interconnections between shop, industry and community.

There is a need for Left-Center and Left forms. When we do not take the initiative to build legitimate Left forms in every area of struggle there is a vacuum into which the phony Left can then move. We have seen this in the trade union movement.

We have to consider carefully our approach and tactics in relation to elected Afro-American leaders. They have a real problem. We can have the very best elected leaders and officials, but they are ineffective unless they they are able to say to the power structure: "Either you make concessions and pass reforms or there's going to be an upsurge." They need the power of the grassroots and the rank and file to back up what they say. They have to be able to say: "Look at this mass movement. How do you expect me to deal with this grassroots movement without concessions and reforms?"

These kinds of forms are not easy to build. It is not always easy to formulate a Left program. Those who want to take a Left position have to have some place to go. This is the problem we face in the trade union movement. Generally, comrades in the shops have concluded, incorrectly, that it is now possible to lead a Left-Center type of movement without an organized Left.

One of our major contributions to the overall struggle must be the building of forms for rank-and-file development and the organization of Left forms. On this question there have been interesting discussions in relation to the National Alliance Against Racist and Political Repression[13] as one of these forms. It does have Left concepts and programs and is especially influenced by Communists in leadership.

We have to keep arguing the point that the Party can not substitute for such Left forms. Grassroots and Left forms have to take up immediate economic and social issues. That has to be their base of operations, although they can not ignore the others. Such grassroots approaches are needed in struggles such as housing, health, school integration and political action.

Another argument for building Left forms is that they are necessary to give leadership to broader forms. And giving leadership to broader forms is one criterion of a legitimate and effective Left, because many of the phony Left sects move precisely into areas where this is not done by the legitimate Left. The fundamental task of the organized legitimate Left must be to lead broader movements.

One more argument that relates specifically to our Party. We can not build the Party without such Left forms. People usually do not make a leap, ideologically or politically, from, for example, a mass movement position to the Party.

However, the transition from a Left form into the Party is a much more natural one. That is not the main reason for Left forms, but they do serve the purpose of preparing people for the Party. One of the reasons we are not building the Party fast enough is that there are not enough Left forms and therefore not enough people in the process of moving toward the Party. We could call this process a "peaceful transition."

(I recall a discussion we had a few years ago with a group of Catholic priests. They said they would join with us in making things as good as possible on earth. They agreed to join with us in the struggle for reforms, to make things as good as possible for people. Someone said this would be a kind of "peaceful transition" to the utopian heaven, without a big leap.)

Our Party does not yet put the major emphasis on the most difficult phase of the struggle against racism. There are tendencies to bypass the problem.

This is decisive for us because our resolve on this question will determine whether we will win over and draw into struggle white workers and white people in general. This is one of the most difficult of all tasks we face. We still tend to slip into the position that the Afro-American community will conduct the struggle and we will support it.

Among our weaknesses is lack of conviction that it is possible to win victories and advance the struggle to higher levels. This is reflected in a surprised reactions—"I didn't expect that," or "I didn't expect so-and-so to take such a good position." If you don't expect to win white people to a nonracist position, then you won't fight very hard to win them.

One reason for this weakness is lack of know-how concerning how to approach the issue, how to find the interconnections and overlapping interests.

I hear examples of white comrades who have taken up and won the struggle to move white workers to a nonracist position. We have to write more about such experiences. No matter how small the successes, they are very significant and the whole Party should know about them and learn from them.

Therefore, in order to strengthen and deepen the struggle and move more forcefully into this difficult area of work we have to develop a plan.

We need consistent, well-planned discussion outlines. We need exchanges of experience that are shared with the whole Party through articles. We need to become more creative in developing a plan that will keep the issue of racism and the fight against it consistently in the forefront of all our work.   □

[Talk at National Seminar on Questions of Black Liberation, 1980]

Reaganomics
And Racism

The policies of the Reagan Administration are not only reactionary, anti-labor, anti-people, pro-Big Business, imperialist and militarist, but also blatantly racist. Reaganite policies and actions on the government level are removing restrictions on discrimination in shops, factories and offices, in housing, education and social services. The Reagan-Stockman Trojan Horse is a racist hack.

The racism stemming from Reaganite policies penetrates all sectors and all processes. It sanctions corporate practices of racism. It encourages two-bit bosses to harass, bankers to red-line, landlords to discriminate, raise rents and evict, real estate operators to gentrify and practice "urban removal," supermarkets to jack up prices, and school administrations to turn the clock back on quality, integrated education.

The root cause of racism is capitalism and, at present, state monopoly capitalism. That is why every racist practice that adds to surplus value and corporate profits is being intensified. This system has created a vicious racist circle. Those last-hired and first-fired are also the first to run out of unemployment benefits, savings and other resources. They are the first to wind up in critical, emergency situations. For increasing numbers the cycle is becoming an economic dead end.

Unemployment among Afro-Americans is now beyond the crisis point of 20 per cent. Joblessness among Afro-American teenagers is a brutal 50 per cent, while overall youth unemployment stands at 21 per cent.

In human terms these grim figures translate into anger, frustration, hopelessness, despair and desperation. The Reaganites call this "downward mobility."

The celebration of Afro-American History Month (February) has become both a national tradition and a time to assess history in the making.

In a longer-range perspective, history moves inexorably forward, in a progressive direction. For example, capitalism is an advance over slavery and feudalism; socialism is an advance over capitalism.

However, the march of history is anything but straight. Its gait is not steady, smooth and consistent. There are leaps forward, but there are also setbacks. And there are periods when history seems to just tread water.

Both long- and short-range patterns of history are basically propelled by the struggle between two opposing classes, two social and political forces. One class fights to block the progress of history—wherever possible, to turn the clock back. The class which feels its position declining fights desperately to halt the march of history. The opposing class, whose historical position is rising, strives to speed up, to advance, to make great leaps in historical progress.

In our time, the reactionary force that fights to halt and reverse forward movement is Big Business—the class of monopoly capitalists. The advancing, progressive class is the working class. The struggle between them is the class struggle.

The class struggle is, in one way or another, involved and intertwined with changes in all areas of social life. The struggle against racism is inextricably linked with the class struggle, the struggle for social progress and the struggle for socialism.

In most periods, long- and short-term historic trends

move in tandem. But there are moments when immediate trends either stand still or move opposite to the main direction of history. The 1982 observance of Afro-American History Month must deal with such an occurrence.

I t is appropriate to celebrate long-range advances in the struggle against racial and national oppression. But it is also necessary to use this February to reassess, to protest, to mobilize and organize an all-people's front against new racist attacks—to protest the open, brutal, racist policies and practices of the Reagan Administration. Using raw state power and blatant racism, the Reagan Administration is in collusion with monopoly capital to turn back the civil and human rights clock.

This same raw state monopoly capitalist power is being used to force the working class to retreat and to defend all that it has won in the past. As a result, setbacks, takebacks and givebacks have become the short-range pattern. For the moment, monopoly capital is on the offensive; the working class and people are on the defensive. This casts a long shadow over all fronts of struggle.

Because racist attacks are geared to driving a wedge between people, they are a critical feature of the overall monopoly offensive. They divide, confuse and disorient a section of the working class and people, thus weakening all fronts. It is undeniable that the working-class and people's movements can not go from a defensive to an offensive posture without going on the offensive against racism.

In all battles, the most critical question is how to develop strategic and tactical plans that focus the total power of one's fighting forces on the central front.

It is important to examine how the reactionary establishment calculates the impact of racism in its overall offensive. The division and confusion racism creates in workers' ranks permits corporations to demand bigger takebacks and concessions from the workers. It emboldens employers to speed up production, to force overtime, to cut piece rates, to ignore health and safety standards.

The Reagan Administration uses racism to cut even more deeply into people's social and economic programs. It uses racism to divide and rule, and it shares the spoils it robs from the people among the monopolies. It pushes racism because it is profitable for the corporations.

In a period of general, all-out, antipeople offensive, the self-interest of the victims of monopoly capital objectively requires a fight against racism. The fight against the general offensive and the fight against racism tend to come together, to become more closely intertwined. To effectively oppose the Reagan-monopoly-capitalist offensive, white workers and people must more clearly see their own interest in the struggle against the racist offensive.

The struggle against racial and national oppression and for equality is based on justice and fairness. It is morally right. It is supported by the United States Constitution and the Bill of Rights. It is also vital to the self-interest of all except the same group which enjoys the extra corporate profits reaped from racism.

The ruling class uses racism, as it uses anti-Communism, to set precedents.

When they get away with deep cuts in housing funds for racially and nationally oppressed residents of the inner cities, they set the stage for cutting funds for housing construction elsewhere.

When they eliminate busing programs and desegregation plans, this is a precedent for an overall cut in the quality of education everywhere.

The same applies to mass transit and medical care—to all services and programs which benefit the people.

In their own interest and in the interests of justice and equality, white workers and people must fight against the detrimental, destructive precedents set by increased racism, discrimination and segregation. To fulfill their class responsibilities and to better their own lives, white Americans need to take on the struggle against racism concretely, to take specific initiatives on all fronts.

Because the all-round character of the reactionary offensive tends to link the various areas of struggle, the struggle against racism must become an inseparable feature of all people's struggles and movements.

The question of how a movement or a struggle affects racially and nationally oppressed people must become a vital consideration in planning strategy and tactics. If this is not the case, even some "general victories" can easily turn into their opposites. In other words, not only can they perpetuate racist patterns, they also can create divisions among the people and obstruct further victories.

Take, for example, the struggle for jobs. A fight in this field "in general," not taking into account the special problems of Afro-American, Chicano and Puerto Rican workers—which means some concrete form of affirmative action—can serve to perpetuate racist employment patterns and divide and weaken the people's forces.

To win an extension of unemployment benefits in general would be a people's victory. However, such a victory would leave out workers who have been jobless for long periods, as well as millions of Afro-American youth who, because of racial discrimination, have never had steady employment. Therefore, the fight for extended unemployment benefits must include the demand for benefits for all who are able and willing to work. To remain silent on this would be complicity with racism.

Likewise with respect to housing. Funds for new housing "in general," without provisions guaranteeing funds for low-income families in the inner cities and for non-segregated housing, would perpetuate and extend racist housing patterns and would be an obstacle to united struggle for new victories.

In every area of struggle there must be special consideration given and special demands advanced to address the problems created by centuries of racial and national oppression. All tactics, demands, slogans and struggles must include provisions to undo and compensate for the effects of centuries of racism and discrimination.

The interests of various sectors of a coalition are not

necessarily identical. Very often differences show up in questions of secondary importance. How these differences are dealt with largely determines the level of unity and, in the final analysis, the success or failure of the coalition.

In the struggle against racism and national oppression, the people who are not the direct victims of racist policies and practices must be the most alert, the most sensitive to and conscious of the need for a people's coalition to take steps against the problems created by racism. It is necessary to seek tactics and programs which unite all sectors in a way that also takes up the struggle against the special problems created by racism.

In any struggle, the people's forces and movements must be on guard not to permit the ruling-class establishment to counterpose the interests of those who are exploited as a class to the interests of the victims of racial and national oppression, most of whom are also exploited as members of the working class. The main fire, the main demands and mass actions, must be aimed at the common enemy—the exploiters, the monopolies, the banks, the landlords, the establishment. Adjustments and compensation must be considered for the special problems caused by racism. But they must be considered within the framework of the struggle against the common enemy.

It is worth repeating: Because of the general, overall nature of the Big Business offensive, winning a victory in any area is now tied more closely than ever to the struggle against racism. Therefore, a new kind of unity of our people is on the agenda.

Under heavy fire from the Reagan-monopoly offensive, the struggle against racism has been momentarily forced a step backward. However, this can be reversed.

To get back on the track of progress requires a mass struggle, a massive people's counteroffensive against the monopoly offensive. And a people's counteroffensive means a united fightback on all fronts. A renewed, determined and unrelenting struggle against racism in every area of life, wherever and whenever it rears its ugly head, is an absolutely indispensable prerequisite for a united fightback of all the people.

History tends toward progressive development, but this progress is sometimes interrupted or reversed. This is precisely what Reagan is working to achieve. The policies, practices and positions of the Reagan Administration are all within the framework of the plan to turn the clock back, to undo the advances won by the people through decades of mass struggle.

There is a rich heritage of Afro-American culture and history. But to observe Black History Month 1982 in words alone, without concrete initiatives against the new racist attacks, is meaningless. It descends to the level of pious platitudes, and serves as a cover for racism.

We must begin now to build an all-people's front that can stop and reverse the monopoly turn-back-the-clock offensive. Then, in a year or two years, we will be able to celebrate both the long- and short-term trends of development. This is a necessary component of the mass upsurge to defeat the overall offensive of monopoly capital.

The racist corporate-Reaganite offensive takes place on all fronts.

The Reagan Administration rejects the concept and is cancelling affirmative action programs, in effect freezing discriminatory patterns and setting back the struggle for equality in employment and job training.

Its blocking and cancellation of busing programs freezes and sets back the struggle for quality, integrated education.

The revocation of a 12-year federal policy denying tax-exempt status to private schools that practice and preach segregation and race hatred is a signal that Reagan intends to dismantle and discard entirely the civil rights enforcement apparatus.

Success of the Administration's attempts to amend and weaken the Voting Rights Act of 1965 would set the stage for cancellation of advances made during the civil rights struggles of the 1960s. The racist Reaganite cuts in funds for mass transit, child and health care, housing, job training, education, aid to dependent children and other people's programs cancel and reverse advances achieved in the struggle against segregation and discrimination.

The Reaganite frontal assault on human and civil rights is waged under the guise of "color blindness," "neutrality," "proving racist intent" and "equal opportunity for every American." These are hypocritical denials of the cumulative impact of more than 200 years of U.S. ruling class racist ideology and racial and national oppression that must be redressed in order to achieve true social and economic equality.

The Reagan offensive presents some new tactical questions which must be considered to halt and turn back the racist attack. Among these considerations is that success in any area of struggle is now more than ever dependent on the unity of forces on all fronts.

Because the main front of the offensive relates to the class struggle, it is necessary to seek issues and forms of struggle that synchronize and coordinate the struggles on separate but related fronts. The fact that the main front of the offensive relates to the class struggle places new responsibilities on the working class in the struggle on all fronts and, in a special way, in the struggle against racism. The new level of multiracial, multinational makeup of our working class adds an important dimension and new strength to the working class in this struggle.

The Reagan Administration's racist offensive creates new legal and constitutional questions. Many of the Reagan Administration's actions violate existing laws, precedents and constitutional provisions. Thus, the struggle against racial and national oppression and against specific racist attacks by the Reagan Administration is a struggle for the legal and constitutional rights of all Americans.

Violation of the legal rights of one group sets a precedent, gives a green light, for the violation of the legal and constitutional rights of all the American people. The racists, inside and outside the Administration, increasingly operate outside legal and constitutional norms. The racists are the violators of the Constitution.

The action of the Internal Revenue Service transferring public funds to private schools that advocate, teach and practice racism, violates existing laws, court decisions and long-standing administrative rulings.

The effort by the Reagan Administration to undo the Weber decision, which upheld the legality of a voluntary affirmative action agreement between a trade union and a corporation, is an attempt to reverse the Supreme Court. The affirmative action agreement challenged by Weber makes it possible for racially and nationally oppressed workers to attain higher skills through access to training programs.

The efforts of the Reagan Administration to make "intent" the legal criterion for proving discrimination violates the accepted legal principle that practices and acts are the primary evidence of crime. This is a legal coverup for racism because to "prove intent" requires mindreading. It invites racists to discriminate with the excuse that their "intent" is not racist. Reagan is already employing this dodge himself. As he claimed after his infamous tax-exempt-hate decision, "I have been on the side of opposition to bigotry and discrimination and prejudice." Knowing Reagan's history and his actions, are we to accept his statement of "intent" as truth rather than his concrete racist actions?

These are but attempts to bamboozle the people of the United States and confuse an issue that is vital to their unity and thus to their ability to win a better life. The "intent" of the Reaganites is clear—to cover up the increasingly intense racial and national oppression. The new patterns of racial and national oppression demand new patterns of struggle against racism. They demand new levels of understanding and unity against racism.

The time has come to put an end to attacks on laws and court decisions advancing civil rights over the past decades, to end the dismantling of government machinery for enforcing these laws and decisions, to end retreats and reversals in the area of civil and human rights. The time has come to put an end to ambiguities in the area of human and civil rights and to protect these precious rights from the malign intent of exploiters, racists and reactionary politicians from the federal to the local level.

This can best be done by adoption of a constitutional amendment that prohibits, in clear, concise and forthright language, all acts of racism and discrimination.

Most of the member states of the United Nations have ratified the International Convention on the Elimination of All Forms of Racial Discrimination. Article 4 of this convention provides that parties to it shall make it a criminal offense to disseminate "ideas based on racial superiority or hatred or incitement to racial discrimination" or to provide "any assistance to racist activities, including the financing thereof." The convention also provides that the parties shall illegalize and prohibit organizations which promote or incite racial discrimination.

Our government, with all its hypocritical prattle about "human rights," has not ratified this convention.

The time is long past due for us to get in step with the majority of nations of the world on this question. We can begin to press now for legislation at the local, state and federal levels unambiguously prohibiting discrimination in all areas of life; for verifiable criteria defining discrimination; for an adequate enforcement apparatus to implement it. We can begin to press now for Congress to initiate the process of adoption of a constitutional amendment—to label as crimes and to proscribe such acts in the highest law of the land.

To set the stage for a Marxist-Leninist assessment, it would be helpful to review some basic concepts. Without taking these fundamental concepts into account it is impossible to forge people's unity or develop winning strategy and tactics in the fightback against monopoly.

First, we should set the record straight. There is no

question that as a result of militant struggles and movements some victories have been won against specific racist practices. However, in the total picture these advances are token. The Black community still remains locked in the same bind, subjected to the same level of economic oppression, without any significant advancement.

Further, during this economic crisis gains made during the up side of the economic cycle are being wiped out in one industry and profession after another. When there is an economic recession there is a Black economic depression. In a depression there is disaster, devastation and desperation in the Black communities across our land.

No one in the United States can take a second step without encountering the iron heel of monopoly capital. The class struggle is an expression of this central, all-encompassing contradiction. The class struggle affects all struggles for social progress. The main force for resolving the class contradiction is our multiracial, multinational working class.

This is the path that is open. To reject this path is to reject the only option available. Such a rejection could lead only to dead ends, to hopelessness, inaction and passivity.

In a very basic sense, the weakness in the struggle against racism and against influences of chauvinism are closely related to the overall influences of Right opportunism in the working class.

Accommodation to enemy ideology is opportunism. In most cases it is Right opportunism. Those who can not see the working class as the major force in the struggle for social progress can not see the possibilities of the struggle against racism either. This leads to passivity and opportunism in the struggle against racism. And racism, in turn, influences and feeds opportunism.

The struggle against racism leads to a struggle against opportunism. The struggle against opportunism clears the board for a struggle against racism. As a rule, wherever there is opportunism there is racism. And wherever there is racism there is also opportunism.

Our emphasis on the basic relationship between the class struggle and the struggle against racial and national oppression has nothing in common with the position that narrows everything down to what is miscalled "the class position." Such a so-called "class position" is a fig leaf to cover up accommodation to racism. Some use a Left-sounding "class position" to deny the racial and national character of the special system of Black exploitation and oppression. We not only recognize the special national and racist nature of this oppression, but we raise the struggle against it to top priority by clarifying its relationship to the class struggle and to capitalist exploitation.

Our position gives us confidence in the possibility of winning victories against racism. We are confident of being able to win against racism because we have confidence in the working class. Our confidence in the working class is not wishful or romantic. It follows from our understanding of the laws of capitalism and their effects on the working class. Developing working-class consciousness is, therefore, the ideological framework for plowing under all currents which support exploitation or oppression.

The sharpening of the class contradiction is the objective propellant stimulating the development of class consciousness. Our Party supplies the subjective propellants. This consciousness, based on real class interests, tends to overcome all alien class ideological influences. Class consciousness leads to a higher level of social consciousness. It leads to higher moral concepts. These higher levels of consciousness are all important factors in the struggle against racism.

There is a dialectical relationship between the struggle against racism and the rise of class consciousness. Class consciousness has a built-in limitation unless it takes up the struggle against racism. This is the meaning of Karl Marx's profound observation, "Labor in the white skin can not be free as long as labor in the black skin is branded." The other side of this truth is that the struggle against racism has a built-in limitation if it is not related to struggles that give rise to class consciousness.

Because we understand the relationship between the class struggle and the struggle against racism, we also understand the crucial importance of the struggle against racism in the ranks of white workers. From this comes our confidence that we can, with consistent effort, win the ideological confrontation.

Racism is a central ideological current diverting white workers from the path of class consciousness. In the ranks of the people as a whole, it is also the poison diverting them from the path of anti-imperialist consciousness and disrupting the necessary unity against the monopolies. In the United States, racism is a formidable obstacle to socialist consciousness. The struggle against racism, therefore, is crucial for the development of working-class consciousness, antimonopoly and anti-imperialist consciousness.

We must see clearly the relationship between these ideological currents and people's struggles. There can be no successful long-range struggle for democracy which does not undertake the struggle against the racist ideology of the anti-democratic forces. There can be no anti-monopoly coalition that does not confront the racist ideology and practices of monopoly capitalism. Thus, the struggle against racism is inextricably linked with the most basic processes of the class struggle, the struggle for social progress and socialism.

We have been temporarily sidetracked from the forward march of history. To get back on the track full speed ahead, we must mount a deliberate, determined and concrete counteroffensive against Reaganomics and racism.

We are in the midst of an explosive mass upsurge. However, only a new level of unity of our multiracial, multinational working class, of our people, can mount a winning fightback.　　　　　　　　　　　　　　　　　　　　□

[*Political Affairs*, February 1982]

The Changing Patterns Of Racism

Racism has deep roots both in the history and in the social and economic soil of the United States. But it is not unchangeable or ineradicable.

Under the pressure of movements and struggles racism retreats, changes channels and constantly emerges in new disguises.

The victory that put an end to lynch terror did not end racism. It took many years of long, hard and bitter struggles for Afro-Americans to win the right to vote, to end the poll tax. But those victories did not put an end to racism.

The battle that put an end to segregation in public restaurants, other public places and on public transportation were important advances. But they did not finish off racism. The breakthroughs in hiring and even promotion in basic industry were very important. But they also did not put an end to racism. The advances in housing, education, medical care and culture are all very important. But they have not eliminated racism either.

Many of the affirmative action programs have corrected some of the inequalities, have compensated for some of the effects of long-term practices of discrimination. But they have not by any means done away with all the existing inequalities.

There have been welcome changes in the thought patterns of millions. But the racist poison, the thought patterns that are influenced by racism and chauvinism, have not been eradicated.

The lessons of the past are twofold: that victories against racism are achievable, but that it takes struggle, unity and persistence.

It is a measure of progress that it is more difficult today for racists to propagate and peddle their wares openly and in the old crude ways. This is the positive side. But in some ways, it is more difficult to fight racism that is camouflaged, racism that is attached as a rider to other complex issues.

The Reagan Administration pursues policies and programs of racism behind demagogy about "equality for all." Reagan claims concern about "everyone's civil rights." But the open, unashamed boasting about how "the South shall rise again" was directed to those in the South who are influenced by the more flagrant, open racism.

During the ten years before Reagan's election, affirmative action programs and agreements started the process of chipping away at the centuries-long, unequal status of Afro-Americans.

The Reagan Administration not only put a stop to this process, but turned things in the opposite direction. It turned antidiscrimination cases into reverse-discrimination cases. The demands of Black firemen and police for equality were turned into charges of inequality by white firemen and police, supported by the Reagan Department of Justice and the courts.

Reagan's anti-Civil Rights Commission proclaimed a victory when its chairman, Clarence Pendleton, said:

> We believe that quotas are a dead issue and we want to keep on course and make certain that we do those kinds of studies and activities that make certain that discrimination is not the only factor in lack of opportunity, and that there is equality of opportunity and not a mandate for positive results.

There can be no equality of opportunity as long as racism remains a factor blocking the path of opportunity to Afro-Americans.

The 1984 Reagan-Bush election campaign was a perfect example of this new, double-dealing approach.

Reagan and the ultra-Right forces are against the very concept of seniority rights. In fact, they are for destroying the whole trade union movement, which fights for seniority rights. They are the main supporters of the anti-union, anti-seniority-rights, open shop laws passed by many states.

They took the issue of seniority rights and turned it into an argument against affirmative action, with a clear racist message to white workers.

The system of seniority rights has never been perfect or unchangeable. After World War II adjustments were made for the period young workers served in the armed forces. Their time in the armed services was added to the time they had worked in the shop.

Thus, adjustments can be made to compensate for the many years of seniority Black workers have *not* been allowed to accumulate. This can be done without destroying the seniority system.

In fact, if adjustments are not made, the ruling class will go around the seniority system and evade it. Useless clauses in contracts that pretend to make up for inequality losses are affecting fewer and fewer workers.

One of the most effective first steps toward equality is a contract that compensates for past hiring practices based on racial inequality. Such contracts can be effective, especially if they are accompanied by adding special seniority provisions for older workers who would be entitled to early retirement with full benefits.

Wherever possible, the adjustments should be made from corporate profits. It is easier to convince workers about the need for adjustments and concessions on their part if the main fire is directed at corporate profits.

This would be a form of takeback from the extra profits that have been made from using racism. This kind of adjustment can prevent the corporations from using the question of seniority to create divisions and friction in the ranks of workers.

Corporations use the question of seniority rights as a vehicle for spreading racism. But they are also chipping away at the concept of seniority. When they shut the doors on industrial plants, they also close the doors on seniority systems for all workers.

Where there are hiring policies that compensate for past inequalities, the struggle for a six-hour day with no cut in pay can become an important instrument in the struggle for equality. Over a period of time, compensatory hiring in filling job openings can become an important step toward equality. It can become an issue, a demand that unites the working class.

Where the trade unions fight for affirmative action programs the fight against compulsory overtime can also become a factor in the struggle for equality. In this case, the hiring of workers to replace those who do not work overtime can be done on the basis of compensation for past inequality.

The food stamp program is a good example of racism in federal programs. What should matter is not the race or nationality of those receiving food stamps, but that people who are poor and hungry are able to eat. But in its drive to get support for cutting food stamps, the Reaganites use a racist pitch. By implication they put over the idea that white Americans should not protest this cut because it only affects Black, Puerto Rican and Chicano people.

This maneuver cuts two ways. It spreads racism and cuts socio-economic programs. It covers up the fact that more whites will lose their food stamps than will Black or other oppressed national minorities.

Even the cuts in funds for housing are put over with the racist subterfuge that housing is only a ghetto problem.

In his State of the Union speech, Reagan did the same thing with the issue of crime. First he said, "All Americans are victims of crime." Then he implied that criminals come from the ghettos, and that the attack on Afro-Americans is justified as an attack on criminals.

On all these questions racism is slipped in as a rider. The intent is to create confusion and divisions, to promote prejudice and biases. The purpose is to keep working and poor people from seeing their common interests, as well as their common enemy.

To begin with, winning the six-hour day with no cut in pay and early retirement, the elimination of overtime, together with special provisions for compensatory hiring—can make inroads into the inequalities from past discrimination.   □

[*Daily World*, February 28, 1985]

1985

What's Behind
The Goetz Case?

The outrageous, shocking and precedent-setting decision of the New York grand jury, which failed to indict Bernhard Goetz for the crime of attempted murder, is itself a crime—against all the people of New York City.[14]

It's bad enough that a criminal who publicly admitted he went out to kill was charged with illegal possession of a gun instead of premeditated murder.

But with this unconscionable decision, the grand jury and the district attorney are also sending an insidious message to society—that in the eyes of the law, murder is a beatable crime, that it is permissible to shoot to kill, that the facts and the evidence will be ignored, that justice will look the other way, especially if the victim is Black.

It is a message that tells the public you can get away with murder if you plead self-defense.

This sets the stage for increased racism and vigilante terrorism, a completely lawless atmosphere in which groups and individuals feel free to take the law into their own hands.

This sets the stage for the ultra-Right and fascist forces in New York City to act more boldly.

This is the same atmosphere in which the death squads operate in Central and South America, in which the fascist stormtroopers operated in Nazi Germany.

It is in keeping with the CIA how-to handbook of world-wide counterrevolutionary murder and assassination.

Why did the grand jury feel it could get away with letting Goetz off? Because the mass media had already exonerated Goetz through a blitz that highlighted and headlined all the forces that applaud and support lawlessness and vigilantism and ignored and suppressed all those who condemned the crime and the criminal.

It was part of the continuing campaign of the Koch forces to take issues of very real concern to people and use them to divide the population of New York City, especially along racial lines.

The public opinion polls showed that although people are deeply concerned and very fearful about street and subway crime, 75 per cent of those polled said they do not see carrying hand guns and taking the law into their own hands as the solution.

The majority said jobs and more funds to meet growing desperate needs are the only real solution.

In spite of these healthy sentiments, the media continued to sensationalize and idealize a killer and his supporters—the same reactionary Right-wing forces who worked for Reagan's re-election and are now working to re-elect the racist Koch.

This is not to say that street crime—assaults on the property and persons of working and poor people—is not a serious problem. But it can not be stopped by officially-sanctioned, premeditated armed attacks.

Crime can not be excused or justified. However, most street crime has its roots in poverty, hunger, frustration, anger and generations of unemployment.

The increase in street crime can be directly attributed to big-time crime—the vicious Reagan cuts in social and economic programs.

While deploring crime in the streets, we have to point the finger at the source of most big city crimes—the big landlords and bankers, the runaway corporations, and a Koch Administration that sees the homeless and hungry as mentally ill burdens, the jobless as lazy, and which does not fight for funds for jobs, education, recreation and cultural centers—the only realistic, effective crimefighters.

In addition, the policies of the Reagan Administration, including its refusal to take action against the bombers of abortion clinics, create the atmosphere for terrorism on the streets.

It is an atmosphere that sanctions police brutality in New York City, including the official murder of Eleanor Bumpers, that permits the city's chief medical examiner to think he can get away with falsifying autopsy reports to cover the brutality of the police.

It is an atmosphere that recalls the days of lynch-terror, bombings, beatings and murder, that breeds racism, anti-Semitism, chauvinism, prejudice, bigotry and anti-youth sentiments, that threatens democracy and the democratic rights of all.

There is a very real relationship between the U.S. invasion and takeover of Grenada in the name of "national defense" and Goetz' plea of "self-defense" for shooting to kill four teenagers.

It is an atmosphere in which brutality against women, pornography, arson for profit, decadence and moral degeneracy invade the very fabric of our everyday lives. It is a lawless, uncivilized, terrorist-like atmosphere, and is created and sustained on all official levels of our capitalist, crisis-ridden society.

What can we do to protest this grand jury outrage and prevent the vigilante-like atmosphere created by such actions?

First, we must begin now to build coalitions against the re-election of Koch.

Second, we must demand a reversal of the New York grand jury decision charging Goetz with gun possession and the re-indictment of Goetz on charges of attempted murder.

Third, we must join in the call for a federal probe into the crime.

Above all, we must join in the struggle for federal funds for job-creation, housing, subways, bridges, tunnels, schools, hospitals and recreation centers.

Street crime and the number of unemployed go up or down together. When people's basic human needs and rights are met, the basic cause of and motivation for most crimes decrease. □

[*Daily World*, January 31, 1985]

5

THE ROOTS
OF OPPRESSION

The Afro-American/Labor Alliance

The events of this past year have set in clear perspective the nature and place of the Afro-American/labor alliance in the U.S. political scene. This community was the core of the mass base that gave a crushing electoral defeat to the ultra-Right Goldwater challenge. It was a roadblock to reaction, swinging the decisive large industrial states into the anti-ultra-Right column, and was also responsible for the qualitative improvement in the composition of their congressional delegations and state legislatures.

In the Southern states reaction still has two weapons that prevent this force for progress from exercising its full potential: continued Afro-American disfranchisement, and white chauvinism and prejudice, reinforced by terror. To the extent that these weapons were nullified, however, the Afro-American/labor alliance also began to play this role in the South. This, of course, was especially true of the contribution of the Afro-American people in the Southern states.

The political influence of the Afro-American/labor alliance hit a new high in the 1964 elections. But this is only a harbinger of what is to come. From now on, the Afro-American/labor alliance is more and more going to be a determining factor in the direction of U.S. political life, the central stimulus and point of reference for forces of progress and the main deterrent to forces of reaction and retrogression.

The cynical, antidemocratic maneuvering over reapportionment of electoral districts reflects this development. Reactionary politicians are trying to gerrymander the Afro-American/labor alliance out of its position of growing political influence. Reaction is alarmed because the democratic principle of "one man, one vote"[1] shifts the political mass base of our electoral process toward the Afro-American/labor alliance just when this community is beginning to exert its new, united power. The gerrymanderers are trying to segregate the Afro-American/labor alliance into separate districts in order to water down its influence.

When it was possible to create artificial divisions in the Negro-labor community, its influence could be dissipated by such gerrymandering schemes. But as the political consciousness and unity of this community grow, the gerrymanderers are having an ever more difficult time.

The Afro-American/labor alliance has been the foundation of progress in American life for a long time, although this has not always been obvious because its influence has been indirect and without organizational form.

This is an alliance of the oppressed and the exploited. It is an alliance based on mutual self-interest. It has deep roots in our history. At each critical turning point it has tended to close ranks and its influence has grown. Within the overall framework of long- and short-range mutual self-interest, there have been and continue to be contradictions. These contradictions create problems, but they do not in any way change the basic essence of the alliance or its role in our history.

The 20 million Afro-American citizens are an oppressed people, subjected to a system of segregation and discrimination which has its historic roots in the plantation system of slavery. U.S. capitalism has adapted this special system to divide the working class and the people, to cut down their resistance to oppression and exploitation. The system of segregation and discrimination against Black people is an instrument for extracting maximum profits from Black and white workers.

As in the case with colonialism on the world scene, the ending of the system of racial oppression has emerged as the most crucial domestic question for the United States. The time for its abolition has arrived and can not be long postponed. All class groups are forced to take a stand on this question; not only the future of 20 million Afro-Americans is involved. The future of the entire country rides on how this question is solved. This includes our democratic institutions, our educational system, the pattern of our economy, the future of organized labor, and so on.

The force that will largely determine the nature of the solution is the Afro-American/labor alliance. While the Afro-American people are all victims of special oppression, there is a growing class differentiation among them. The Afro-American workers, who are part of both the U.S. working class and the oppressed Afro-American people, are of cardinal importance.

The destruction of the evil system of discrimination and segregation, directed against Afro-American citizens but used to divide all the victims of monopoly capital, has emerged as an absolute condition for progress. The mass movement that now fights for its elimination has therefore emerged as the generative force that sparks the struggle for progress on all fronts.

Class societies inevitably produce one class whose self-interests propel it to become the leader of all forces of progress. In our time life has assigned this responsibility to the working class. On its broad shoulders rests the advance of civilization.

The opposite side of this historic coin is that simultaneously there arises a class that embodies all that is reactionary and backward. In modern times, the sewer that carries all this refuse and dirt and sickness is the capitalist class.

One class leads the struggle for progress; the other creates obstacles to it. One is constructive; the other is destructive of all human values. One propels social advance; the other attempts to turn back the wheels of history. One class covers its resistance to progress with an ideology of cynicism, demagogy and appeals to prejudice and backwardness. The other inscribes on its ideological banners concepts that guide and support mankind in their rise to a higher form of civilization.

The development of these class forces is a distinct historical process in each country. With time each of the classes increasingly takes on its specific role, until this leads to a qualitative shift which completely discards the reactionary class and the system that gave rise to it.

This class framework determines the course of affairs in the United States as much as anywhere else in the world. With all its weaknesses, our working class in the United States has fulfilled its historic responsibilities and is continuing to do so. The fact that it has not fully taken on what history demands of it, or that it has not carried the struggle to its final conclusion, does not in any way disqualify it as the most advanced sector of our society.

It is only on the basis of understanding this objective class relationship that one can give leadership to struggles to end the evils of capitalism. Any attempt to deal with social or economic problems while ignoring or rejecting this class reality will lead up blind alleys. The very heart of capitalist propaganda is the denial of the class nature of capitalism and the role of the working class. The influence of such ideas penetrates even the ranks of the progressive movement.

Only an understanding of class forces and their role in society makes it possible to understand alliances, coalitions and united front formations. These relationships are built around parallel and mutual self-interests, which can and do cut across class formations. Because of its objectively designated role in history, the working class attracts all sectors of the population whose self-interests are served by a progressive direction. In some cases, these self-interests run along parallel lines only for brief periods. Coalitions, in such cases, are of brief duration and are usually around very specific issues. But this does not in any way minimize their importance. The history of human progress is in fact a history of the rise and fall of coalitions and alliances based on parallel self-interests.

There are also coalitions based on long-range mutual interest. Such coalitions run the course of whole historic epochs.

With these things in mind, I want to deal with the historic role and nature of the Afro-American/labor alliance in the United States. This is a very distinctive kind of alliance, one that runs the course of the epoch. Without an understanding of this central phenomenon of our society, one can not fully understand the American scene.

In a sense, the Afro-American/labor coalescence is more than an alliance or a united front. It is a political and economic community, an overlapping, interlinked unit. As the consciousness of this grows in its ranks, this community will become the power that will determine the direction of events in our country.

On a world scale, the working class is emerging as that class on whose shoulders the future of civilization rests. Because it is the leading element in the world socialist, anti-imperialist, peace community, it is now the decisive force determining the course of world events. Hence the elements in the community are more than allies; they are parts of one historical revolutionary process, of one progressive community—an interlinked unit. And one can understand the nature and role of this community only if one understands the nature and role of the working class.

A distinctive feature of the historic formation of the U.S. working class is that it is composed of Black and white workers; it is a class of many national backgrounds. This has provided U.S. capitalism with a special ideological weapon to create division and dissension: the weapon of prejudice. Nevertheless, nothing is so inevitable, so absolute, in capitalist society as the emergence, growth and political maturation of the working class. The development of class consciousness, class unity, class struggle is rooted in the very process of exploitation. To deny the historic role of the working class is to deny the very class nature of capitalism.

And so, in spite of the obstacles created by the system of discrimination, by the practice of keeping Afro-American workers out of some industries altogether and confining them to the hardest, lowest-paying jobs in others, and by constant infusions of the poison of white chauvinism—an inseparable component of capitalist ideology—a united, integrated working class is taking shape and assuming its designated historic place. Indeed, the process of formation of an integrated working class of Black and white workers as the basis of the Afro-American/labor alliance has paved the way for an integrated nation in which all of our people live in equality.

The historic path to a united, integrated working class has been marked by many obstacles and setbacks. It is a slow process because it is fundamentally a process of development of a class ideology and class outlook. Ideology is the result of experience upon experience. For long periods white workers could not see their overall class interests because of the heavy fog of chauvinism and prejudice. The fog has slowly dissipated, though much of it remains.

With the lifting of the fog, the process of unification takes place through a series of qualitative leaps. The unionization of the basic mass production industries remains a modern landmark, one of those qualitative leaps. It went a long way toward destroying the ideology behind the craft unions—one which hides the class nature of society. Craft union ideology long divided Black and white workers.

The CIO, and especially the Left-led unions, made historic contributions to this development. Their formation firmly established the concept that all workers, Black and white, of all trades and professions, belong in united industrial unions.

A graphic illustration of both processes—the formation of an integrated, united working class and the development and rise of the Afro-American/labor alliance—was the Conference to Organize Negro Steel Workers into the new Steelworkers Union, held in Pittsburgh, Pennsylvania, in 1937. All sectors of the Negro people and their organizations were represented at this meeting, together with the leaders of the newly emerging steel union. This participation was a clear indication that the leaders of the Afro-American people's organizations understood the role of a united, integrated working class in defending both its own class interests and those of the Afro-American/labor alliance in the struggle against discrimination. This conference was an important step in the development of both these processes.

The process of integration and unification of the working class is continuing. Afro-American workers have become part of the most militant and union-conscious sector of the U.S. working class. This process and the growth of class consciousness in the ranks of the working class are parts of the same development. Class consciousness is the most formidable antidote to the poison of chauvinism and prejudice.

The process of class integration has made its clearest advances where the need for class unity has been most obvious. Thus each economic struggle has been a classroom for integration and unity. In such struggles, class and individual self-interest rise to the surface and the evil, divisive role of chauvinism becomes more obvious and therefore more easily eliminated.

The influence of the rising, integrated, united working class on the struggles of today is not always fully appreciated because this influence is not always direct or dramatic. But as the fog lifts, as workers get a qualitatively new sense of their class position, they will increasingly have a greater influence on the character of all mass cur-

rents and movements. The methods of mass struggle today already show the influences of working-class experience. The sit-ins, boycotts, picket lines, mass demonstrations, combining economic struggle with political action,
and the tactic of alliances and united front relations, are
all variations of methods originally developed in the fires
of the class struggle. Leaders and spokesmen of religious
and social organizations take a more forthright stand for
civil rights where they sense the influence of members of
the working class in their organizations and communities.

The vote for the Civil Rights Bill was a barometer of
how elected officials assess the mood of the people in general. But above all it was an assessment of the mood of the
Afro-American/labor alliance in the big industrial centers. Workers are usually not the spokesmen or leaders of
reform movements. But invariably the Afro-American/la-
bor alliance is their mass base.

Therefore, to fully appreciate the present role and influence of this community, one has to study its grassroots
base, the details of relations and forces that never appear
in headlines and are not immediately evident. But all
movements get their staying power and their militancy
from this base. Movements without this mass base are
usually very short-lived.

Racial oppression and unorganized shops are closely
related twin evils in the South. They are, in fact, two
faces of one policy designed for one purpose—maximum
profits for Big Business and the landowners. The net result
of this policy is a "Southern differential" of lower wages,
longer hours, mass poverty, mass misery. The brutal oppression of Afro-Americans, combined with an open policy
of violence against unions and progressive organizations—
this is the strategy of Big Business for keeping the South a
sort of semicolonial preserve of extreme exploitation, high
profits, cheap labor, runaway shops and disfranchised
people, ruled by a racist, fascist-like gang through terror
and murder. Big Business wants this kind of South not only

because of the immediate profits it yields, but because it is a bulwark of reaction throughout the nation. The ultra-Right Goldwater attempt to use the South as a base in his bid for power strikingly illustrates the point.

The heart of the forces that will break this stranglehold of reaction on the South is the Afro-American/labor alliance. Toward this end, it is necessary to find links that bring together the drives to end segregation and discrimination and to organize nonunion shops. The trade unions will have to understand that they will never conquer one evil by ignoring its inseparable twin. Racism is antiunion; antiunion policies are instruments to perpetuate racism. These are the two sides of the coin. The struggle against the common enemy in the South demands a new level of unity and integration of the working class and a new quality of relations within the Afro-American/labor alliance.

This is the central challenge facing the leaders and the rank and file of this community nationally. There is a great need for a national conference of the Afro-American/labor alliance to map out a joint mass plan to end segregation and discrimination, to end the brutal terror against Afro-American citizens and against unions and union organizers, and to bring equality, the right to bargain collectively and equal protection under the law to all citizens of the South. Such a common drive would be the greatest stimulus to progressive forces on all fronts.

The history of the American people is full of examples of objective forces in our society pressing toward the formation of both the Afro-American/labor alliance and an integrated, united working class. That these early efforts did not result in a fullblown product and that there were numerous setbacks is no reason to call them failures. Nor are these grounds for rejecting the idea that these things are in the process of development. Each of these experiences in our history has added something to this development. And each new development has in turn made the objective conditions more ripe, and has thereby slowly increased the pressure of the objective screws of history.

In the last century, the Knights of Labor constituted the first real attempt to organize a national working-class union. They were outlawed and condemned. But even these early class formations had in them the seeds of the unified, integrated class of Black and white workers. The objective forces were just beginning to turn the screws. In the South Afro-American workers led the heroic efforts to organize unions under the conditions then existing.

In 1885 these efforts were recorded as follows: "They are now everywhere joining the Knights of Labor. Do not discriminate against them. They are considered amongst their most faithful members." At about the same time a union leader reported from Richmond, Virginia: "The Negro workers are with us heart and soul and have organized seven assemblies [locals] in this city and are in Manchester with large memberships."

Long-range and permanent assemblies in the South of today can be most meaningful if they rest on an integrated working class in large industrial union locals which have put an end to discrimination in their shops, which have outlawed discrimination in the union contract and union constitution. This relationship can then become the basis for a Afro-American/labor alliance that can determine the direction of union affairs in the South.

It was during the Civil War that the Afro-American/labor alliance first left its indelible mark on our history, and the post-Civil War period is evidence of the fact that it did not take long for the capitalist class to realize the potential danger to its selfish aims which the development of such a community presented. It quickly unleashed a campaign of murder and terror.

The capitalist class allied itself with the forces opposing Southern slavery only so long as it served its narrow interests, and not one minute longer. They were not motivated by ethical, moral or humanitarian considerations. So long as Northern capital profited from slavery, they supported slavery in the South. Ships owned by New England capital sailed to Africa loaded with rum, and there exchanged the rum for Black slaves, whom they carried to Southern states to be sold in the slave market. In turn, they bought molasses from the plantation owners and returned to New England, where the molasses was turned into rum to start the cycle all over again.

This is a clear indication of the nature of capital's interests in this earlier period. Only later, when the slave system became an obstacle to the expansion of their profit-making empire, did the capitalist class give its support to the struggle against the slave society of the South. This was a very brief period, because capital was interested in doing away only with those features of slavery that were adverse to its narrow interests. In fact, it adopted as its own those practices that aided the drive for profits. This is the background for the present system of segregation and discrimination, of white chauvinism and terror practiced against Afro-Americans.

The relationship of the working class to the Civil War was quite different. How different our history might have been if the British working class had not stopped the English Government from entering into armed struggle against the North when the outcome of the Civil War hung in the balance. Only the working class opposed an armed attack. It put up a historic battle. Abraham Lincoln regarded this attitude of the English working class towards Afro-American slavery as "an instance of sublime Christian heroism which has not been surpassed in any age or in any country." (Letter to the workingmen of Manchester, January 19, 1863, *Senate Documents*, 3rd Session, 37th Congress, 1862-1863.) It is true that the working class was motivated by its own long-range interests. But these were also the interests of human progress.

In 1830 Thomas Wentworth Higginson, a New Englander, wrote: "The antislavery movement was not strongest among the more educated classes, but was predominantly a people's movement based on the simplest human instincts and far stronger for a time in the factories and the shops than in the pulpits or colleges." (*Cheerful Yester-*

day, 1898, pp. 115-117. Quoted by Herman Schlüter, *Lincoln, Labor and Slavery*, New York, 1913, p. 38.) One of the first political parties to declare in its platform the need to abolish slavery was a newly-formed political party of labor.

The Civil War period is also rich in lessons on the nature of alliances based on parallel interests. The victorious alliance against slavery finally included the slaves, the workers and the frontier farmers, as well as sections of the capitalist class, and the clergy and professional people, mainly in the Northern states. Though they were allied against slavery, the contradictions between these classes did not disappear. The advanced sections of the working class fought to combine the struggle against wage slavery with the struggle against chattel slavery. The capitalist class fought against all concepts of classes and class struggle within capitalism. Most of the popular abolitionist leaders took a favorable position toward the struggles of the working class. These were swallows heralding the future course of development of the Afro-American/labor alliance.

But not all of the antislavery forces could see the relationship of the rising working class and its aims to the struggle against the slave system. Even such a militant fighter against slavery as William Lloyd Garrison[2] argued:

An attempt has been made—it is still in the making—we regret to say, with considerable success—to inflame the minds of our working class against the more opulent . . .

And further:

There is a prevalent opinion that wealth and aristocracy are indissolubly allied; and the poor and vulgar are taught to consider the opulent as their natural enemies. Those who circulate this pernicious doctrine are the worst enemies of the people. (*Lincoln, Labor and Slavery*, pp. 40, 43.)

These differences in the alliance created stresses and strains, but the objective screws pressed the alliance against slavery. The precursors of the labor/Afro-American community of today were present in even the earliest actions of the organized labor movement in the South. As early as 1831 organized white mechanics petitioned the Virginia legislature to abolish the competition of slave mechanics. They complained that "the wealthy owners of slave mechanics were in the habit of underbidding them in contracts." (*Lincoln, Labor and Slavery*, p. 100.) Their protest meetings were brutally smashed.

Not all of early labor understood the urgency, from the standpoint of their own interests, of ending the slave system. Some argued that an end to "wage slavery" would then force an end to the slave system in the South. But then, as now, the special oppression of Afro-Americans constituted a roadblock to progress. Then, as now, it was in the interest of all exploited and oppressed to join in an alliance to end that oppression.

Thus, the Afro-American/labor political and economic community is a specific U.S. historical development. It is rooted in history, and formed by present-day objective factors. In the very center of this community is the developing, united, integrated Black and white working class, ever more conscious of its class nature and its assigned role in our present and future.

It is important to understand the nature of this community and the role of the working class in it, because all progress emanates basically from this source. It is important because all who try—for whatever reason—to divide this community are dispersing and dissipating the main driving forces of progress. We are called upon to find the issues and organizational forms which, based on objective conditions, will unite this community.   □

[*Political Affairs*, February 1965]

The Root
Of Social Evil

Let me begin with an expression of my appreciation for the opportunity to present the Communist viewpoint on matters facing our nation today.

I especially value this invitation because the Black people of Tuskeegee have carved out an important outpost in the Deep South in the struggle for freedom and democracy. I feel a deep sense of humility because I know so many of you are veterans and heroes of the struggle for equality and democracy. Indeed, many of you have earned your war medals, battle ribbons and citations in this epic struggle in the courts and jails of the South.

The recent landmark decision against gerrymandering in the case of *Gomillion v. Lightfoot* (364 U.S. 339, 1960) remains an important legal marker on Freedom Road. The resurgent efforts of white supremacist terrorists to nullify the historic results are doomed to fail, although the dastardly murder of your fellow student, Samuel Younge, Jr., has imposed great suffering. Those of us who did not know Mr. Younge join you in honoring him and in the declaration that his death will not be in vain.

In order to explain the Communist viewpoint as it relates to current events I would like to provide a general framework of how we approach problems.

A few weeks ago a delegation of three American peace

fighters, Dr. Herbert Aptheker, Professor Staughton Lynd and Thomas Hayden,[3] made a personal fact-finding trip to Vietnam. After seeing, first hand, the horror and devastation wrought by saturation bombings, the attempt to depopulate and defoliate an entire nation, Professor Lynd, expressing the bewilderment of millions, asked: "How can people do a thing like this?"

What makes men send bombers 5,000 miles from their own country to napalm, burn, gas and gun down a whole people? Why does man do this to his fellow man?

This same question is asked by the millions who suffer want in the midst of plenty, by the millions who go hungry while there are food surpluses rotting in warehouses,

This same question is asked by the millions of Americans who are not hired, promoted or permitted to vote, who are insulted, vilified, clubbed, killed, lynched and jailed because of the color of their skin.

Professor Robert S. Browne of Fairleigh-Dickinson University in New Jersey, who has also borne witness to the crimes against humanity which our government is committing in Vietnam, who was a government aide and economics adviser and has participated in many teach-ins, public meetings and seminars, was able to tie the two "wars" together.

In his article, "The Freedom Movement and the War in Vietnam" in the autumn 1965 issue of *Freedomways*, Prof. Browne declared,

Indiscriminate burnings and bombings of Vietnamese villages are often gleefully confirmed in morbid detail by sadistic Americans boasting with obvious satisfaction of the number of "yellow bastards" they have "bagged."

In this same article, Prof. Browne described the mounting protest movement in the United States:

As American involvement in Vietnam has grown more massive and as aerial bombing has expanded into neighboring Laos, Cambodia, North Vietnam and up to the very frontiers of China, a groundswell of protest and indignation has arisen.

Still the question was repeated everywhere: How can they do this? Why are they doing this?

This baffling question is also asked by the thousands of U.S. workers who are suddenly laid off, thrown aside like discards, after a lifetime of loyal service—replaced by automated machines.

The same question is asked by a frustrated generation of youth, a generation whose life pathway is blocked by the automation curtain, a generation without any perspective—an excess generation.

The same question is asked by the impoverished farmer, being evicted from his land, by the half-starved, half-clothed, homeless migrant farm workers.

It was also echoed in the gas chambers of Hitler Germany.

Why does man practice this most vile kind of inhumanity, this brutality against his fellow man?

The answer to this seemingly abstract and philosophical-sounding question goes to the very heart of how we react to the acts of inhumanity of our day. It determines whether we are going to continue to accept inhumanity or to resist it.

Wherever men have discovered the cause of these evil practices they have rebelled against it, with the aim of removing the evils themselves.

The fundamental answer to the question is rooted not in the "inherently evil nature of man," but rather in the inherently evil nature of social systems that man has built.

There are evil men because there are evil classes. There are evil classes because there are social systems built around evil concepts of the inherent right to enslave, to exploit, and to subjugate one's fellow man for private gain. The root of all social evil is the right to exploit, which is the right to steal the fruits of another man's labor.

As long as social systems are based on the inherent right to exploit for private profit there will be pressure for the right to oppress and subjugate. This has been and remains the source of man's inhumanity to man.

Human progress is like a beautiful clear stream that got bogged down in a swamp of social systems built on the inherent right to exploit one's fellow man for private gain. It is a swamp of greed and violence, flowing from that inherent right. Humanity became contaminated in this swamp. It is only now beginning to find its way out and is again heading toward the stream of progress.

Feudalism, slavery and capitalism are all swamp-types of social orders. These swamp societies are all class societies. They all have two classes: the great mass who work, who produce all the wealth; and the other, always the minority, that lives in luxury on the fruits, the profits from the exploitation of the first.

The swamp has diverted civilization and social systems from the noble design of serving man. It has replaced this exemplary purpose with social systems whose main effect is the accumulation of wealth for the ruling class. In turn, the feudal lord, the slave master and now the capitalist class are the enforcers of and the recipients of this exploitation.

General Motors does not manufacture cars because it is motivated by the needs of people. There is no human consideration in their plans. Its sole aim is the $2,100,000,000 in after-tax profits it made by exploiting the hundreds of thousands of auto workers it employed in 1965.

Man's inhumanity to man is based on the swamp society's concept of the inherent right to exploit, to accumulate private wealth from the sweat and labor of one's fellow man. With each succeeding new swamp society the rate of this exploitation has increased.

The moral code of such a society justifies murder, including mass murder, in the quest for more profits. It justifies the wanton destruction of food when millions go hungry. It breeds wars of aggression. It is always on the prowl for more raw materials, for more cheap labor, for greater profits. It justifies the annihilation of a people.

Historians will find it difficult to explain to future generations the criminal contradiction of our stage of civilization: Nature is abundant and science and technology have reached the point at which humanity can now produce enough of everything for every soul on this earth, but more than half the world's population goes hungry. Thousands die daily for lack of food, clothing and shelter.

National boundaries were created to defend the accumulated private wealth of a privileged class. There were no other reasons for such artificial fences. But the self-interests of the exploited were not involved in the defense of such boundaries. They were not ready to die defending the very wealth that was stolen from them.

National chauvinism, animosity and prejudice were necessary ideological poisons fed to the working and poor people to get them to defend the boundaries that actually enslaved them. A sense of group superiority had to be created. This chauvinism reached its zenith in Hitler's master race theories.

Under the spell of the maater race potion, the fascists were able to get the German people to commit history's most heinous crimes, crimes to further the right of German capitalism to exploit the German people and people beyond Germany's borders. National and racial differences became a convenient form, a mask for this ideological narcotic.

Of all these monstrous theories, white supremacy became the most widespread. It has become one of the main ideological weapons by which the minority class of exploiters holds the power to exploit and rule the majority. The fostering of prejudice in order to divide and rule is the oldest of all social shell games.

In the swamp of human existence, one social system of class rule, of class exploitation, was replaced by another. But their inherent class nature and exploiting essence remained.

Only now is civilization breaking out of the bounds of class exploitation. History is at floodtide. The dam that has held back mankind in the polluted swamp of class societies is collapsing. We are at history's dividing line.

The new society emerging has eliminated the source of man's inhumanity to man. It has ruled out man's right to accumulate private wealth by exploiting another. It has cancelled out all concepts of the "divine right" of some to lord it over others. It has discarded the inherent right to enslave, to exploit. The new society does not need the ideological drug. It can proceed on the basis of brotherhood.

All of today's social explosions—the uprisings, the mass upheavals, the waves of national liberation, the political turmoil and stress, the socialist revolutions—are related to this central historic revolutionary process—the transition from societies of class exploition to societies without class exploitation, to socialist societies. This moment is so explosive because it is not just the transition from one society to another. Civilization is moving to a new level, a new kind of society, a society without exploitation for private gain.

The current running through all of the struggles of today is freedom from oppression, freedom from exploitation. It is the hallmark of this revolutionary period of transition from one kind of social concept to another.

As with everything in life, social systems have life spans—a birth, a period of growth, the flowering of maximum potential, followed by a period of decline and demise.

Again, following life's pattern, solutions to problems come easy when the system is on its upward spiral. But as the lengthening shadows of decline set in the solutions are ever harder to come by.

Capitalism is now suffering from ailments of old age. We are now witnessing the decline of capitalism. It is on the way out.

During its period of growth it was possible to solve the social, economic and political problems of society. But in the declining phase of the life cycle, a system increasingly loses its recuperative and regenerative powers, its ability to find fundamental solutions to new problems, because it does not have the forward thrust to draw on.

So the solutions become bandaids. Problems begin to overlap and to pile up. Moments of crisis come more often and last longer. The difficulties and the crises become chronic. Capitalism now suffers from such a chronic crisis.

As the old system declines it gives birth to a new social order. As Marx said, the new social system is formed in the womb of the old.

The new system emerges as an historic necessity, as a solution to the social problems the old could not solve. However, the old does not leave the scene until it is forced out, and the new order does not arrive until its time has come. The old system of capitalism is being forced off the stage of life. The new system, socialism, is replacing it. Over one-third of humanity is now reconstructing its life along socialist lines.

The complex of unsolved problems not only gives rise to a new social order, it also predetermines the nature of the new system.

Capitalism is preparing the soil for socialism, which discards the basic flaw in capitalism: the right to exploit, to enslave a fellow man.

From this it follows that our opposition to capitalism does not rest only on a subjective feeling, but is rooted in our firm conviction that capitalism, like an old, beat-up car, is beyond repair and must be thrown onto the scrap heap of history. Mankind needs a new car.

Thus, the struggle for socialism, the struggles for national liberation, the struggles for equality, are not man-made conspiracies or foreign inspired. They are the inevitable, logical counterpart to oppression and exploitation. They also inevitably move closer to the task of removing the cause of evil, of changing the system that produces it.

Allow me briefly to present the main currents of struggle in our country as they relate to this overall framework. They are the struggles of the working class, because of the effects of automation, the civil rights struggle, the struggle of the Afro-American for equality, and the struggle against the policy of U.S. aggression in Vietnam. The basic cause of all these struggles is the system of oppression for the purpose of exploitation. That is the very heart of a capitalist system. This is its inherent inner nature.

Automation and cybernation are scientific breakthroughs. They are not the achievement of any class, least of all of corporate executives. They are the accomplishment of humanity. But why have these brilliant breakthroughs turned into their opposites, into nightmares of insecurity, into layoffs for millions of Americans? Why are they closing the door of opportunity on the new generation?

Here again the advance in technology is in the control of a class which has always taken the riches of nature and confiscated the products collectively produced by man, as its inherent right, as private profit. In the same way automation has become an instrument for greater corporate profits and in turn a threat to the economic security of the masses.

This is bringing the working class into ever sharper conflict with the exploiters. This is the issue in every new labor strike. This is the issue in the conflict over Section 14B of the Taft-Hartley Act.[4]

It is this objective process that is forcing the working class to fulfill its historic role as the fountainhead of all human progress.

The special oppression of Black people in the United States spans all three of the swamp-type social systems. Capitalism has adopted and refined the oppression of a people into its specific, capitalist form of exploitation.

The system of oppression of Afro-Americans, with all of its chauvinistic, ideological drapings, continues because it is profitable for Big Business. It is a revealing aspect of our history that the capitalist class of New England continued to give its support for the institution of slavery in the South so long as there were profits in the transportation of slaves to America. This same motive was reflected in the words of Abraham Lincoln when he said, "If I could save the Union without freeing the slaves, I would not free them."

We are still too close in time to the events of the past years to be able fully to assess the effects of the civil rights movement on history and the course of our nation. It has served as the catalyst and well-spring of the overall struggle for democracy. The struggle to end racial and national oppression is a struggle for a democratic U.S.A.

The forces on both sides of this epic struggle are related to the two sides locked in the historic world struggle for or against the right to exploit.

The Dixiecrat racists are the forces of oppression and discrimination. But they are also the most vocal support for the policies of U.S. imperialist aggression, from the Dominican Republic to Vietnam, from Cuba to the Congo. They are the spearhead of all antidemocratic, antilabor elements. They are the shock troops for all reaction. Labor should draw the full lesson from the fact that the Dixiecrat Senators are the backbone of the drive to preserve the antilabor Taft-Hartley Act.

On the other hand, the civil rights movement has an interest parallel to the forces of world peace, with the national liberation movements, and with the overall forces of democracy, decency and progress.

These sides and these issues were clearly enjoined in the cynical ouster of Mr. Julian Bond from his seat in the Georgia legislature because he symbolized the unity of the struggle for civil rights with the struggle against the U.S. policy of unjust military aggression.

This is the new stage of all of the three currents of struggle. They are all moving to new levels, influencing and drawing strength from each other. They are drawing closer together to make up a powerful progressive current.

The Watts explosion signalled the new questions in the struggle for civil rights. Watts raised the cover that exposed a deeper layer of the miseries of the system of oppression and discrimination.

It exposed also how close to the surface is the nerve, the fuse of social explosion. Watts exposed not the poverty resulting from a plantation system, but rather the generations of poverty and rejection, the exploitation and discrimination of the industrial capitalist system.

It put the spotlight on how closely related are the problems and the victims of racial oppression, exploitation and automation. It exposed how pitifully small and meaningless is the antipoverty program when applied to the big problems of the ghetto and raised the question of economic equality to a new level of importance.

The struggle for civil rights has now reached the barriers to economic and political equality. For the victories of past years to have meaning and lasting value the struggle must now break down these barriers.

Afro-Americans are demanding an end to the status of being the poorest sector of the poor, the longest unemployed of the unemployed, getting the lowest wage of the low-wage earners, living in the worst houses of the slums, getting the longest prison sentences of all prisoners.

There are ghettos because of segregation. But the ghettos are slums because of the economic barriers, because of the walls of economic discrimination.

This is a new stage in the struggle, because this is the crossroads where the civil rights struggle meets the class struggle, where the demands for equality and for a greater share of economic abundance become joined.

Here is where the demand for equality comes in contact with and challenges the profit structure. Here it is easier to see the roots of racist oppression in the class structure of capitalism.

For this phase of the struggle there is a need for new demands and new alliances. Some Americans who could see the immorality of discrimination in what they considered the public domain are not ready to place that label on discrimination in the private profit domain. Therefore, they will not be as reliable as allies as in past stages. Besides new alliances and demands, no doubt new forms and new methods will also arise. It is clear that here the role of the working class becomes crucial and the Black-labor alliance decisive and imperative.

For Attorney General William Katzenbach, big talk about new laws has become the smokescreen for taking the token road in enforcing the laws that exist. How long can the Department of Justice continue the practice of bringing up test cases? They are still bringing up test cases in the school desegregation struggle. The "test case road" is the path of token enforcement.

It is an irony of the epoch that our government speaks about freedom, the rights of man, government by law, all over the world. But in one-half of our nation and after 300 years of government by hoodlums, countless political murderers go free and laws are nullified by terror and torture. Our federal government does nothing beyond claiming it doesn't have the right to stop this wrong. When the juries cynically release murderers, Katzenbach just as cynically states, "That's how things are. That is what we pay for a government by law." But that is just the point. That is government by murder and terror. In the name of "government by law" the federal government must move in and enforce these laws.

The fundamental concepts that are the points of reference for our viewpoint were eloquently expressed years ago in a now-historic letter written by the scholar, editor, historian, novelist, poet, philosopher, organizer and fighter against all injustice, Dr. W.E.B. DuBois.

Let me conclude my remarks with a quotation from that letter:

> On this first day of October 1961, I am applying for admission to membership in the Communist Party of the United States. I have been long and slow in coming to this conclusion, but at last my mind is settled. . . .

Today I have reached a firm conclusion. . .

Capitalism can not reform itself; it is doomed to self-destruction.

Communism, the effort to give all men what they need and to ask of each the best they can contribute, this is the only way of life. In the end communism will triumph. I want to help bring that day.

[Speech at Tuskeegee Institute, February 1966.]

The Roots
Of Afro-American Oppression

What are the basic, primary causes of Afro-American oppression? Who is responsible? What forces in our society sustain and perpetuate this evil system of special oppression of 20 million of our people? What forces make Afro-Americans victims of discrimination and segregation in every phase of life, special targets of police brutality and fascist terror?

The rebellion of the poor—intense, militant struggles centered in the big-city ghettos—has thrown these basic questions into sharp focus. The rebellion has brought a deep national crisis to the surface. Detroit, Newark, New Haven are but sparks on the surface of a developing, deepening confrontation.[5] They are sparks from a movement, a cause, that is demanding progressive solution of a question which history has placed on the order of the day. To a great extent, the speed and completeness of that solution will be determined by the understanding and consciousness of the forces fighting for it.

Therefore, to know the primary causes of oppression, to pinpoint the enemy, is a matter of very practical importance. It is necessary to develop correct tactics and alliances, without which victory is impossible. The purpose of this article is to probe these causes. In the space of one article, of course, it is possible to deal with only a few of the many sides of this question.

The people of our land want honest answers. Their inquiry is sincere. Increasing numbers of our people are ready to draw the necessary conclusions. They can be won for progressive solutions.

The same can not be said about the ruling circles of our country. The corporate establishment is hell-bent on misdirecting the inquiry, on covering up the real causes. These people are for a whitewash. They are out to create an atmosphere, a mass state of mind, in which reasoned inquiry is not possible. Instead of inquiry to combat racism, they are for heightening racist tensions. They want to turn the rebellions into a "white-Black" riot.

The corporate brass have always regarded racism as an instrument of their rule. The men of Big Business create it. They perpetuate it. The ghettos are of their making. Now they intend to use the struggle by the victims of their racist policies to heighten racial tension, increase racial prejudices, to continue to divide and rule.

In addition to extracting superprofits from its victims, racism also serves capitalism by diverting workers from the struggle against their real enemy. The South is the clearest example of this. For generations large sections of Southern whites have lived in utter poverty, only because injections of racism by the rich landlords divert their attention from the responsiblity of the government and the rich for their miserable status.

A most important feature of the long, hot summer is the failure of the deliberate efforts of the ultra-Right, both in and out of police departments, to turn the rebellions into racial conflicts. The mass media view every remark or act which tends to heighten racial tension, no matter how insignificant, as "big news" and blows it up. But the mass actions have not been struggles between Black and white. In fact, there have been increasing signs of Black-white unity in action. These significant developments, however, have not appeared in the news.

Without understanding the root causes and social forces

that lead people to rebel, it is impossible to wage a successful struggle. One must know the enemy in order to defeat him.

One can not help but admire the groups which get together and go into the ghettos to "clean up a block." The clergy who inititate such actions do so with the best of intentions. But such efforts are not solutions. In fact they are misleading, since ghettos are not the result of people failing to clean up their neighborhoods. These well-meaning efforts are fruitless because they do not come to grips with the underlying causes of the problem. Any action that does not lead to a search for basic causes will not result in even temporary solutions. Mass actions must lead to inquiry that in turn can lead to even more meaningful mass struggles. Such is the path to victory.

What line of inquiry do the corporate powers want to obstruct? The one that asks: What makes ghettos? Why should tens of millions of Americans be forced to live in rat infested, dilapidated, rundown tenements without elementary conveniences or facilities? Why is this the lot of Black Americans in the first place?

If the answer is poverty, what then is the cause of poverty? Why is there such poverty in the midst of plenty?

If the answer is unemployment, low wages, high prices, rents and taxes, what then is the reason for unemployment and low wages? And again, why is the percentage of Black Americans among the unemployed and low-paid so large? This line of inquiry leads to the very doorstep of the real culprit. It guides one to the real enemy—the exploiting class—and its accessories.

For Marxists this is not a new discovery. But for the millions it is a necessary line of inquiry and an important and necessary discovery. This line of inquiry will lead from actions on the spontaneous level to a conscious line of struggle focused on the basic cause of the oppression.

At the end of such a line of inquiry the people will find the culprit: the corporate system of capitalism, a system in which the few rob the many. It is this system that creates unemployment and low wages, jacks up prices, rents and taxes. This system, this capitalist structure, adapted from slavery the special system of oppressing the Afro-American people and fitted it to its system of exploiting workers. The express purpose of this system is to rob the poor. The entire corporate structure exists for the sole purpose of squeezing as much as possible from the people and giving as little as possible back to them. It thus makes the handful of rich richer and the millions of poor poorer.

Exploitation is the economic basis of capitalism. The basic function of capitalist ideology is to justify and to facilitate exploitation of the workers by the capitalists. The basic politics of capitalism is the politics of exploitation. It is a politics that preserves and perpetuates this exploitative system. In short, the whole capitalist establishment is an instrument of exploitation.

But why repeat such elementary truths? Only to point out the special responsibility of Communists, of Marxists. These truths are not known by the millions who are in struggle. This side of capitalism remains hidden to them. It is very carefully camouflaged. All "establishment" inquiries stop at this border. It is a safe bet that the presidential commission appointed to investigate the summer rebellions in the ghettos will not enter this arena of inquiry.

This crisis forces all Americans to re-examine their responsibilities. That white Americans have a special responsibility there can be no doubt. How this responsibility is placed is a very important question. Our purpose in placing it is to win white Americans to the goal of putting an end to the system of discrimination against their Black fellow Americans and thereby create a united people's force for overall progress.

By and large, Afro-Americans are, to one degree or another, in this struggle. The challenge at this point is to win a larger section of white America. Black-white unity is one of the keys to victory over discrimination and segregation.

A correct understanding and acceptance by white Americans of their special responsibility is a primary factor in building such unity.

A *New York Times* editorial states the question as follows:

> White Americans, of course, must share the greater burden of responsibility. They are the majority group and *they control most of the levers of political, economic and social power in this country.* Moreover, it is the white man's sins and commissions that are the root of much of this summer turmoil. (Emphasis added.)

It is progress that this organ of monopoly capital does not place the blame on the victims of oppression. But this does not mean that the *Times* is now ready to print the truth. In fact, it has done nothing but exchange one camouflage for another.

The *Times* is twisting a half-truth into a protective shield for the real culprit. The half-truth is that white Americans do have to face up to a special responsibility for the continuation of the system of racial oppression. The responsibility does not, however, result from the fact that "they control most of the levers of political, economic and social power in this country." This is the *Times'* way of covering up the fact that a small group of white Americans control the monopoly corporations, which in turn control the "levers of political, economic and social power." The *Times* is covering up for the system of capitalism. What direct power do the mass of white Americans have over jobs, prices, taxes and rents?

The *Times*, an ideological voice of capitalism, wants to cover up capitalism's sins by referring to the sins of white Americans. The *Times* tries to cover up the capitalist, corporate, dictatorial control of the "levers of political, economic and social power" by making it appear as if an undifferentiated, classless, mass of white Americans has such power and control. The *Times* is for everything—as long as it in no way weakens the real power and control of the capitalist monopolies.

Now what is the special responsibility of white Americans in the struggle to end all practices of discrimination and segregation against Afro-Americans? One must start from the fact that the system of special oppression of the Afro-American people continues only because white Americans have been and continue to be accessories in the crime. They are the human force through which the system of oppression operates. Some by choice, others by force of circumstance, have become participants and accomplices in the deeds of racism.

The *Times* editorial is a vivid example of how the crimes of U.S. capitalism are carried out in the name of white Americans. Therefore white Americans have a special responsibility to end this shame. Equality must become the cause of all Americans.

The perpetuation of the system of racial oppression is possible only because a small section of white Americans support it by acts of racial violence, and because a larger number are seemingly neutral and thereby passively support the evil. Without this, the oppression of Afro-Americans could not continue for long. White Americans are responsible for the system of special oppression of Afro-Americans in the same sense that all Americans are responsible for the dirty, unjust war being conducted in their name against the people of Vietnam. When white Americans do not join in the struggle to end discrimination, they are as responsible for the acts of oppression against Afro-Americans as Americans in general are for the continuation of the war in Vietnam when they do not act to end it.

But the primary responsibility for the imperialist policies of aggression in Vietnam and discrimination and segregation against Afro-Americans is not that of a "whole people." The roots of these policies are in the system of capitalism. They are in the very inner nature of capitalism. For capitalism, the oppression of Afro-Americans is an additional instrument of exploitation. It is a source of extra profits. The people, either by support or silence, may become accessories to this crime.

No ideological struggle is easy. But for forces on the right side of history, no ideological battle is hopeless. White chauvinism has deep roots in our society, but it is not unconquerable. In fact, considerable progress against it has been made. It will be burned out with the rest of the clutter of capitalist class ideology.

For progressive white Americans to give up the struggle against the ideology of white chauvinism "because it is hopeless" means that they themselves have become victims of this ideology. The aim of bourgeois propaganda is exactly to create a feeling of hopelessness.

No, it is not hopeless. Rather, to win victories in this ideological contest is a matter of continuous struggle, a matter of developing ever new approaches, a matter of using the new experiences of people to deepen their understanding.

What are some of the general features of this struggle?

The purpose of an ideological struggle is to win people to action. The aim of the struggle against the ideology of white supremacy is to win white Americans to do battle against the practices which that ideology fosters. An ideological struggle abstracted from action limps.

It is a many-sided struggle. It is many-sided because the poison of white supremacy penetrates and affects every facet of our lives. It poisons the moral climate. It affects our moral and ethical standards as a nation and as individuals. Thus it is a moral issue. Further, the concept of white supremacy rests on a complete falsehood; therefore it is a matter of fighting for scientific truth. It is also a legal and constitutional question because the oppression tramples the very premises on which the constitution rests. The cruel practices of racism and discrimination contradict the accepted practices of all civilized people. Hence it is a matter of basic human rights.

The fight against white chauvinism must become the cause of all progressive forces in society because the system of racial oppression is a primary obstacle to all social progress. It affects the immediate and long-range interests of the bulk of the American people. It is a matter of our many-sided and urgent self-interest as a nation. The struggle must be related to each of these facets.

To relate the ideological struggle against racism to people's material interests does not in any way minimize the need to conduct the struggle on more general grounds. Double standards, the conflict between the statement of generally-accepted concepts by trade unions, religious bodies and other democratic organizations, on the one hand, and racist practices, on the other, give rise to shame and moral dissatisfaction. This sense of shame is an important ingredient of the atmosphere in which the ideological struggle can be successfully waged.

But when white Americans can be concretely shown, on the basis of their own experiences, how the ideology that sustains the system of oppression of Black Americans also cuts against their own interests, the battle is on solid ground. Their commitment to equality will be firmer with the realization that this moral and ethical position is in harmony with their deep self-interest.

To win white Americans to the struggle for equality, an understanding of the basic roots of the system of oppression and the ideology of racism is of primary importance. As class consciousness grows, as more Americans come to understand that capitalism is the primary cause of all social evils, the understanding that it is also the root source of the special system of oppression of the Afro-American people increasingly becomes a vital element in the struggle.

This basic understanding is key in winning white workers to the fight. The realization that their problems can be traced to the same source, to the same class, can go a long way toward burning out racist concepts. The multiracial composition of our working class is an important factor in this struggle, and, in fact, will increasingly become the pivotal element in it.

Progressive Americans must never tire of seeking new ways to explain that the ideology of racism is deliberately perpetuated, artificially maintained, with a very specific purpose. Workers can understand the explanation that it is designed to divide the working class, to weaken it. Democratic-minded Americans can be concretely shown how racism serves as the primary instrument of the reactionary forces seeking to destroy the democratic rights of all Americans. It is a means by which the Dixicrats and the ultra-Right have subverted and corrupted the democratic process for generations.

These are some of the facets of the struggle against the ideology of racism. In this struggle, it is obvious that one of the special responsibilities of Marxists-Leninists is to expose racism's class roots, to expose it as a class weapon, a weapon whose specific purpose is to extract ever bigger profits.

White Americans who are progressive, who are in the ranks of the Left, who are members of our Party, are not immune to the influences of the ideology of white chauvinism. I do not agree with those who say it is always present in all white Americans. But it is clear that there must be continuous struggle, perpetual alertness against the penetration of this poison.

Because Communists and many others on the Left do understand the class nature of the roots of racism, because of their general world outlook, they reject it. So it does not appear among them as a fullblown ideological position, but rather as an influence. Ideology influences action, for better or worse. Even a slight influence of a false ideology can have negative effects.

In the Party and in the ranks of the Left, chauvinist influences result in a lack of participation in the struggle for equality. They lead to a cutback in political initiatives, especially initiatives to move white Americans into the struggle. They give rise to paternalism, to lack of sensitivity to the problems resulting from the everpresent ideology and practices of white supremacy. They dull the ability to detect or grasp the character of acts that arise from the influence of white chauvinism. Racist influences result in a failure to see the special reponsibilities of white progressives and Communists in the struggle against chauvinism.

In the Party, ideological struggles can and do take place on a higher level than in broader circles. But even in the Party and on the Left, such struggles, if they are conducted only on the level of internal discussion, are bound to limp.

The influence of white chauvinism in the ranks of progressives can be most effectively fought when such forces are actively engaged in the struggle against all acts of racism and discrimination and when they are participating in the struggle against the ideology of white supremacy among the millions. These struggles should never be placed in separate compartments.

The most effective way to fight smoke is to also fight the fire. If one doesn't fight the fire, he will be engulfed by the smoke. In a sense, it can be said that one's seriousness about eliminating smoke can be measured by how seriously one fights the fire.

Such, then, are the responsibilities of progressives and Communists in the all-important struggle against white chauvinism.   □

[*Political Affairs*, October 1967]

The Path
To Revolution

There is a feature of the positions and programs of many Left groups that is basically different from ours.

While hiding behind phrases about "achieving Black and white unity in the future" or "under socialism," they have, in fact, given up the struggle for unity of Black and white. In our view, Black and white unity, unity of the working class, Black and white, the alliance of the Afro-American people's movement and the labor movement, are the foundations of progress. Not to fight racism, not to fight for Black and white unity based on the elimination of racism, is to retreat. It is to give in to racism.

Just as these groups avoid coming to grips with the centrality of the class question, so they avoid coming to grips with the crucial question of racism.

Our program is a challenge to these wrong concepts.

Our program can serve as a guidepost, a marker in the stream of political and ideological currents.

Our program is a reflection of the realities of this moment. It does not opportunistically skirt difficult questions. Our concepts are based on an understanding of how the laws of capitalist development operate on the American scene. It is the product of the application of Marxism-Leninism to our specific reality.

The section of our draft program on Black liberation has

created more discussion than any other.

Since the question of Afro-American equality is crucial for our country, it is crucial for our program. It has a bearing on all other sections of the program.

It is understandable that we are having some difficulty formulating this section. In an area where there is continuous struggle and daily change, it is more difficult to generalize experiences. Because of this, there are some differences in the estimation of exactly which are the main trends, in what direction some of the present mass currents will go and how they will develop.

But the basic reason for the difficulty is that Black oppression in the United States has a number of unique and distinct features. It is a special system of oppression within a special set of circumstances.

It is a system of special oppression of a people within a nation. The oppression is racial. The oppression is of a national minority. The oppressed by and large are of the working class. Their exploitation as wage workers at the point of production determines the class status of the great majority of Afro-Americans. Thus the main economic issue is not land. There is discrimination in housing, education, every phase of life. But the main economic issues are encased in the structure of U.S. capitalist production. It is a special system of oppression woven into the fabric of capitalist exploitation. The oppression is economic, political, cultural and social. It is a ghettoized oppression.

The struggle is as manysided as the oppression. The struggle is for national expression, but it is also to break down the walls of segregation and discrimination. Thus the struggle is both for national identity and for equality and freedom within and as a part of the nation.

The struggles to break the chains of special oppression have developed movements both toward integration and toward separation. What is important is that both are movements of struggle. They are both directed at the system that creates inequality. These trends are not necessarily contradictory. They are interrelated and interwoven.

Neither tendency is one of resignation or acceptance of the status quo.

The present tendency of the Afro-American community is a reaction to 300 years of struggle to break the chains of special oppression.

It is a reaction to 300 years of effort to break the racist barriers that bar Afro-Americans from the mainstream of national life.

It is a reaction to years of violent resistance and indifference by the majority of white Americans to the efforts to break down the walls of segregation and discrimination.

It is a reaction to 300 years of cruel persecution, indignities and injustices. This struggle has now reached a qualitative turning point.

The future of Black and white unity, as well as how the struggle of 25 million Afro-Americans will develop, will in large part be determined by how fast white America, and especially white working-class America, moves to break down the walls, the system that oppresses 25 million of its fellow Americans. It depends how quickly white America realizes that this is necessary in its own interest. It depends to a large degree how quickly white America extricates itself from the net of racism.

This is why the question of the struggle for equality is an American question. This is why it is a crisis of the nation. How this crisis is solved will be a big factor determining how all trends in the Afro-American community develop.

There are differences on just how some of these unique features of the struggle against the special system of oppression are going to develop in the period ahead.

Some of these problems will be with us for some time. But our discussion of the draft program shows basic agreement on most questions. This provides a solid basis for our program, even if we are not able to formulate some questions in detail at this moment.

How the program should state the question of the right to self-determination has come up in our discussions.

It has been said, "We must stand unalterably for the right of self-determination." This is one of those statements that lead one to ask, "Just how do you mean that?"

If it is a restatement of our basic Leninist position regarding the liberation of oppressed nations or developing nations, then it is a statement of a truth. Of course that is our position. And as far as I know, no one in our Party has challenged it.

No one challenges the correctness of the position of self-determination of nations. But the application of this Leninist principle to the unique situation arising from the oppression and struggles of 25 million Black Americans is a different matter.

It is always important to determine whether all people in a discussion are using terms and words in the same manner. New experiences can, and often do, change the meaning of old expressions, old concepts. When we use an old expression in a context which gives it a new meaning, we have to say so.

The concept of "the right to self-determination" has an accepted political meaning. The accepted meaning is very closely related to relations between nations and states. It is a demand for a nation to have the right to decide its own affairs and to determine what relationship it will have with other nations—especially what relations it will maintain with the nation that has oppressed it. Above all, it includes the right to separate or to establish some other relationship, such as federation of equal nations and states.

This accepted meaning of the concept of self-determination is of necessity linked to the existence of a common territory and separate economy, expressed in a political and state structure.

Our strategic concepts must flow from our reality. If our reality does not fit into some generalized concept drawn from other experiences, then we must make our own generalizations. There are many similarities between the reality of Black oppression and other experiences. To the extent that there are, we should draw on them.

Strategic concepts are based on estimates of trends. Therefore, we have to ask: On the basis of present-day trends and currents, can we conclude that the Afro-American community is developing in the direction of a separate territory and a separate economy? I don't think the trends sustain such a conclusion. To reach such a conclusion would be overdrawing the separatist tendencies that exist.

When we consider strategy in the struggle to end racial and national oppression, a number of other specific factors must be taken into consideration. Among these factors the class question is very important.

In a basic sense Afro-Americans are working-class Americans. By and large they are victims of exploitation in the production process. They approach the solution to the economic problems they face, as a result of both racial oppression and class exploitation, in the context of the class structure of society.

To formulate strategic concepts based on a realistic evaluation of trends, one would have to ask: How would Black steel, auto or rubber workers or coal miners respond to the slogan of the right of self-determination, in the accepted usage, as a solution to their problems? They are tied to the production process of U.S. capitalism. This is the arena of their struggle for freedom and equality.

Our program must start and end with the thought that to fight for Black liberation is to fight against racism.

Our approach to the concept of Black and white unity is a struggle against chauvinism, against all forms of discrimination. Ours is not only a moral plea. It is an argument based on the reality that social progress can be won only with Black and white unity, based on a struggle against racism.

Our program must be a witness to the unique quality of our Party. It must speak about and for a working-class party uniting Black and white.   □

[Report to Special 18th Convention, CPUSA, July 1968]

1978

The Biggest Obstacle
To Social Progress

Like most pollutants that poison our air, water and food, racism is not something you can see most of the time. It penetrates us like a poisonous, invisible gas. And, as with other pollutants, it is the effects that become visible.

In the United States racism against Black Americans has the deepest roots and its effects are the most open, blatant and devastating. It is a chronic disease in our society that has been infecting our people's lives for 300 years.

The other hideous forms and patterns of racism and chauvinism, such as the discrimination against the Chicano communities, are fed by the same source, the same sewer that continues to carry this disease throughout our land.

The capitalist ruling class has used this poison of racism and discrimination to exploit and oppress, to divide and rule, in order to reap huge profits and superprofits. They know that "in unity there is strength," and that a working class divided against itself is unable to unite against its common enemy.

The ruling class is united in its determination to perpetuate racism and it will use any method to wield this weapon of division to keep the working people from uniting.

Through its control of the mass media, the ruling class

daily belches out clouds of racist distortions, half-truths, little and big lies. It is not always easy to see through this fog, to avoid being trapped and sucked in by the continuous lies.

The lies are tricky, insidious. They follow well-thought-out campaigns, well-thought-out strategies for misleading the people. Humor and satire on TV have become a vehicle for insidious racism. The ruling class uses its best brain trusts and think tanks to work out these campaigns.

Besides using the media to brainwash us, the ruling class also manipulates and distorts history for its own purposes. Just as it controls the mass media, so it dominates the educational system. It makes sure that history is written in accordance with its selfish class interests. To distort or ignore history is itself a manifestation of racism.

Until the upsurge in the Black liberation movement of the '50s and '60s, historians and the whole educational system all but ignored Black history. "Why study the history of Black people? Black people aren't supposed to have a history worth knowing and understanding," was the rationale.

Racism is and continues to be the biggest drag, the biggest obstacle to social progress in this country. Slavery held back economic development. Since then, the poison of racism has distorted the entire political, economic and social fabric of our lives.

How many racist, reactionary, ignorant, antilabor and antidemocratic senators from the South and from California, in control of key congressional committees, have we had to suffer through; senators elected because the right to vote was stolen from Black people in the South; senators who blocked everything progressive and democratic?

It is impossible to measure the damage done to the U.S. working people of all colors and backgrounds, to the working-class and trade union movement of our country, by the vicious venom of racism.

Karl Marx saw this over a hundred years ago. "Labor," he said, "can not emancipate itself in the white skin where in the Black it is branded." This was true when Marx said it, and it is just as true today.

The fight to include the history of Black Americans in our educational system is part of the long, hard struggle of Black people for their dignity, for their human rights, for their rightful place in U.S. society.

But this step forward, this victory, does not mean ruling-class historians now give a true picture of Black history. This change does not mean that our schools and universities now tell the whole truth about Black history.

These historians, bending to the pressure of mass struggle, decided that where they could not ignore Black history they would promote it, institute it in the educational system as a way to control and manipulate what is taught and how it is taught, to keep the true lessons from being drawn by those who study it. They do this by hiding the true cause, the roots, of racism, by covering up who profits from racism and whose interests are served by it. They promote ideas that divide Black and white.

Knowing this, we must study Black history to look for its true lessons for our people, not the false ideas the ruling class is peddling.

To cover up, to justify their monstrous racist crimes, they have developed monstrous, racist theories.

The second important lesson to be learned from Black history is the need for unity of all working people and for a coalition between workers and all progressive peoples who suffer under the iron heel of monopoly domination, a coalition against the common enemy.

It was a coalition of these forces against the slaveholders that won the Civil War and the emancipation of the slaves.

It was a coalition of the Black liberation movement with all other progressive forces in the '50s and '60s that forced the ruling class to make concessions in the area of civil rights.

While there have been gains, the great struggle against racism must continue today because the racist patterns persist. We know that the income gap between Black and white households has now reached over $4,500 yearly. And if you multiply this by the number of Black households, and add in the wage gap between Chicano and white households, you can see that this superexploitation results in extra profits of about $50 billion every year—almost every dollar of which goes into the coffers of Big Business. Racism is the most profitable business!

This is the main reason why the federal and state governments will do nothing to end racist discrimination.   ☐

[*Daily World*, March 9, 1978]

1979

Labor
Up Front

There are Supreme Court decisions, executive orders and periodic reports and studies by presidential commissions. Presidents, their wives and vice presidents appear at conventions of Afro-American organizations to make speeches about vague, abstract progress and advances, and make even vaguer promises concerning the future struggle against racism.

In spite of all the talk that "there is no special system of racism," and while there is some progress, the basic system, the basic patterns of racial and national oppression remain intact.

While there is a decline in racist attitudes among the people in general, there is no basic change in the racist attitudes of corporations. While there is growing working-class, Black and white unity, there is also an increase in racist activity by ultra-Right and fascist groups. The KKK has been emboldened to march. While more Afro-Americans are elected to public office, there is also a well-organized attack against those already holding office.

There are changes and shifts, but the basic patterns of racial and national oppression have not been broken. The proof is in the economic arena.

Because racism is an instrument of capitalist exploitation for superprofits, both its use and the struggle against it are affected by overall developments and trends.

While the present economic situation is a serious problem for most people and for all workers, its impact on Afro-Americans is even sharper due to the racist economic gap that existed before the crisis. For Black youth the crisis starts from the precrisis level of 60 per cent unemployment, passed on from one generation to the next. Inflation cuts into the living standards of all workers, but for Afro-Americans it cuts into an existing economic gap that continues to widen.

Black family incomes have declined in relation to white family incomes, from 62 per cent in the early 70s to 57 per cent today. The Black unemployment rate, including those who have given up looking for work and those who hold part-time jobs because they can not find full-time employment, is 23.1 per cent, or roughly one out of every four workers. Twenty-eight per cent of Black families are poor, compared to 7 per cent of white families. The proportion of Black families in middle- or upper-income brackets actually declined from 37 per cent to 34 per cent in the years 1972-1978.

One dollar per gallon for heating oil is a crisis for most working-class families. But for Black families in Harlem, Chicago, Detroit and other cities it comes on top of a situation in which tens of thousands have gone without heat in below zero weather in past winters.

Afro-Americans need no proof. They live with the proof every day. We have to keep updating the proof because the new deception is that racism is "something in the past," that "Blacks have made it," and that "the problem is now reverse discrimination."

The peddlers of the "reverse discrimination" line do not expect people to buy the full line—and most don't. These peddlers expect their line to disarm and demobilize people. On this, they are right. For the peddlers of racism, this is only a first step. Their longer-range goals are to reverse the historic trend, to undo the victories that have been won against racism.

Racism adds a special weight and a brutality to the national oppression of Afro-Americans. It is an ideological drug. Those addicted to it need outside help. For workers, the understanding that the drug pushers are supplied by and come from the corporate suites is a most important starting point.

Affirmative action has emerged on center stage in the struggle against racism. It raises the struggle from talk to concrete action. The Supreme Court decision in the Weber case is a significant victory for affirmative action and a tribute to the broad coalition of trade unions, Black and Hispanic organizations, and other progressive groups which fought in unity to secure a reversal of the lower court decision.

The response of the trade union movement, spurred on by rank-and-file organizations like Trade Unionists for Action and Democracy and the Coalition of Black Trade Unionists, has been historic. The United Steelworkers of America called a conference on Weber, expecting 600 delegates. More than 900 showed up.

Weber marks a setback for the racist opponents of affirmative action. Under the false slogan of "reverse discrimination" they had hoped to consolidate the success they had won in the Bakke case. The effect of the Weber decision is to validate the consent decrees and collective bargaining agreements for affirmative action in steel, as well as similar agreements in other industries.[6]

However, the victory in Weber is no cause for complacency. The decision is narrow in scope. It applies only to voluntary affirmative action programs—that is, to plans on which both the employer and the union agree, and then only if a court finds the plan to be "reasonable." It does not deal with the power of the courts to order such a program as a remedy for discrimination, no matter how rampant the discrimination may be. It has no application to situations such as the construction industry, where both employers and unions adamantly oppose affirmative action.

It was to limit the decision in this way that the AFL-CIO leadership joined the anti-Weber coalition and argued in its brief that courts are powerless under Title VII to impose an affirmative action program on an unwilling employer or union. Thus, preservation of the gains won in the Weber case—let alone further advances—must still be fought for.

There will doubtless be efforts in Congress to overturn the decision by amending Title VII. These must be countered by an amendment to Title VI overturning Bakke. It will take the greatest possible unity in struggle of all anti-racist forces, particularly in the ranks of labor, to win the upcoming fight. The Supreme Court decision in the Weber case can be used to raise the struggle for affimative action with teeth (quotas) to a new level.

This year marks the 25th anniversary of *Brown vs. Board of Education*, which held that segregated education in public schools violates the 14th Amendment's guarantee of equal protection under the law.

A quarter-century after *Brown*, segregated education remains the rule. The situation in Columbus, Ohio, site of one of the most recent school decisions, is typical.

In 1954, when *Brown* was decided, all Columbus schools were openly and intentionally segregated. Twenty years later, half of its 172 schools remained 90 per cent Black or 90 per cent white. The Court, however, did not order immediate, or even prompt, correction of the Constitutional violation it found in *Brown*, but ruled that desegregation should be accomplished "with all deliberate speed." Predictably, the entire accent has been on "deliberation."

Moreover, the Burger Court has backed off from its predecessor's commitment—if only in theory—to the principle of desegregation. It reversed the lower court order in the Detroit school case on the ground that an entire metropolitan area can not be treated as a unit since, according to the Court, the inhabitants of the white suburbs bear no responsibility for inner-city segregation and hence should not be "burdened" with Black children in their schools.

These and other rulings jeopardized a number of desegregation orders issued by the lower courts after years of litigation and inspired grave fears for the future of court-ordered desegregation.

These fears have been somewhat allayed by Supreme Court decisions in June, upholding the desegregation orders for Columbus and Dayton and relaxing somewhat its requirements for proof of a discriminatory purpose.

However, desegregation remains subject to the whims of a Supreme Court which has the power to delay, dilute or halt it by inventing and manipulating complex legal formulas not so blatantly racist, but not much less deadly that "separate but equal."

Desegregation faces an even graver threat from Congressional initiatives in the form of legislation or a Constitutional amendment prohibiting busing.

The fight for equality and quality in education remains, as it did before *Brown*, a major battleground in the war to eradicate racism and rid our country of this poison.

It should be clear that the struggle against racism has emerged even more as a key element in every area of struggle. It is a key factor in the class struggle, in the struggle for working-class unity, in the struggle for democracy, for detente, for SALT II, and in the struggle for socialism. It is a struggle that can be won, but it is a struggle.

Over generations, the catastrophic effects of the economic and social onslaught of monopoly on the living conditions of the Black population have created special obstacles to their ability to achieve equality, even to rise from the status of the most oppressed. In so doing, it has also placed the Black worker, and consequently Black women workers, in a special position. In their struggle to achieve equality, Black women force monopoly to make concessions benefiting women as a whole.

A phenomenon characteristic of the Afro-American population has been the fact that Black women have always participated in production in greater percentages than their numbers in the population. Black women have traditionally shared as breadwinners in their families, from slavery to the present, because it has always taken two wages to sustain life in nationally oppressed families.

Black women were the first women to enter heavy industrial production. Prior to that they shared equally with men in agricultural production. Their labor has ranged from unpaid and underpaid to domestic and often unrecorded labor.

Frequently, the fact that they are in the labor force at all has been unrecorded because their employers have not done so. This is especially true of domestic labor. Consequently, because of their special victimization and exploitation in the work force based on class, race, nationality and sex, Black women have accumulated a certain collective experience resulting from the struggle against oppression that has been passed down from one generation to another—through tradition, culture and in the upbringing of children.

This special consciousness includes the understanding that this is a system that breeds racism, discrimination and injustice and that the source is the profits made by the rich resulting from unequal wages, education and living conditions.

The very nature of their living conditions and inability to overcome the barriers of discrimination over generations have served as a collective lesson, whose conclusions have been adopted by the community as a whole. The "American Dream" has never been realizable for Black people, and certainly not for Black women.

Consequently, the unique role of Black women in the fight for women's equality has been to raise the basic economic issues of the right to equality on the job, the right to safe and healthy conditions, the right to child care, the right to quality, integrated education for children, the right to health and decent housing—the right to a life that establishes equality.

At the very height of the feminist movement, when Black women were being criticized for not participating, they raised these issues as the key to equality foɪ Black people, and for women in general. This concept has ɪargely been accepted.

There have also been some changes in the arena of Chicano-Mexican-American equality. But the basic chauvinism, the basic policies of national oppression and discrimination against the Chicano-Mexican-American community, continue.

In most Chicano-Mexican-American communities the per capita income remains below the poverty level. Therefore, the present economic crisis for the majority means moving downward from the already existing poverty levels. For most of the young people the prospect for a bilingual, quality education remains on the drawing boards. Because of the lack of bilingual education the dropout rate of Chicano-Mexican-American students is 50 per cent. Because of the extremely racist conditions in cities like Houston, Texas, the rate is 85 per cent.

The housing construction boom has bypassed the barrios. The high unemployment rate, work in low-paying and seasonal jobs, discrimination in housing, education, medical care and culture, and vicious police brutality all fire the struggles and movements for Chicano-Mexican-American equality.

Much of the chauvinism affecting the whole community is centered around the drive against people without legal documents. Every so often there are widely publicized "roundups" and "dragnets," as in the days of slavery. These "roundups" and deportations continue to be a convenient way of getting rid of excess labor when the harvest is in, without paying unemployment or social security benefits.

People without documents are blamed for the economic ills of the system. They are projected as an economic burden, while in reality most of them are workers who produce and pay taxes, but don't receive social security and unemployment benefits

Because they are forced to work in low-pay industries, these workers continue to be a source of extra profits. Any solution must start from the premise that the superexploitation, which results in extra profits, must stop.

Chicano-Mexican-American communities are basically working-class. Some 50 per cent of Chicano workers are blue-collar workers in metal, mining, aerospace, longshore, steel and auto, and laborers in a variety of other industries. Some 20 per cent are agricultural workers.

These workers are therefore an integral part of the multiracial, multinational U.S. working class. They are the key section of the working class in many industries and shops. These Chicano members of the U.S. working class have a unique role in the alliance of the working class and the Chicano-Mexican-American liberation movements and struggles.

The struggle for Chicano-Mexican-American equality has unique features because it develops mainly in regions that straddle the United States-Mexican border. Hence, it shares the history and traditions of both countries.

But the exploitation and oppression are an integral part of the U.S. capitalist system of exploitation. This determines the trends, the social and economic outlook, the relationships and class forces within the movements for Chicano-Mexican-American equality. These movements are struggles against patterns and policies of discrimination in industry, in the system of education and culture. They are struggles against the policies of national oppression by U.S. corporations and by the U.S. government.

There has always been an ongoing conspiracy between the U.S. corporations and some of the ruling-class circles of Mexico on how to exploit the border situation. Mainly it has been at the expense of the people and workers of Mexico. In the past it involved agriculture. Now the conspiracy includes industry and trade.

This conspiracy includes low wages and tax ripoffs on both sides of the border, the aim of which is to extract more profits for the multinational corporations. Only a united movement of the peoples of Mexico and the United States, especially a united movement of the trade unions on both sides, can put an end to the profit conspiracy.

In the Chicano-Mexican-American communities there is a growing movement of independent political action. There is a growing sense of affinity and alliance with the working-class and trade union movement, and a strong anticorporate, antistate sentiment. There is a need to create a mass democratic human rights campaign to force the U.S. government to end the harassment and brutality inflicted on people without legal documents.

We must do more to mobilize a movement, especially by the U.S. trade unions, to take the superprofits out of the exploitation of undocumented workers. There is a need for a campaign to secure prevailing wage levels and to secure all the benefits and social services to which the Chicano-Mexican-American people are entitled. This is both a human rights campaign and a struggle that will serve the self-interests of the whole U.S. working class.

In the struggle for Chicano-Mexican-American equality we can make an important contribution by helping to find the forms and the programs that will come together in a broad Chicano-Mexican-American front that will have working relations with the trade unions and the organizations of the other racially and nationally oppressed peoples. The objective situation for such a front exists now.

It is one of those contradictions in life that less than 100 miles from our shores there is a thriving, independent country building socialism and another country suffering under the heel of U.S. colonial domination.

Socialist Cuba is in the midst of the most explosive building boom in history. Without unemployment, without racism and at an unprecedented pace, Cuba is eliminating slums and solving its housing problem. It is guaranteeing all its citizens free education, medical care, child care and old age security. It is creating a new society that provides prosperity, security and happiness for its people from the cradle to the grave.

Socialism in Cuba is only 20 years old. Twenty years ago Cuba was at the lowest level of economic and social development in the hemisphere. What a dramatic contrast!

Puerto Rico is staggering under the weight of colonial exploitation and domination—with the highest rate of inflation, with food stamps in place of wages on a large scale, rising unemployment and spreading slums. Medical care and education are now out of reach for the majority, while the U.S. corporations pile up huge profits as a result of low wages and poor working conditions. Without regard for the rights and welfare of the people or the ecology of the country, the monopoly monsters plunder and pollute the island.

The continuing bombardment of Vieques stands as a blatant example of the arrogance and inhumanity of U.S. imperialism towards the Puerto Rican people.

U.S. imperialism has turned this beautiful island into one of the largest U.S. military bases in the world, one with nuclear arms.

Cuba is a showcase for socialism in the Americas, for national liberation. Puerto Rico is a showcase for capitalism, for colonial oppression.

Cuba is independent and free to build relationships with the rest of the world based on its self-interests. Puerto Rico is oppressed and tied to U.S. imperialism. The independence that Cuba has won remains the goal of the Puerto Rican independence movement.

At the moment the struggle is focused along the lines of the United Nations resolution passed last year, and on the upcoming September world solidarity conference in Mexico to which we must give our full support.

Every year tens of thousands of Puerto Rican people, impoverished by colonialism, are forced to migrate to the United States in search of a livelihood. They are oppressed and exploited from all sides.

In Puerto Rico they faced colonial oppression and exploitation. Here in the United States they face racial and national oppression, as well as class exploitation. Here they are forced to accept lower wages, inadequate housing and education, and high rates of unemployment. However, millions have also become an important component of our multiracial, multinational U.S. working class. They have become the key section of the class in some industries and shops, such as the garment industry in New York and the National Steel Company plant in Lorain, Ohio.

The South Bronx in New York City is a dramatic example of the dimension of the housing crisis, the hopelessness and poverty in which the Puerto Rican community is forced to live. The crisis of the cities, the crises of education, medical and child care, and mass transit, have special meaning in terms of the suffering and impoverishment of the Puerto Rican community.

Big Business would like to return to the past, when the people from Puerto Rico were treated as a labor pool for temporary, cheap labor, without the benefits of social services. But the rising struggles among the Puerto Rican people for full economic and social equality are rejecting that approach.

There are growing movements for Puerto Rican representation in public office, and an important element in the development of the whole movement for political independence.

The question of Puerto Rican independence and the struggle against racial and national oppression in the United States are very closely linked. They are struggles and issues that must be of deep concern to the people of the United States as a whole, and especially to the U.S. working class.

With the developments in Nicaragua, Jamaica, Grenada and other islands of the West Indies, the struggle for Puerto Rican independence is coming into sharper focus. Puerto Rico is part of the new Caribbean "arc of crisis."

The movement for independence within Puerto Rico fights under very difficult conditions. The FBI functions there as a foreign para-military force. The Communist Party of Puerto Rico, the Socialist Party and many others are victims of constant harassment and provocation. The FBI uses groups as provocateurs under a Left cover.

We must give greater priority to supporting and aiding the struggles that will turn the Caribbean "arc of crisis" into an arc of national liberation and socialism.

A special resolution to this convention on Native-American liberation states:

> A crisis exists for Native Americans. The American Indians and Alaskan Native peoples and nationalities are fighting for their very survival. They are victimized by the wanton exploitation and destruction of their lands and energy resources by powerful multinationals, by the U.S. government's policy, by astronomical unemployment, and by extreme social and economic deprivation.

The resolution correctly states the essence of the question. The growing struggles of the Native American Indian peoples' movements are, in the main, directed against the corporate monopolies such as Peabody Coal, Gulf and Shell Oil. Because of the special role of the state in perpetuating genocidal programs based on concepts of governmental chattel, these struggles have a sharp antigovernment, antistate focus.

The extreme poverty in the slums of the reservations forces increasing numbers of Native Americans into the new reservations of poverty in the urban centers.

The search for new sources of energy has opened a new war against Native Americans, a new brutal campaign through legal means and plain trickery to force the people off their lands and allow corporate takeover.

This new war, this new campaign of genocide, must find a new response in the ranks of the people's democratic movements. There is a crucial need for the trade union movement to take up the struggle, both as a human rights issue and because the struggle is in the self-interest of all U.S. workers.

The struggle for Native American Indian equality is a complex one. One side of the struggle involves land rights and old treaties which the U.S. government has violated and ignored. The struggles involve fishing and hunting rights. The land rights have become more critical because these lands are rich in minerals and sources of energy.

The struggles are against the bureaucratic, dictatorial rule on the reservations by government-appointed people who are steeped in corruption. The struggles also involve the fight against the policies of discrimination against Native American Indians who have, in increasing numbers, become a part of the U.S. working class and face severe discrimination in industry.

The issues are complex, but the class forces are not. The enemy is state monopoly capitalism. The struggle is against all forms of racial and national oppression. The key forces increasingly are the Native Americans who are part of the U.S. working class.

We will be able to make an effective contribution in this struggle only if we keep in mind who the forces are and the relationship of these struggles to the class struggle.

Unity has become the key necessity of this movement. Unity, a mass approach to struggle, and the seeking of allies are the main ingredients for advances and victories.

Citizens and nationals of Asian and Pacific origin are subjected to racial discrimination and chauvinist abuse in jobs, housing, education or any other aspect of life. They are the victims of a discrimination which cuts across class lines. At the same time, a large proportion of these peoples are workers who suffer class exploitation as well as racial and national oppression.

We are champions of the economic, political, social and cultural equality of every people and support the struggles of the peoples of the different Asian and Pacific nationalities for an end to all manner of chauvinism and national humiliation.

The unfree peoples of Asia and the Pacific Islands continue the struggle for their national rights, their independence and socio-political progress.

We stand for ending the trusteeship role assumed by the

imperialist powers, the United States in the first place, and for their freedom and right to self-determination. We particularly protest the use of the Pacific Islands for U.S. nuclear testing in violation of the health and national rights of their peoples.

Our task is to support their just democratic demands and to study these questions more deeply, develop the applications of our basic policies in order to assure a working-class approach, and to achieve greater mass involvement and Party building.

Racial and national oppression has been and is a built-in feature of world capitalism's drive for superprofits. It became an effective weapon especially in imperialist expansion.

Socialism marks the end not only of class exploitation, but of racial and national oppression and exploitation as well. It also marks the beginning of the end of racism as an ideological pattern of thought.

In the capitalist world it is very much a fact of everyday life. There is brutal, fascist oppression of the majority Black people in South Africa. There is oppression of the Irish and now oppression of Black immigrants in Great Britain. There is racist discrimination and policies of genocide against Indian populations in a number of South American countries and Canada. There is brutal oppression of the two or more million Arab peoples and the darker-skinned immigrants in Israel.

To one extent or another, racial and national oppression is a phenomenon within most of the capitalist countries. But with the exception of South Africa, Zimbabwe and a few other countries, nowhere is racial and national oppression practiced on the scale it is in the United States.

Racial and national oppression are an encrusted inner lining of corporate operations. Even as new nationalities arrive they are immediately classified on the ladder of national oppression, as the refugees from Vietnam are finding out. This mark will affect their employment and their children's advancement, culture and social life.

In the United States we may not have the largest number of nationalities. But there is no question there are more racially and nationally oppressed people here than in any other country. There are so many different nationalities that speakers and writers have difficulty determining how to deal with the total scope of the problem without always mentioning all of the racial and national groups who are victims of the oppression.

In addition to the Afro-Americans, Chicanos, Puerto Ricans and Native Americans, there are many other national groups and millions of others who, to one extent or another, are victims of national and racial oppression. There are Native Alaskans, who are now the victims of the fuel wars. There are growing numbers of Spanish-speaking peoples and nationalities from various countries of South and Central America. There are Chinese, Japanese, Hawaiian peoples, and increasing numbers of Vietnamese and Arab peoples, Filipino, Korean, East Indian and Pacific Island peoples.

There are millions of Jewish Americans, who at this point do not sharply feel the cutting edge of economic discrimination, but anti-Semitism continues as a very active, reactionary force, and poverty is growing.

And there are some 115 Native American Indian peoples, nations and nationalities.

The total number of people who are, to one extent or another, racially and nationally oppressed in this country is 50 million.

It is very important to have a clear understanding and appreciation of different forces and their interrelationships. This deeper understanding is necessary in the struggle for working-class unity, antimonopoly unity, and in the struggle for democracy.

First, we should be clear that the struggle against national oppression and racism is of necessity an integral feature of every struggle. The victories and advances in the struggle for economic and social progress are inextricably tied to the struggle against national oppression and racism. Without this struggle, the struggle for democracy, the class struggle, the antimonopoly struggle and the electoral struggle will have built-in limitations.

Second, we should be clear that not all nationalities are oppressed.

Third, there are different levels of oppression. Not all are of the same scope or intensity. There are differences in the level of chauvinism. Not all are discriminated against on the same level in the economic arena.

I received some letters which refer to the question of national oppression of a specific nationality and compare it with the oppression of Afro-Americans, using phrases such as "it is the same as," or "there is no difference." These comparisons don't stand the test of reality.

The main root and the sharpest expression of racial and national oppression in the United States is that which is directed against Afro-Americans. All other forms and systems of racial and national oppression are related to and are fed by the racism directed against Black Americans. Any attempt to equate or substitute this concept with another is a misrepresentation of reality and becomes divisive.

Racism, white supremacy, adds a brutality, a deadly pervasive ideological poison, a scope and a depth to the oppression of Afro-Americans that can not be compared to any other section of the oppressed nationalities. That is why the main blow in the struggle against national oppression and racism must be struck where the root is.

Victories on this front will result in victories on the other fronts. When racism against Black Americans abates, the national oppression and chauvinism against all other oppressed peoples will also abate. In all cases, unity and struggle is key.

Our task is to find the avenues, the issues that will unite the 50 million racially and nationally oppressed peoples in alliance with the working class.

We should not play numbers games. These are political

concepts. Quantity, by itself, is never a *determining* factor in political assessments. We must not use numbers either to upgrade or to downgrade an oppressed national group. This serves no purpose except to divide.

Our task is to give our very best in the struggle against racial and national oppression in every arena of struggle and to find the forms and issues that will bring the struggles together into a single stream.

We must fight against the increasing, unceasing efforts of the ruling class in this moment of crisis to divide, to set one group against another. Unity must be our watchword.

A correct understanding about the relationship between the struggle against racial and national oppression and the class struggle is a most important question. This is one of the very special contributions our Party makes to this struggle.

A proper understanding of the class struggle, the working class and the forces of national liberation provides a powerful base for the progressive movement in the United States.

This understanding rests on a correct understanding of the class struggle, the role of the working class and the forces in the struggle for national liberation.

The class struggle is the controlling phenomenon of capitalist society. It determines the nature of all processes. Any attempt to ignore this leads to floundering and going around in circles. ☐

[Report to 22nd Convention, CPUSA, August 1979]

Notes

Part 1—The Most Dangerous Pollutant

1. My Lai (Song My), a Vietnam village, was destroyed and its population massacred by U.S. troops in 1969. The atrocity aroused worldwide condemnation.
2. In 1967 Israel, with the backing of the U.S. government, launched a war against its neighbors, seizing and occupying territory belonging to Egypt, Syria, Jordan and the Palestinian people. The occupation resulted in a permanent state of tension and conflict.
3. Students for a Democratic Society (SDS) was a radical student organization which opposed the Vietnam War and supported the civil rights movement during the 1960s. At the end of the 1960s it splintered into several ultra-Left factions. The Progressive Labor Party was a small sect of U.S. adherents of Maoism. Troskyites, followers of Leon Trotsky, are organized in numerous small parties and groups. Trotskyites habitually employ splitting tactics in people's movements, and promote anti-Communism in pseudo-radical guise.
4. George Meany was then president of the American Federation of Labor-Congress of Industrial Organizations.
5. Earl Browder, one-time general secretary of the Communist Party, USA, proposed in 1945 that the Communist Party be dissolved and replaced by a "political association." He was later removed from leadership and expelled for trying to dismantle the Party.
6. William Z. Foster was a prominent leader of the CPUSA for 40 years, from the time of his joining in 1921. He was a well-known trade union organizer and theoretician of the working-class movement.
7. The Young Workers Liberation League (1970-1982), a Marxist-Leninist youth organization, was the predecessor of the Young Communist League.

Part 2—Working-Class Unity

1. A mobilization of Right-wing elements in support of the Vietnam War. The demonstrators violently attacked peace activists.
2. I.W. Abel had been elected president of the United Steel Workers of America on a reform program, but later abandoned the right of the union to strike and based union policies on improving the financial health of the steel companies.
3. The Fairfield decision, a ruling by a U.S. district court, found the U.S. Steel Corporation (in collusion with the United Steel Workers of America) guilty of discriminatory hiring and promotion practices. In a consent decree, April 12, 1974, the company was compelled to institute an affirmative action program and a more democratic seniority system.

4. See note 3 above.
5. Ben Chavis, a minister of the United Church of Christ, and ten others (all but one of whom were Black) were framed up and railroaded to prison following civil disturbances in Wilmington, North Carolina. A national and international campaign for their freedom developed.
6. South Africa and Rhodesia were both ruled by white settler minority regimes which denied the Black majorities any political and economic rights. The Rhodesian regime was overthrown in 1980, and the country's name changed to Zimbabwe.
7. Gus Hall and Jarvis Tyner were the presidential and vice-presidential candidates of the Communist Party, USA, in 1972 and 1976.
8. See pp. 69-72 for a commentary on the Bakke and Weber cases.
9. Bull Conner was a notoriously racist chief of police of Birmingham, Alabama. In 1965, his police, using clubs and dogs, viciously attacked a peaceful civil rights march.

Part 3—Strategy and Tactics

1. The Scottsboro (Alabama) case was the focus of a 17-year nationwide mass struggle for the vindication of nine Black youths framed on a false rape charge in 1931. The struggle was led by the Communist Party and the International Labor Defence.
2. Charlayne Hunter and Hamilton Holmes were the first Black students admitted to the University of Georgia in 1961 under court order.
3. Dixiecrats were the rabid segregationists in the Southern wing of the Democratic Party.
4. An act to prohibit discrimination based on race, religion or sex in hiring. Some executive orders restraining such discrimination had been in effect since World War II.
5. Organizations advocating "white supremacy" and engaging in violence and intimidation against Afro-Americans and other democratic-minded people.
6. A well-funded, conspiratorial group of ultra-Rightists, founded and led by millionaire Robert Welch, seeking to seize power in the United States.
7. Senator Barry M. Goldwater of Arizona, an ultra-Rightist, was presidential candidate of the Republican Party in 1964.
8. Laws passed during the cold war years after World War II which reversed many of the legal gains of labor codified in the Wagner Act of 1937.
9. Major General Edwin A. Walker, an ultra-Right activist, was arrested in 1964 for assault of federal officers assisting in the desegregation of the University of Mississippi in Oxford, Mississippi.
10. The Reverend Martin Luther King, Jr., Julian Bond and Floyd McKissick were leaders of the civil rights movement. King headed the Southern Christian Leadership Conference (SCLC); Bond was from the Student Nonviolent Coordinating Committee (SNCC); and McKissick led the Congress of Racial Equality (CORE).
11. An open letter to the President issued by the CPUSA calling for an end to U.S. aggression in Vietnam and massive programs to wipe out poverty and discrimination.

12. Whitney Young and Roy Wilkins were leaders of the National Urban League and the National Association for the Advancement of Colored People (NAACP) who supported the war in Vietnam.
13. A Black labor leadership organization.
14. See note 2 above.
15. See note 13, above.
16. A federal youth jobs program begun as part of antipoverty legislation.
17. A federally-funded preschool program for children of low-income families.
18. The Black Panther Party was the target of a nationally-coordinated campaign of police repression, including numerous shootings and frameups. Bobby Seale, a Panther leader, was singled out for flagrant persecution at the Chicago conspiracy trial of antiwar activists. The Plainfield Seven were falsely convicted of the murder of a police officer in Plainfield, New Jersey.
19. Albert Shanker, president of the American Federation of Teachers.
20. Marcus Garvey, a Jamaican by birth, led a movement which advocated migration of Afro-Americans to the African nation of Liberia.
21. Angela Davis, a member of the CPUSA, was dismissed as a teacher at the University of California and then framed on a murder charge as part of a campaign of political persecution. In 1972 she was acquitted of all charges.
22. Fleeta Drumgo, John Clutchette and George Jackson were prisoners at the Soleded Prison, Salinas, California, who were falsely accused of the murder of a prison guard.
23. Jonathan Jackson died in a shootout with police while attempting to free his older brother, George Jackson, a long-term prisoner in California.
24. The Montgomery boycott in 1955 was a mass refusal by the Afro-American men and women of that Alabama city to ride in segregated public buses. Their victory sparked the sit-in and freedom ride movements of the '50s and '60s.
25. Eldridge Cleaver was a leading figure in the Black Panther Party. George Wallace was a former segregationist governor of Alabama.
26. Carl Stokes was the first Black mayor of Cleveland.
27. See note 24 above.
28. The Supreme Court ruling came in the case of Brown v. Board of Education of Topeka, Kansas, 1954.

Part 4—Against War and Reaction

1. The National Negro Congress, formed in 1936, was dedicated to enlarging and speeding up the campaign against discrimination. It had a broad representation from religious and fraternal organizations and from unions.
2. See note 24, Part 3.
3. William L. Patterson (1891-1980), a leader of the civil rights movement for many decades, was National Executive Secretary of the Civil Rights Congress.
4. The Voting Rights Act of 1965 was designed to abolish legal and extra-

legal practices which prevented Afro-Americans from voting, especially in the Southern states.

5. Clement F. Haynsworth, Jr. was nominated for the Supreme Court by Richard Nixon. The Senate refused to approve the nomination when it became known that he knowingly belonged to a private club which barred Black members.

6. An anti-civil rights coalition of Republicans and Dixiecrats. Stror. Thurmond was a U.S. senator from South Carolina.

7. See note 2, Part 3.

8. Site of police killings of Black college students.

9. A national gathering of 3,000 Black elected officials and political activists chaired by Mayor Richard Gordon Hatcher of Gary, Indiana.

10. A radical, independent political grouping based in Chicano communities in the Southwest and West.

11. A California ballot initiative, inspired by Right-wing forces, to sharply lower property taxes. Its passage forced sharp cuts in social services.

12. A Soviet physicist who has issued numerous statements, pamphlets and other materials which make him a favored "dissident" of the Western mass media.

13. A national legal defence organization which developed, in large part, from committees formed to wage a mass political defence of Angela Davis.

14. Bernard Goetz gunned down four Black youths in a New York subway train, and was hailed as a "hero vigilante" by racist groups and individuals. Subsequent to the appearance of this article, a new grand jury did indict him for attempted murder.

Part 5—The Roots of Oppression

1. The Supreme Court struck down as unconstitutional the longstanding practice of apportioning some legislative bodies according to principles other than population. Such violations of "one man, one vote" had long been used to partially disfranchise Black, labor and urban populations.

2. An outspoken advocate of Abolitionism prior to the Civil War, and a supporter of other progressive reform causes.

3. Dr. Herbert Aptheker is a member of the Central Committee of the CPUSA; Staughton Lynd was a historian and peace activist; Thomas Hayden was a leader of Students for a Democratic Society.

4. Section 14B of the Taft Hartley Act permits states to outlaw closed shop provisions of contracts making union membership universal.

5. Detroit, Newark and New Haven were among the cities which were scenes of violent protests against oppressive ghetto living conditions and for political power and real equality for the Afro-American peo ple.

6. See note 8, Part 2.